Shugendō

Shugenja (yamabushi) in traditional attire blowing a conch in the mountains.

Shugendō:
Essays on the Structure of Japanese Folk Religion

MIYAKE HITOSHI

EDITED AND WITH AN INTRODUCTION BY H. BYRON EARHART

This book was financed in part
through a generous grant from Keio University.

Ann Arbor
Center for Japanese Studies
The University of Michigan
2001

Published by the Center for Japanese Studies, The University of Michigan
202 S. Thayer St., Ann Arbor, MI 48104–1608

Michigan Monograph Series in Japanese Studies, Number 32

Library of Congress Cataloging-in-Publication Data

Miyake, Hitoshi, 1933–
    Shugendo : essays on the structure of Japanese folk religion / Miyake Hitoshi ;
edited and with an introduction by H. Byron Earhart.
        p. cm. — (Michigan monograph series in Japanese studies ; 32)
    Includes bibliographical references and index.
    ISBN 0-939512-05-X (cloth : alk. paper)
    1. Shugen (Sect). 2. Japan—Religious life and customs. I. Earhart, H. Byron.
II. Title. III. Series.

BQ8822 . M582 2001
299'.56—dc21   00–060286

This book was set in New Baskerville.

Jacket design by Heidi M. Dailey

This publication meets the ANSI/NISO Standards for Permanence of Paper
for Publications and Documents in Libraries and Archives (Z39.48–1992).

Printed in the United States of America

Contents

Illustrations

Tables

Acknowledgments

The chapters in this book were previously delivered as papers or printed in Japanese and/or English in a number of works, and are reprinted here with thanks to the original publishers. All chapters have been edited for consistency and continuity for the present volume.

Chapter 1 was originally published in part as "Rethinking Japanese Folk Religion: A Study of Kumano Shugen." In *Religion in Japan: Arrows to Heaven and Earth*, edited by P. F. Kornicki and I. J. McMullen, 120–34. Cambridge: Cambridge University Press, 1996.

Chapter 2 was originally published as "One Aspect of the Japanese Idea of God—around the Kumano Gongen." *Tenri Journal of Religion* 13 (August 1979): 118–37.

Chapter 3 was originally published as "Religious Rituals in Shugendō—A Summary." *Japanese Journal of Religious Studies* 16.2 (June–September 1989): 101–16; previously published as the concluding summary chapter of Miyake's *Shugendō girei no kenkyū.* 2nd. ed., rev. Tokyo: Shunjūsha, 1985. Translated by Paul Swanson.

Chapter 4 was originally delivered as a paper at the Center for the Study of World Religions, Harvard University, December 1975.

Chapter 5 was originally delivered as a paper at the Center for the Study of World Religions, Harvard University, November 1975.

Chapter 6 was delivered as a paper at the Center for Japanese Studies, The University of Michigan, February 1996; previously published as the concluding summary chapter of Miyake's *Shugendō shisō no kenkyū.* Tokyo: Shunjūsha, 1985.

Chapter 7 was originally published as "Shugendō to shamanizumu—gohō o chūshin to shite." In *Shamanizumu no sekai,* edited by Sakurai Tokutarō, 200–14. Tokyo: Shunjūsha, 1978.

Chapter 8 was originally published as "Female Prohibition at Mt. Sanjo, the Omine Mts." *Tenri Journal of Religion* 21 (December 1987): 55–67.

Chapter 9 was originally delivered as a paper at the University of Illinois, February 1975.

Chapter 10 was originally published as "Nihon no minzoku shūkyō ni okeru shizenkan." *Shūkyō kenkyū* 304 (1995): 91–111, and subsequently published as "The Idea of Nature in Japanese Folk Religion." *Tenri Journal of Religion* 26 (1995): 55–82. Translated by W. Edwards and Tsumoto Kōichi.

Chapter 11 was originally published as "Nihonjin no shūkyō seikatsu to genze riyaku." In *Nihon shūkyō to genze riyaku,* edited by Nihon Bukkyō Kenkyūkai, 24–37. Tokyo: Daizō Shuppansha, 1972.

Chapter 12 was originally published as "Revitalization of Traditional Religion—Belief and Practice of Gedatsukai." *Tenri Journal of Religion* 18 (November 1984): 141–63.

Chapter 13 was originally published as "The Cycle of Death and Rebirth." *Echoes of Peace, Quarterly Bulletin of the Niwano Peace Foundation* 37 (April 1992): 4–7.

Preface

Until quite recently, Japanese religions have been studied mainly from the standpoint of established religions, such as Buddhism and Shinto. In the history, thought, and ritual of specific religions there are many excellent studies. However, these works have stressed the distinctive character of each individual religion. But usually when Japanese people actually practice and experience religion, they go to a Shinto shrine with a newborn child to pray for blessing and growth, they may attend a Christian church for a marriage ceremony, they may participate in a new religion for personal counseling, and then they may rely on a Buddhist temple for funeral ceremonies and memorial services. In this fashion Japanese people select from these several religious traditions what is helpful and necessary for living their everyday lives. Moreover, they carry out various religious activities themselves in observing everyday customs, without resorting to any leaders of established religions. I call this kind of religious practice "folk religion." Therefore, according to my definition, folk religion is the religion that emerges from the necessities of community lives. It consists of annual observances, rites of passage, rites of affliction, oral traditions, and images connected with these rituals.

Japanese folk religion has been studied mainly by folklorists. These folklorists tried to sift out the folk religion that formed a synthesis from the various religious traditions such as Shinto and Buddhism, and that survived as the customs of the local community; then, analyzing the folk elements of this synthesis, they arrived at a pure archetype that they saw as the indigenous Japanese pattern of belief. Specifically, they identified ancestor worship, or repose of souls (*chinkon*) as the core of Japanese indigenous faith. However, the Japanese people, who have dwelled for so many centuries in their island country, were not content to limit their religious heritage to one or more elements indigenous to their insular setting; rather, they came to adapt elements from various traditions of the Asian continent, and combined them with indigenous elements to create a complex belief system that they felt enabled them to live their lives more fully. Therefore, in

order to understand Japanese religion and culture, it is necessary to explore the logic of the syncretism that is central to Japanese religion.

In Japan, one typical product of this syncretism is Shugendō, a unique
religion that took the form of an organized religion about the ninth and
tenth centuries, when ancient Japanese religious beliefs and practices in
the mountains were influenced by religions such as northern shamanism,
Taoism, Buddhism, and Shinto. The practitioners of this religion acquired
supernatural powers through ascetic practice in the mountains, and utilized these powers mainly by performing magico-religious activities that
attracted widespread support among the Japanese people. As a result,
Shugendō, like Buddhism and Shinto, exerted pervasive influence on the
religious life of the Japanese people.

This book has as its general purpose the clarification of the logic of
the religious syncretism of the Japanese people, by investigating Shugendō
and folk religion. Toward this end, the first half of the book is on Shugendō,
the typical syncretic religion of Japan; in this part we explore the logic of
syncretism in Japanese religion from the viewpoint of transmission. The latter half of the book includes chapters concerning Japanese folk religion, which
is the receiving tradition crucial in the formation of this syncretism.

Concretely, in the first half of the book, which treats Shugendō, I first
introduce the history of Shugendō's religious organization (and its importance for the study of Japanese folk religion). This is followed by a
description of the belief in the Kumano Gongen (avatar), which is typical
of Shugendō's conception of deity. Next, I provide an outline of Shugendō's
religious rituals and interpret the nature of mountain austerities, which
form the most important rituals in Shugendō. The following chapters discuss Shugendō rites of exorcism—a typical Shugendō salvation rite, the
outline of Shugendō thought, and the cosmology of Shugendō in connection with shamanism. This section closes with a consideration of the religious rationale for the prohibition of women at Mt. Sanjō.

In the second half of the book, the discussion of folk religion is introduced with a structural analysis of Japanese folk religion that analyzes annual observances and rites of passage—which are at the heart of Japanese
folk religion. Following this general subject, I take up the more specific
topics of the idea of nature and worldly benefits. Then I consider how
traditional Japanese folk religion is revitalized within new religions, using
the case study of the new religion Gedatsukai. This part closes with the
timely issue of death and rebirth in the setting of brain death and organ
transplants.

As mentioned above, this book's central theme is to make clear the
logic of syncretism both from the viewpoint of transmission and reception: we accomplish this by looking first at Shugendō as an example of the

transmission of syncretic religion in Japan, and then by turning to the reception of religious traditions and elements within Japanese folk religion. Therefore, it will please me if these chapters help the reader arrive at a greater understanding of the makeup of Japanese religion, and also the nature of Japanese culture and the Japanese people.

Some readers will start at the first chapter and read through the final chapter, to better understand Shugendō, folk religion, and Japanese religion in general; toward this end, the individual articles have been edited to maintain a consistency and continuity for the book as a whole. Other readers, who wish to view only one or a few scenes of the larger picture—such as one aspect of Shugendō (for instance, shamanism, or prohibition of women), or one aspect of folk religion (for example, the idea of nature, or worldly benefits)—will prefer to start "in the middle" and not read all of the preceding chapters in order to comprehend a single article.

This book consists of articles in English gathered together from various earlier publications and presentations. My position as Toyota Visiting Professor at the Center for Japanese Studies, the University of Michigan, provided the opportunity to present some of these articles as lectures, and also to edit these articles for publication. I would like to thank Professor Hitomi Tonomura, Director of the Center for Japanese Studies, who made my stay at the Center possible, and to the staff of the Center who provided valuable assistance. I wish to acknowledge the help of Professor H. Byron Earhart in editing these essays, and the support of Bruce E. Willoughby, Executive Editor of the Publications Program for the Center for Japanese Studies, and Ellen Hartigan-O'Connor, Assistant Editor. Thanks go to Eriko Watanabe and Keio University Press, who kindly agreed to compose the List of Characters. Appreciation also is extended to the Fukuzawa Foundation of Keio University for its generous financial subsidy for this publication.

Introduction

BY H. Byron Earhart

In Japan Hitoshi Miyake is recognized as one of the leading scholars in Japanese religion. His reputation is linked especially to Shugendō and folk religion, two fields in which he has published pioneering studies. Although some of his shorter pieces have appeared in English in various journals and books, his major works have not been translated from Japanese, and his significant contributions are still not widely known outside Japan. The purpose of this book is to bring together in one volume a representative collection of his scholarly work, and to enable the international audience to better appreciate Shugendō, folk religion, and Japanese religion in general.

Miyake, a native of Okayama Prefecture, graduated from Keio University in 1956, received his M.A. in religious studies from Tokyo University in 1959, and completed the Ph.D. course at Tokyo University in religious studies in 1962, the same year as his appointment to the sociology department of Keio University. His master's and doctoral dissertations both had focused on Shugendō; his subsequent publications on Shugendō, especially his massive *The Structure of Religious Rituals in Shugendō*, was the basis for Keio University to honor him with a Doctor of Letters degree in 1969. Since that time he has continued to publish monumental works on different aspects of Shugendō, and groundbreaking treatments of folk religion. His extraordinary scholarly achievements were recognized in 1997 when he was honored with membership in the Japan Science Council.

Miyake's many publications have helped advance greatly the field of "Japanese religion," a simple rubric for a very complex subject. Japanese religion is comparable to the related terms of the Japanese people, language, and culture: each can be recognized as a distinctive entity today, but the exact origins and nature of each is debatable. Although in prehistoric Japan there were beliefs and practices that may be called "religion," and even though this prehistoric heritage—especially centering around the worship of *kami*—became the foundation for Shinto, there is disagreement

1

about whether we can reconstruct what this prehistoric tradition was, and whether we can find a continuity between this "indigenous" tradition and the religious tradition continuing down to the present.

The greatest difficulty in identifying exactly this prehistoric tradition is the fact that the transition to historic times is marked by a wave of influence from the Asian continent: Buddhism from distant India, as well as Taoism and Confucianism from China, often mediated through Korea. These "foreign" influences quickly became so interwoven with the native heritage that they gradually became integral parts of the Japanese landscape, making it almost impossible to unweave the various strands at this late date. Indeed, because the Japanese language first was written with Chinese characters, the very language used to record the early tradition is colored by the same cultural blending.

In other words, the complexity behind the term "Japanese religion" is not limited to the variety of religious practices, but also refers to the ambiguity of what is "Japanese" about these customs. The study of religion in Japan has revolved around these two pivotal issues: first, exactly what is "religion" and what materials should be investigated to comprehend it; and second, what is it that is distinctively "Japanese" about this set of materials? Partly because of the vastness of the subject, it is difficult for any one researcher to cover the entire range of religion in Japan. Most scholars have concentrated their work on one strand of the fabric of Japanese religion—most numerous are the scholars of Buddhism, and also of Shinto, and these scholars, naturally, have tended to emphasize the centrality of either Buddhism or Shinto to Japanese religion. While the debate continues as to whether Japanese religion is Buddhist or Shinto in character, most scholars of Buddhism are more concerned with the intrinsic character of Buddhism, and most scholars of Shinto are more interested in a "pure" Shinto free from foreign/Buddhist influence. Although fewer scholars have focused on Confucianism and Taoism and have been less apt to place their subject matter at the heart of Japanese religion, nevertheless, everyone acknowledges the pervasive influence of this double Chinese legacy. The question that is left begged is how can we conceive of Japanese religion as a whole? Miyake's contribution has been to show how not only Shugendō and folk religion, but also the cultural and national heritage of Japanese religion in general, can be treated as syncretic products with their own unity.

One reason Shugendō is so significant for the study of Japanese religion is that its development involved a process of the interacting and combining of many influences, and its study does not allow avoidance of the complex character of Japanese religion. Shugendō became an organized religion about the ninth and tenth centuries when ancient religious beliefs and practices in mountains were influenced by shamanism, Taoism, and Buddhism. Ancient beliefs in *kami* and customs related to sacred mountains were coupled with Taoist notions about spiritual practices in sacred mountains and Buddhist ideas of ascetic practices in mountain retreats. The result of this interaction was the hybrid or syncretic tradition of Shugendō, which blended such diverse elements as *kami* and buddhas, Shinto and Buddhism, worship and asceticism, into one overall pattern. On hundreds of Japanese sacred mountains, Shugendō centers were established; they shared this compound heritage and general hybrid tradition, while maintaining highly distinctive legacies of their own. The practitioners of Shugendō, known alternatively as *shugenja* or *yamabushi*, while developing their religious qualifications within rigid austerities on one or more sacred mountains, also carried out extensive ministries, first spreading this heritage to the people and then serving their immediate religious needs.

In fact, what many scholars consider as the distinctively Japanese mixture of many religious lineages into one common worldview was in large part created at the Shugendō centers. As packagers and disseminators of a mixture of indigenous, Shinto, Buddhist, Taoist, and Confucian elements, the *shugenja* or *yamabushi* were deeply involved in the creation of what we know today as Japanese religion. That this worldview—created, propagated, and maintained by *yamabushi*—continues to be important down to the present moment is demonstrated by the fact that its influence is continued in many of the new religions of contemporary Japan. Some of the founders of new religions had revelatory experiences while performing religious practices on sacred mountains, and some of the rituals created by new religions bear the imprint of Shugendō rituals; indeed, the highly syncretic character of Shugendō laid down a precedent for the syncretic pattern of most new religions.

In short, much of what is "Japanese" about Japanese religion is the distinctive blend of beliefs and practices developed within Shugendō; and the religious content of much of Japanese religion is the selection of beliefs and practices found in the worldview created and spread by Shugendō.

Of Miyake's two major areas of scholarship, the label "Shugendō" obviously indicates an idiosyncratic Japanese development, but the term "folk religion" seems to be a more commonplace and self-evident category. Unfortunately, the notion of folk religion is not a clearly defined concept when applied to most cultures and regions, and it has also had a checkered history in Japan. Japanese intellectuals generally, and scholars within Buddhism and Shinto more often than not, have either ignored or looked down on folk religion. However, a smaller number of folklorists, usually without academic posts and pursuing their study from personal interest rather than for professional advancement, have maintained a lively concern for folk subjects such as folk arts (including the performing arts) and folk religion. Phrased negatively, Japanese folk religion is the beliefs, customs, and practices of lay people *not* specifically included in the formal institutions of Shinto and Buddhism and their priestly activities; in more positive terms, folk religion is the heritage handed down orally among the people.

Because most Japanese people, especially in recent times, participate in both Shinto and Buddhism, and believe in or take for granted Taoist notions and Confucian ideas, and do so usually with little or no institutional and clerical assistance, much of the average person's religious life is lived outside the boundaries of institutional religion, beyond the scope of clerical procedures. Given this situation of multiple affiliation and lay initiative, the category of "folk religion" has a more prominent position in the discussion of Japanese religion than in the treatment of most religious traditions. As Winston Davis has put it, borrowing Robert Redfield's concept of the "little tradition," "In Japan the 'little tradition' is the 'great tradition.'"[1]

Some of the confusion over Japanese folk religion is directly related to the ambiguity about the concept, origins, and nature of Japanese religion. One assumption of folklorists has been the notion that there is an indigenous Japanese (folk) religion, preceding both Shinto and Buddhism, and remaining even today as the heart of these formal traditions. This assumption usually was not stated so directly and boldly, but it provided the motivation for much work on folk religion; the fact that such publications were rather impressionistic and intuitive, and their writers often lacked formal academic positions, meant that generally they were not taken seriously by most scholars. Even the work of the major founder of folklore studies, Yanagita Kunio, has been recognized more among popular readers than within academic circles.[2]

In current work on folk topics, there has been less emphasis on trying to recover and reconstruct an "original" or "indigenous" Japanese tradition, and greater concern for simply studying the beliefs and religious activities of lay people, and attempting to make sense of the function of these phenomena. One clear conclusion to be drawn from a consideration of folk material is that much of the content and texture of Japanese folk religion was produced and shaped after the pattern created and diffused by Shugendō. Indeed, much of the substance of folk religion was spread and maintained by *yamabushi* through their dramatic performances in festival settings.

Hitoshi Miyake stands at the forefront of Japanese scholars working in the fields of Shugendō and folk religion for a number of reasons, especially because of his extensive publications, meticulous scholarship, and methodological rigor. The best of Japanese scholarship is noted for its erudition—complete mastery of all relevant material—and Miyake has demonstrated this erudition in his mastery of the entire field of Shugendō. The subject of Shugendō may appear to the nonspecialist as a tiny subfield within Japanese studies, but actually Shugendō is a panorama of as many local variations as the sacred mountains where it was located. Although Shugendō is a blend of a handful of religious traditions, there was no single formula for combining all these ingredients into uniform institutions, doctrines, and rituals. Miyake has reviewed the history and literature of the major Shugendō centers, and in fact he has edited Shugendō materials and reference works. However, not content to work in his library and office, he has traveled to these centers and observed the Shugendō practices that survive in altered form today.

Miyake has not stopped at merely collecting and describing the history and practice of Shugendō in its many permutations: in all his work he has insisted on assessing these materials systematically. His succession of publications on Shugendō reveals an agenda of a series of comprehensive treatments of key aspects of the system of Shugendō. After bringing out his early major work on the structure of religious rituals in Shugendō, he proceeded to publish subsequent volumes on the practice and organization of Shugendō, and the belief system underlying Shugendō; he also brought out studies of important Shugendō centers, and wrote general introductions to Shugendō. All future scholarship on Shugendō will have to take into account the corpus of Miyake's work.

The eight essays on Shugendō in this volume cover the range of Shugendō—the history and organization of Shugendō, its religious rituals, mountain austerities, the practice of exorcism, religious thought, cosmology, and the idea of divinity, as well as the prohibition of women at Shugendō sacred mountains. Reading these articles will enable one who does not handle Japanese to sample the breadth and depth of Miyake's scholarship, and gain a new appreciation for the richness of Shugendō.

While Miyake was creating a corpus of Shugendō publications, he was also deeply involved in the study of folk religion: he carried out his own fieldwork, much of it in areas of research related to Shugendō, such as festivals and folk arts; he trained researchers and supervised their fieldwork on folk religion; and he was publishing works both on the results of his fieldwork, and on the methodology and theory needed to conduct and interpret folk religion.

In Japan the study, or at least the recording, of local customs, goes back to ancient times, and in more recent history folklorists and scholars have continued and advanced this Japanese penchant for chronicling regional and local customs and ceremonies. Indeed, scholars and folklorists were often linked in tandem with regional and local people and institutions in accentuating the distinctive or singular character of that locale's beliefs or folk tales or observances. For example, almost every region of Japan has a wealth of publications on its own "annual ceremonies" (*nenjūgyōji*). Western scholars and Japanese scholars sometimes debate whether Japanese studies generally and Japanese religion should be framed in terms of the "uniqueness" of things Japanese, or their commonality with other cultures. In the instance of folklore studies, however, the definition of uniqueness is raised to an even higher level, predicated on the assumption of a uniqueness for each regional heritage. Many of the publications on folklore and folk religion were intended for the preservation and appreciation of local color, and were not presumed to qualify as scholarly analyses.

Even when folk religion has been taken up with more scholarly intent, usually it has lacked a clear methodology for gathering material and a solid theoretical framework for synthesizing it. As a result, much of the work on folk religion has been fragmentary and inconclusive. It is instructive that one of the earlier terms for "folk religion" in Japanese was *minkan shinkō*, literally, "folk belief(s)"; this term could be neutral, or could carry a pejorative connotation, closer to "superstition." The major drawback to the term "folk belief" (*minkan shinkō*) is that it construed beliefs and practices either as bits and pieces of curious customs, or as outmoded superstitions that were studied in order to eliminate them.

One of Miyake's major contributions to this field has been to focus on the concept previously referred to as *minzoku shūkyō*, literally, "folk religion," and to make its study respectable by using a clear and consistent methodology, and a straightforward theoretical framework. His major work advocating the systematic study of folk religion is titled *Shūkyō minzokugaku*, which is an inversion of the term *minzoku shūkyō*, and might best be translated "religious folklore." Central to Miyake's work is a commitment to alloying the Japanese concern for erudition with a cosmopolitan attention to comparative materials and theoretical insights. Especially profitable has been his insistence on employing a structural analysis of each aspect of his fieldwork, and linking the various aspects of a subject into an overall structural or systematic unity. For Miyake, the elements of folk religion are not curious customs or isolated fragments, but meaningful parts of a coherent unity. Miyake has established a high level for methodological and theoretical rigor in the study of folk religion, and all future work on Japanese folk religion that lays claim to academic intentions will have to deal directly with these issues.

The five essays on folk religion in this volume cover a wide range of materials—from broader treatments of the nature of folk religion and how to go about a structural analysis of folk religion, to more particular case studies—the idea of nature, the cycle of death and rebirth, the notion of "worldly benefits," and the revitalization of traditional religion in a new religion. Together, they provide a sample of the methodological approach and theoretical framework of Miyake's scholarship, and testify to the significance of viewing folk religion as a meaningful worldview.

This volume of essays provides to those who do not read Japanese a new window for viewing not only the nature of Shugendō, but also the richness and diversity of Japanese folk religion and Japanese religion in general.

NOTES

1. Winston Davis, *Toward Modernity: Developmental Typology of Popular Religious Affiliations in Japan* (Ithaca, NY: Cornell China-Japan Program, 1977), 6.
2. For several decades Yanagita has been the focus of an extended discussion of the nature and significance of his prolific writings: he has been praised for helping record and preserve Japan's distinctive culture, especially culture of the common people or folk; and he has been criticized for helping create or invent the category of "folk" or a common Japanese identity as an expression of Japanese "uniqueness." For a sample of this praise and criticism, see J. Victor Koschmann, Ōiwa Keibō, and Yamashita Shinji, eds., *International Perspectives on Yanagita Kunio and Japanese Folklore Studies* (Ithaca, NY: Cornell China-Japan Program, 1985), and H.D. Harootunian, "Disciplinizing Native Knowledge and Producing Place: Yanagita Kunio, Origuchi Shinobu, Takata Yasuma," in *Culture and Identity: Japanese Intellectuals During the Interwar Years*, ed. J. Thomas Rimer (Princeton: Princeton University Press, 1990), 99–127.

Part One: Shugendō

Shugendō: Its History and Organization

Shugendō and folk religion[1] are closely interrelated, so it is useful to provide an outline of folk religion as a context in which to treat the history and organization of Shugendō.

Japanese folk religion is centered around belief in, and rituals focused on, the *kami* of places such as mountains and the sea—thought to be an "otherworld"—as well as the myths and traditions concerning these figures. The religion known as Shinto came into being through the process of welcoming, enshrining, and celebrating the *kami* of sacred places (*reichi*) and accepting them as guardian deities of the family (*ie*) or village (*mura*). The influence of religions introduced from abroad was also an important factor, and as a result of this influence some people entered the holy spiritual regions of the mountains and performed ascetic practices under the guidance of "mountain men." These people were able to draw on the power of the *kami* and became religious figures who performed magico-religious activities. The ascetics (*genja*) of the esoteric Buddhist Shingon and Tendai traditions are representative of these figures. During the Heian period (794–1185), people who had cultivated such practices and attained magical powers were called *shugenja*.[2] This marks the beginning of Shugendō as a distinct religious tradition.

Folk religion in Japan, based on belief in *kami*, involves nature worship. The notion of the divine, or of spirits/gods, is a two-layered structure: the indigenous local spirits (*kami*) and those that were introduced from the outside (*kami*) and conferred power on the indigenous *kami*. In earlier times people enshrined and celebrated the indigenous *kami*, and sought to control and protect their lives through magically manipulating these spirits. Then even more powerful figures in the form of buddhas were introduced from abroad. At the same time many techniques for manipulating and controlling these forces were also introduced in the forms

11

of shamanism, Taoism, and esoteric Buddhism. Around the ninth and tenth centuries, *shugenja*, people who had cultivated these techniques and followed ascetic practices in the mountains, began to appear in large numbers, and eventually formed the religion called Shugendō.

Around the twelfth and thirteenth centuries, the way of thinking called *hongaku shisō* (the idea that all things are inherently enlightened) became very popular among the members of the Tendai school on Mt. Hiei. It was assumed that all things have the nature of the Buddha, that even the plants and earth possess buddhahood. It is no exaggeration to say that this way of thinking is animism in Buddhist garb. Tamura Yoshiro has proposed that all of the so-called new Buddhist movements of the Kamakura period (1185–1333) were based in some way upon this Tendai idea of *hongaku shisō*: Zen and Shugendō sought to realize buddhahood within this life through various practices; the Pure Land schools of Buddhism sought to attain buddhahood in the next life by chanting the Buddha's name (*nenbutsu*); the Nichiren school sought to establish a Buddha-land on this earth.[3]

Ancestral veneration took root later, in the sixteenth and seventeenth centuries, with the establishment of the social structures of the family (*ie*) and village (*mura*), and funerary practices and rites for the ancestors assumed an important social role. Eventually, the Buddhist establishment came to be responsible for such matters, and in the Edo period (1600–1868) the lives of people in local societies were structured around a number of religious "authorities": clan or local guardian spirits for regional security (Shinto); the family or clan temple for funerals and ancestral rites (Buddhism); and Shugen[4] or esoteric Buddhist establishments for the healing of disease or avoidance of misfortune. One can identify these religious figures who performed magico-religious prayers (*kajikitō*) as *yamabushi* (*shugenja*), Buddhist priests (*sōryo*), or Shinto priests (*kannushi*), but in fact the three types were all combined. However, after 1868 the Meiji government ordered a separation of "Buddhist" and "Shinto" elements, and outlawed Shugendō, because it was a typical case of the admixture of Buddhism and Shinto. The government sought to establish a State Shinto with Ise Shrine as its center and all the local clan deities with their own places within this overriding structure. One result of the outlawing of Shugendō was that many new religions sprang up to take its place and respond to the human need for fulfilling worldly aspirations. After the Second World War, Shugendō regained its independent status and once again began an active role in the religious life of the Japanese people.

The study of folk religion in Japan has so far taken one of two major standpoints. The first is to seek an indigenous Japanese folk belief that remains even today among the Japanese people; this approach is best represented by the work of Yanagita Kunio (1875–1962). The attempt to seek an ancient prototype for Japanese culture in the practices and texts of ancient Japan is best represented by the work of Origuchi Shinobu (1887–1953). The recent work of Takatori Masao, which emphasizes the distinction between Buddhist and Shinto customs can also be classified under this approach.[5] As we can see from the fact the Yanagita himself referred to his studies as *shin-kokugaku* (new National Learning), this approach is an extension of the *kokugaku* (National Learning) of Motoori Norinaga (1730–1801) and Hirata Atsutane (1776–1843).

The second approach is to focus on the beliefs of ordinary people who do not limit their religious affiliation to any one religious tradition, and thereby attempt to grasp the function of these religious practices. Studies based on this approach include the archaeological examination of artifacts and relics and the study of poetry and literature in works such as the *Man'yōshū* and traditional diaries and tales, which can all be taken as material for the study of folk religion. In such an approach, the content and function of folk religion become the focus of attention, and there is no attempt to find a kind of "indigenous" element.

In light of this analysis, I believe we can say that the Japanese, in response to their perceived needs, have absorbed various religious traditions from abroad and blended them to create their own particular kind of syncretistic folk religion. From this perspective, it is necessary to examine the process and the ways in which the Japanese have absorbed various foreign religions, blended them with indigenous elements, and created a particular kind of folk religion. For this purpose it is necessary to study this blending/syncretism of Shinto and Buddhism *(shinbutsu shūgō)* and the religious traditions that are most representative of this kind of syncretistic religion, that is, Shugendō and the new religions.

My concern is to examine the formation of Japanese folk religion within the thought patterns, rituals, and organization of these syncretistic religions. The rest of this chapter will be devoted to a study of Shugendō history and organization as a specific example of the kind of research I have outlined above.

SHUGENDŌ AND THE ORIGIN OF THE THREE MOUNTAINS OF KUMANO

Shugendō is a religious tradition that took the form of an organized religion around the ninth and tenth centuries. Its practitioners gained supernatural powers through ascetic practice in the mountains, and utilized these powers mainly through performing magico-religious activities.

Shugendō was found at sacred mountains throughout Japan, but the form that was most influential throughout the country was the Shugen that first developed in the Kumano region of the present Wakayama prefecture and around Mt. Kinbu (Kinbusen) in the Yoshino region of the present Nara prefecture.

Kumano consists of the three areas of Hongū, Shingū, and Nachi, and thus is referred to as the "three mountains of Kumano" (Kumano Sanzan). Kumano Shugen was at first connected with the Tendai temple of Onjōji (also called Miidera), but from the fourteenth century it came under the control of the Kyoto temple Shōgoin. This branch of Shugendō eventually came to be known as the Honzanha.[6]

Mt. Kinbu was also known as Kane no Mitake (hills of gold) and is well known as the focus of a pilgrimage made by the Heian period aristocrat and politician Fujiwara no Michinaga (966–1027). The central object of worship in the Shugen of Mt. Kinbu is Kongō Zaō Gongen, a figure venerated by En no Ozunu (En no Gyōja), the Nara period thaumaturge and legendary founder of Shugendō. This Mitake faith spread throughout the country, and at the present time Yoshino is the headquarters of the Kinbusen Shugen Honshū organization.[7] Around the fifteenth century, *shugenja* of 36 temples in the Kinki area founded an association of 36 leaders (*sendatsu*), the Tōzan Sanjūroku (thirty-six) Shōdaisendatsushū, with its headquarters at Ozasa deep in the mountains of Mt. Kinbu. By the sixteenth century, those leaders and their *yamabushi* followers had shifted their headquarters to Sanbōin, a subtemple of Daigoji in Kyoto and were known as the Tōzanha (branch) of Shugendō. This and the Honzanha discussed above formed the major branches of Shugendō.

There are many more famous sacred mountains connected to Shugendō, including Mt. Katsuragi in Nara Prefecture (where En no Ozunu is said to have practiced), Mt. Haguro in the Tōhoku region in northern Japan, Mt. Hiko in Kyushu, and Mt. Ishizuchi in Shikoku. Today there are many independent Shugendō organizations: Honzan Shugenshū (formerly the Honzanha), Shingonshū Daigoha (formerly the Tōzanha), Kinbusen Shugen Honshū, Hagurosan Shugen Honshū, Ishizuchi Honshū, Goryū Shugendō, and so forth. As we can see from this brief history of Shugendō, Kumano Shugen with its offspring—the Honzanha—has been the main stream running throughout. Therefore, in this chapter I will take up Kumano Shugen first, and then consider the Honzanha and Tōzanha.

Kumano is mentioned in the *Kojiki* as the burial place for Izanami no Mikoto, one of the *kami* who, in Japanese mythology, gave birth to the land of Japan. As we can see from this myth, Kumano has from ancient times been considered an "other" world. There are three major shrines in Kumano: Hongū Taisha, Hayatama Taisha in Shingū, and Nachi Taisha.

Figure 1. The three mountains of Kumano: Hongū

Figure 2. The three mountains of Kumano: Shingū

Figure 3. The three mountains of Kumano: Nachi

The central *kami* of Hongū shrine is Ketsumiko no Kami, known as a tree deity. The corresponding Buddhist figure was believed to be Amida Nyorai. The central *kami* of Shingū's Hayatama shrine is Kumano Hayatama no Kami, believed to have come from the other side of the sea. The corresponding Buddhist figure was believed to be Yakushi Nyorai. The central *kami* of Nachi is Kumano Fusumi no Kami, with the corresponding Buddhist figure believed to be the Bodhisattva Senju (thousand-armed) Kannon. In later times, however, each of the shrines enshrined the *kami* of the others, and they are as a group referred to as the Kumano Sansho Gongen (avatars of the three Kumano shrines).

Nachi is also the location of the temple Seigantoji, which enshrines another form of Kannon: Nyoirin ("wish-fulfilling jewel"), and the temple Myōhōzan Amidaji. Also, in medieval times there were many people who boarded boats from the beach of Nachi, setting out to sea to the west in hopes of reaching Fudaraku, the paradise of Kannon.

According to the *Kumano Gongen gosuijaku engi*, which is the oldest extant written record on Kumano and was included in the *Chōkan no kanmon* of 1163, the *kami* of Kumano was originally Shin, the "divine prince" of the land deities of Mt. T'ien-t'ai in China.[8] These *kami* are said to have flown to Japan, stopping first on Mt. Hiko in Kyushu, Mt. Ishizuchi in Shikoku, Mt. Yuzuruha in Awaji, and so forth, until finally arriving at places in the Shingū area, such as Kannokura and Asuga, and the Hongū area. Here they were discovered by a hunter named Chiyosada and were first enshrined as the avatars of Kumano.

From about the eighth century a large number of *shugenja* gathered in the Kumano area and were active there throughout history. They practiced at Kumano and healed diseases through the use of magical powers. Some of the most famous include the figure of Eikō, who was considered a bodhisattva; Jōzō, who first conducted ascetic retreats at Nachi Falls in the tenth century; Ōsho, who sacrificially burnt his body at Nachi; Zendo of Hongū, whom tradition credits with being the first to practice asceticism on Mt. Ōmine; and Ragyō, who practiced at Kannokura and is said to have discovered the Nachi Falls with the guidance of Kannon.

SHUGENDŌ AND THE DEVELOPMENT OF THE THREE MOUNTAINS OF KUMANO

Pilgrimage to the Kumano area (Kumano *mōde*) by members of the imperial and aristocratic families became popular during the period of *insei* (retired emperors, 1086–1192). The Retired Emperor Uda participated in a Kumano pilgrimage in 907, and another pilgrimage was undertaken by Emperor Kazan who visited Nachi in 987. When Retired Emperor

Shirakawa went on a pilgrimage to Kumano in 1090, he visited all of the areas of the Kumano Sanzan under the guidance of the monk Zōyo of Onjōji. Shirakawa later granted the temple Shōgoin to Zōyo. Also at that time the steward (*bettō*) of the Kumano Sanzan was appointed to the official government rank of *hokkyō*. As a result the Kumano Sanzan area became bound up with the central authorities in Kyoto. According to the *Kumano bettōkeizu* (lineage of the Kumano stewards), this line of Kumano stewards continued until the time of Shōtan in 1284.

Pilgrimage to Kumano continued to be popular after the time of Retired Emperor Shirakawa. Shirakawa himself made the pilgrimage 9 times, Retired Emperor Toba 21 times, Retired Emperor Go-Shirakawa 34 times, and Retired Emperor Go-Toba 28 times. Go-Shirakawa was an especially devout pilgrim, and in 1160 he enshrined the Kumano Gongen at the Hojujiden sanctuary on the imperial palace grounds in Kyoto. He renamed the sanctuary Imakumanosha (new Kumano shrine), and appointed Kakusan, the head priest (*kengyō*) of the Kumano Sanzan, as *kengyō* for this shrine. During this year Go-Shirakawa also had the temple Zenrinji of Higashiyama in Kyoto enshrine the Nachi avatar (*gongen*), and also renamed this temple Imakumanosha. Later it was known as Nyaku Ōjisha.

There were Shugen practitioners throughout Kumano Sanzan. Those centered at Hongū used for ascetic practices the long and narrow shrine buildings known as *nagatoko*. The *yamabushi* who used those buildings were called *nagatokoshū*. The *nagatokoshū* of Hongū practiced all along the long path from Kumano, past Ōmine, and into Yoshino, but they centered their activities at the sites known as Jinzen and Zenki. They were organized around the elders of five temples known as the Nagatoko Shukurō Goryū. The Shugen centered at Shingū included unmarried Buddhist priests (*shuto*), Shinto priests (*shinkan*), and men formally known as "Buddhist" priests but who served at "Shinto" shrines (*shasō*); there were also ascetics among the *shasō* who were called *nagatokoshū*.

The Kannokura *hijiri* practiced on the mountain overlooking Shingū known as Kannokura. The Shugen at Nachi included those who held retreats at one or more of the forty-eight waterfalls of Nachi. They were called Nachi *takigomori-shū* ("those who hold retreats at a waterfall").

THE RITUALS AND THOUGHT PATTERNS OF KUMANO SHUGEN

As the pilgrimage to Kumano became more and more popular, the *kami* enshrined at Kumano also increased in number. By the middle of the twelfth century, the *kami* had increased to twelve and were called Kumano Jūnisho Gongen (the twelve avatars of Kumano). These twelve avatars and

the other objects of worship and practices associated with them will be
treated in the next chapter.

Kumano Shugen was slightly different at each of the three areas. There
was no site for ascetic practice close to Hongū, so the Shugen of this area
performed their "entering the mountains" by traveling as far as Ōmine
and Yoshino. Two of the characteristic practices of Hongū Shugen are
spending a retreat in the mountains over the New Year by the *misoka
yamabushi*, and the Jinzen consecration (*kanjō*) performed at Jinzen. At
Shingū there was the practice of the Kannokura *hijiri*, who fasted and kept
watch over the "eternal flame" in preparation for the fire festival of the
New Year. At Nachi there was a retreat near a waterfall for practicing austerities by sitting under the waterfall.

THE REGIONAL DISPERSION OF KUMANO SHUGEN

As the practice of the Kumano pilgrimage spread among the retired
emperors, aristocratic families, and members of the *bushi* (warrior) class,
an increasing number of manors (*shōen*) were donated to Kumano organizations. During the period of the retired emperors, many manors in the
Kii area were donated by members of the imperial or aristocratic families.
During the period of the northern and southern dynasties (1336–92 in a
dispute over imperial legitimacy), both the northern and southern fac-
tions sought the military support of those in the Shingū area, thus leading
to the donation of a number of manors. Such donations gradually dwindled
after that time. Areas in which there were three or more manors belonging to Kumano authorities were as follows: Kii, twenty-two; Tōtōmi, eight;
Bizen, six; Ise, Suruga, and Mimasaka, four each; Mikawa, Tajima, and
Awa, three each. Manors belonging to the Imakumano and Nyaku Ōji
shrines in Kyoto included eight in Bitchū, five in Yamashiro, four each in
Settsu and Harima, and three in Awaji. It should be noted that the manors
belonging to Kumano and Imakumano were mostly places conveniently
located by the sea—Awa and locations along the Seto inland sea—Ise,
Mikawa, Tōtōmi, and Suruga. This indicates that Kumano authorities favored manors that were conveniently located for the transport of goods by
sea. The Kumano Gongen were enshrined at those manors and became
centers for the activity of Kumano *sendatsu*. During the Sengoku period
(1467–1568), however, members of the warrior class seized the manors,
and eventually they became economically unprofitable to maintain.

At this point the Kumano organizations found it better to depend on
"tourism" rather than the manors for economic subsistence, that is, on patrons (*danna*) who visited Kumano on pilgrimage from around the country,
because they received income directly from the pilgrims. These patrons

were led to Kumano by *sendatsu*, and their specific religious needs, such as the performance of prayers and arrangements for lodging, were taken care of by escorts known as *oshi*. The first *oshi* made their appearance during the pilgrimage of Fujiwara no Munetada in 1109, as recorded in the *Chūyūki*.[9] The retired emperors and aristocrats who made pilgrimages to Kumano during the period between 1090 and 1221 had their needs taken care of by certain *bettō* (steward) families, but from around the end of the thirteenth century, as pilgrimage became popular also among the warriors and ordinary people, priests from Kumano began to fulfil the role of *oshi*. There were *oshi* affiliated with each of the three Kumano regions, but the *oshi* from the Nachi area, affiliated with temples such as Rōnobō and Jippōin, were particularly active during the fourteenth and fifteenth centuries.

Sendatsu would lead their patrons to certain *oshi* of the Kumano area, and then would be responsible for taking care of various tasks, such as ritual purification before departing, and rituals to be performed at sacred sites such as Ōji (the small shrine near the road), and for acting as guides along the way. During the period of retired emperors, these duties were performed during the pilgrimage of a retired emperor or member of the aristocracy by a high-ranking priest of a famous temple. From around the end of the twelfth century, however, more pilgrimages to Kumano were undertaken by warriors, their servants, and ordinary people, and a variety of types of *sendatsu* developed in response to these new needs. When a *sendatsu* brought his patron to an *oshi*, he would present a petition (*ganmon*) listing his own, and the patron's, name and address. Thus the *sendatsu* acted as a go-between for his patron and an *oshi*, and henceforth a relationship was established whereby this patron's family would always depend on this *oshi* for services such as lodgings and religious rituals. The *oshi* would then receive financial support from the *sendatsu* and patron on the occasion of each pilgrimage. Such *sendatsu* and patrons thus became the source of economic support for those in the Kumano area. Eventually, among the *oshi* the rights to patrons became the object of transfer and sale, and collateral for loans. In such cases the *ganmon*, containing the name of the *sendatsu* and patrons, would be used as a legal document. An *oshi* also kept records and a register of the names of the *sendatsu* and patrons affiliated with him. Such historical records, such as deeds of transfer or sale, collateral for loans, petitions, and registers, are called *oshi monjo*. About 1,500 such records are preserved at the Kumano Nachi Taisha, and about 250 at Hongū Taisha.

A look at those *oshi monjo* shows that the number of patrons steadily increased between the fourteenth and sixteenth centuries. Once the Sengoku period began at the end of the fifteenth century, however, rights to serve patrons were frequently sold. At this time Rōnobō and Jippōin at

Figure 4. A Kumano *sendatsu* and his patron

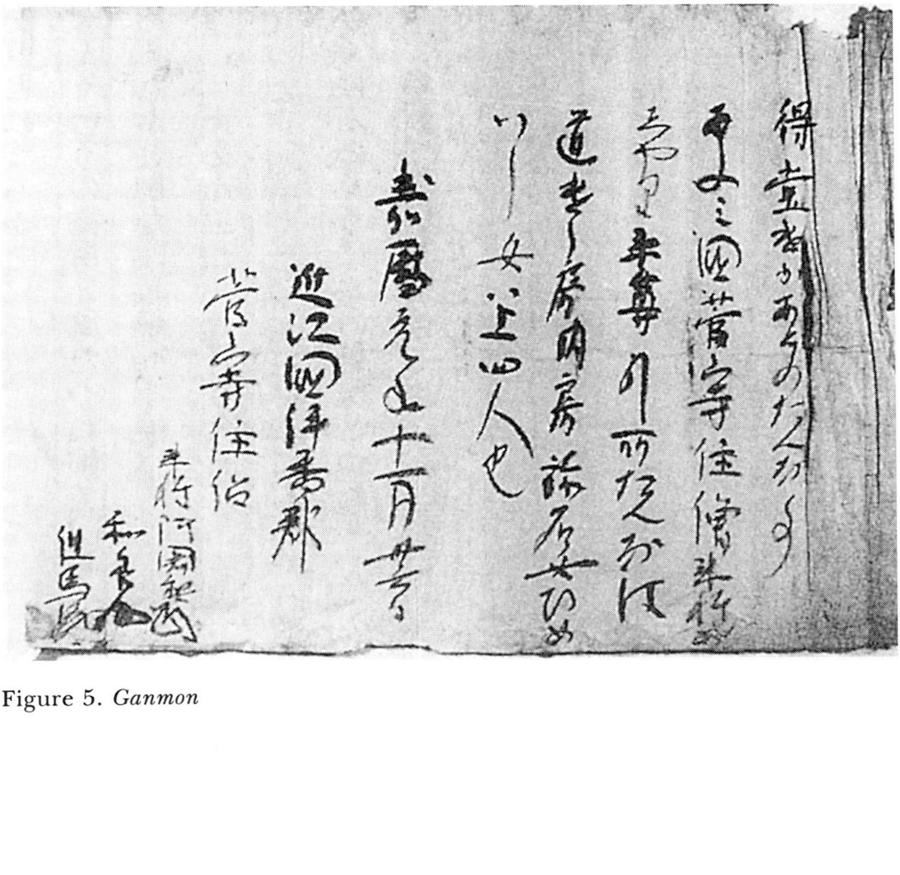

Figure 5. *Ganmon*

Nachi bought up many of the rights to the *oshi* patrons and increased their influence in the area. Areas of medieval Japan from which the largest number of such patrons and *sendatsu* hailed are as follows: 92 patrons and 78 *sendatsu* from Ōmi; 90 and 55 respectively from Mutsu; 75 and 42 from Musashi; 69 and 76 from Iyo; 67 and 28 from Ise; 53 and 22 from Echigo; 50 and 36 from Awa; 46 and 18 from Kōzuke; 44 and 7 from Suruga; 40 and 22 from Yamato; 36 and 22 from Sanuki; and 36 and 21 from Settsu. Note that these areas are in the northeastern part of Japan (Mutsu, Kōzuke, Musashi, Echigo), areas that can be reached conveniently by sea (Ise, Suruga, Settsu, Shikoku), and geographically close areas such as Yamato and Ōmi.

Historically, the earliest centers for such activity were among the *sendatsu* of the Kinki and Chūbu areas, later spreading to the Chūgoku and Kantō areas, and finally to Echigo, Tōhoku, Shikoku, and Kyushu. The activities of the *sendatsu* in the Kantō and Tōhoku areas continued well into the Sengoku period in the early sixteenth century.

Next, based on the *oshi monjo*, let us look at the different types of *sendatsu* and patrons. First there were *sendatsu* directly affiliated with *oshi* from the very start, such as the Jippōin *sendatsu*. These were only a minority, however. The second type were *sendatsu* who came to Kumano from another area and then traveled around the country inviting and soliciting patrons to go to Kumano on pilgrimage. These are called *yugyō* (wandering) *sendatsu*. The second type were also called Ise *ajari*, Wakasa *ajari*, and so forth depending on their place of origin. The third type were called *zaichi* (regional representative) *sendatsu* because they stayed in a certain local area, such as a sacred mountain like Nikkō, a certain large shrine or temple, or a Kumano manor, and served there as Kumano *sendatsu* and representatives of Kumano Shugen. The fourth type were Honzanha *sendatsu* affiliated with places like Imakumano or Shōgoin in Kyoto, or members of the thirty-six Tōzanha *sendatsu*. These were called Shugen *sendatsu*. The fifth type were religious figures other than Shugen *sendatsu*. These include the *nenbutsu-hijiri* of the Jishū, *yin-yang* masters, and lay people who served in the role of *sendatsu*.

Patrons included priests and nuns of regional shrines and temples, family members of warrior families or their servants, and common people such as farmers and merchants. In general, at first wandering *sendatsu* would lead religious members of a regional temple or shrine on a Kumano pilgrimage. Then the religious members of a regional temple or shrine would become "representative" *sendatsu*. This pattern can be found in many areas. In the Kantō and Tōhoku areas, however, most of the patrons were from warrior families or their servants, whereas in the Kansai area (which was more highly developed), many of the patrons were merchants or artisans.

Finally, let us take a look at developments in the organization of *sendatsu*. There were various special types of *sendatsu* and their disciples. First, as we can see in the *Ise ajari monteihiki* (Guide by Ise *ajari* Disciples), it appears that it was the disciples who actually accompanied the pilgrims to Kumano. These *sendatsu* and their disciples are referred to, respectively, as the *honsendatsu* and *toki no sendatsu*; the person who actually accompanied the pilgrims to Kumano was sometimes called *michi no sendatsu*. Second, as this kind of sharing of responsibilities developed, titles such as *daisendatsu* and *shōsendatsu* that distinguished superior and inferior ranks began to be used. Third, there appeared hereditary *sendatsu* families, wherein the role of *sendatsu* was handed down from generation to generation. These families would often place members of their family in various regions, and these would act as *sendatsu* for patrons in those regions. For these *sendatsu* families, the original, first-generation *sendatsu* was called *konpon sendatsu*. The Mochiwatatsu *sendatsu*, who were active in the northeast part of Japan (Ōshū) from the end of the thirteenth century and into the fourteenth century, are representative of these families. Fourth, the subtemples of a hereditary temple (*inge*) of Shōgoin were appointed the regional representatives as *sendatsu*. These formed the base of the later Honzanha organization.

In addition to these types of organization, there were also groups of ascetics who gathered around Kumano *sendatsu* in areas such as the northeast part of Ōmi, the Shirakawa area of Mutsu, and in Sagami. The Tōzan Sanjūroku Shōdaisendatsushū, an organization of *sendatsu* in the Kinki area, is thought to have been an outgrowth of such a group. In places such as Ōmi, Kyoto, Osaka, and Sakai, groups of lay people gathered around *sendatsu* to organize pilgrimages to Kumano.

Branch shrines of the Kumano Gongen, like those of Hachiman, Ise, and Inari, sprang up across the country. A map of their distribution shows that these shrines developed along the sea coast following the Kuroshio Current to the northeast from Mie and Aichi to Shizuoka, Kanagawa, Chiba, and Fukushima; and to the southeast to Kōchi, Kagoshima, and as far as Okinawa. There are also many Kumano shrines along the Seto inland sea coast. This reveals that the dissemination of Kumano Gongen was closely related to sea travel. Also, during the period of retired emperors, the Kumano Gongen were enshrined as the guardian deities of the manors that belonged to Kumano. There are records of enshrining the Kumano Gongen among the warriors in the period of the Northern and Southern courts, and such enshrining was conducted by Kumano *yamabushi* and Kumano *bikuni* (nuns) from the Sengoku period up to the Edo period. In any case it is clear that the Kumano Gongen enshrined across the country were the focus of activity by Kumano *sendatsu*.[10]

THE ORIGIN OF HONZANHA

The *bettō* system began to lose its authority in Kumano from around the end of the Kamakura period. In its stead the Kumano Sanzan *kengyō* officials gained political power owing to support from the manors, and eventually came to dominate the Kumano Sanzan area. The post of Kumano Sanzan *kengyō* had been held by the high temple (*monzeki*) of Onjōji since the time of Zōyo. In the latter half of the fourteenth century, however, Ryōyu of Jōjūin (the Onjōji high temple) was appointed *kengyō*. Ryōyu was very active: he began the practice of the *Jinzen kanjō* (consecration) in Ōmine, and 16 times filled the central role of *chūdan* (central priest) in *godanhō* ceremonies sponsored by Ashikaga Yoshimitsu. Eventually his successors at Shōgoin were appointed to the post of Kumano Sanzan *kengyō*. The temple Jōjūin of the Imakumano Nyaku Ōji *bettō* in Higashiyama was appointed as Kumano Sanzan *bugyō* by Ashikaga Takauji, assisted the *kengyō*, and eventually came to be responsible for control over the Kumano Sanzan and the Kumano *sendatsu*. From around the end of the fourteenth century, Nyaku Ōji guaranteed the position of *sendatsu* to Kumano *sendatsu*, and in exchange received part of the fees that the *sendatsu* were paid by their patrons.

Dōkō (1465–1501) of Shōgoin, seeking to organize all of the Kumano *sendatsu*, especially those in the Mutsu and Kantō areas, left Kyoto in 1486 and traveled around through the Hokuriku and then the Kantō and Tōhoku areas over the next year. During those travels Dōkō visited a large number of Kumano *sendatsu*, staying at the lodgings of the major *sendatsu*. He also practiced mountain austerities at the major sacred mountains such as Hakusan, Tateyama, Fuji, and Nikkō, made pilgrimages to shrines and temples throughout the country, and enjoyed the hospitality of the local governors of these places.[11] It should be added that Dōkō was the elder brother of Konoe Masaie, the current *kanpaku*, and was retained by the shogun Ashikaga Yoshimasa. Thus the Kumano *sendatsu* in the local areas expected his protection, and joined his group.

From around the middle of the sixteenth century (1532–55), the head monk of Shōgoin began to grant the status of *nengyōji* to important local Kumano *sendatsu*. In turn the *nengyōji* were given responsibility for organizing the local *yamabushi* of a certain area and the *sendatsu* who would guide patrons to Kumano and other sacred sites. They were also responsible for the distribution of charms and other religious activities. Shōgoin received a portion of the income from this activity. The area controlled by one of these *nengyōji* was called *kasumi* (territory for religious activity). Moreover, the local governor permitted Shōgoin to appoint the *nengyōji*, and guaranteed the activity of the *nengyōji* in the part of his *kasumi* that belonged to the domain.

Figure 6. Procession of *shugenja* leaving the gate of Shōgoin

This method of governing by Shōgoin is a different style from that of the Kumano *oshi*. The Kumano *oshi* stayed in Kumano and received offerings directly from their patrons who visited Kumano. Shōgoin, on the other hand, appointed Kumano *sendatsu* as *nengyōji* and guaranteed their control over the *yamabushi* and their right to conduct prayers and purification rites, as well as to guide their followers in their *kasumi* to sacred places. In turn Shōgoin received a part of the income that the *nengyōji* and *yamabushi* earned through these activities.[12]

In sum, the organization of Kumano Sanzan consisted of the relationship between the *oshi* and *sendatsu*/patrons. In contrast, the Shōgoin organization emphasized direct control of the *sendatsu* by the headquarters (Shōgoin), and did not include the patrons.

In the Edo period, the head of Shōgoin (the Kumano Sanzan *kengyō*) left the general management of the Kumano organization to the Nyaku Ōji (Kumano Sanzan *bugyō*) and the temple families directly related to Shōgoin. They controlled the 27 *sendatsu* (i.e., the religious rulers of the *kuni*), the *nengyōji* of *gun* (districts), the assistant *nengyōji* (*jun nengyōji*), and the subordinate *yamabushi* under the authority of Shōgoin. In this way the organization of Kumano Shugen that used to be based on a relationship between *oshi* and patrons eventually developed into the Honzanha, the centralized organization of *yamabushi*.[13]

Kumano Shugen exerted a great influence on Japanese folk religion. Especially significant are the stories about the origin of the Kumano deities as avatars of divine personalities from China and India. In Japan, there were traditionally twelve figures identified as the *kami* of mountains (*yama no kami*), and those stories gave character and content to the twelve deities and provided them with authority. With regard to organization, what is important is that the Honzanha that developed out of Kumano Shugen put down deep roots in local areas around Japan during the premodern era. It responded to the needs of the local villagers by providing religious festivals, prayers, rituals, and leaders for pilgrimages to sacred sites. In its organization of pilgrimages and ascents of sacred mountains, it took as its model the organization of *oshi*, *sendatsu*, and patrons that originated in Kumano. In addition, *shugenja* have had a great influence on Japanese folk religion through their participation in village rituals, folk arts, annual observances, rites of passage, and prayers and incantations.

THE SHUGENDŌ OF MT. KINBU AND THE ORGANIZATION OF RELIGIOUS LEADERS
OF TŌZAN SHŌDAISENDATSUSHŪ

Another important Shugendō center comparable to Kumano is Mt. Kinbu in the Yoshino area. During the latter part of the seventh century, priests such as Shin'ei at Gangōji (temple) maintained ascetic practices at Yoshino Temple on the north side of the Yoshino river. These priests practiced the rituals of Kokūzō seeking to strengthen their memory. Kūkai (774–835), the founder of the Shingon sect who opened Mt. Kōya, also practiced the Kokūzō Gumonji rituals at Mt. Kinbu. Also, Saichō (785–822), who founded the Tendai sect at Mt. Hiei, practiced mountain asceticism. After that, Shōbō (832–909), a Shingon monk, provided a ferry boat at Yoshino river and built a temple at Mt. Yoshino, and then established an ascetic practice site at the summit of Mt. Sanjō. Recently the archaeological remains of this religious practice were excavated at the Ōmine temple of Mt. Sanjō.[14]

In the tenth century, the area from Yoshino to Mt. Sanjō came to be called Mt. Kinbu, and Mt. Kinbu Temple was established. Then Kongō Zaō Gongen was worshipped at three Zaō temples that were built at Mt. Yoshino, Aone Peak, and Mt. Sanjō. In 1052 (the seventh year of Eishō) as the time of the end of the world (*mappō*) drew near, Mt. Kinbu was considered as the place where Miroku would descend to this world in order to rescue the Japanese people.[15] Many aristocrats, such as Fujiwara Michinaga, climbed Mt. Kinbu and created *kyōzuka* (sutra mounds) where sutras were buried as offerings to Miroku. The temple organization of Mt. Kinbu was managed by the *kengyō* (head priest) who oversaw the temple affairs. From the twelfth century, this position of *kengyō* was held by the monk of the temple Kōfukuji who controlled the entire Yamato area. But the *kengyō* usually lived at Kōfukuji; therefore, the position of *shikkō* (administrator), who was chosen from among the Yoshino monks, managed the religious affairs of the Kinbu temples. From the latter half of the thirteenth century, the position of Ichijōin *monzeki* of Kōfukuji took over the duties of the Mt. Kinbu *kengyō*, and the positions of *shikkō* took over the affairs of the two temples Yoshimizuin and Imakumanoin at Mt. Yoshino. The temple organization of Mt. Kinbu consisted of the *jisō* (scholars) of the Tendai sect and the *mandō* (regular monks) of the Shingon sect. The *jisō* group took charge of business affairs, Buddhist services, and studies. The *mandō* group took charge of daily maintenance and management of the halls, and also observances at Zaō Temple on Mt. Sanjō. This *mandō* group is considered as Yoshino Shugendō. The temple organization of Mt. Kinbu possessed great military power in order to protect its properties and rights. In the fourteenth century Emperor Go-Daigo depended on its power when founding the southern court at Yoshino.

In the Edo period, Mt. Kinbu Temple belonged to Rinnōji *monzeki* of Nikkō and Tōeizan, and the high priest of Tōeizan or Hieizan was appointed as *gakutō* (head priest) of Mt. Kinbu Temple. However, the *gakutō* stayed at his own temple. So the management of Mt. Kinbu Temple was handled by the *gakutō dai* (the proxy of *gakutō*). This position was passed down within Yoshimizuin. The Mt. Kinbu Temple officials consisted of the *jisō*, *mandō*, and *shasō* (shrine priests) who managed Komori Shrine, Katte Shrine, and Kinbu Shrine. Sakuramotobō and Chikurinin, which were main temples of the *mandō* group, took an active part in Yoshino Shugendō. Each temple on Mt. Yoshino also had its own traveling priests, who were called *kidan*, throughout Kinki District. These temples offered lodging to *kidan* in summer, and in winter the *kidan* traveled around the area where they lived, to distribute talismans.[16]

From the middle of the Heian period (794–1160) to the end of the Muromachi period (1336–1573), many temples of the Yamato area were under the influence of Kōfukuji. At these temples, in the same manner as Mt. Kinbu Temple, there were *jisō* or *gakuryo* (scholar monks) and *doshū* (regular monks); most of the latter were *shugenja*. These *shugenja* who were also Kumano *sendatsu* walked the Ōmine ridge from Yoshino to Kumano, and then visited Kumano Gongen (avatar). They also solicited money for their temples. Gradually, the *shugenja* who belonged to such temples formed a group called Tōzan Shōdaisendatsushū, and they worshipped the legendary founder Shōbō (872–909), who had reopened the austerities of Mt. Ōmine. They entered Mt. Ōmine twice a year, i.e., *hanaku no mine* (flower offering peak) in summer, and the reverse peak (pilgrimage from Yoshino to Kumano) in fall. In both instances, they assembled at Ozasa, deep within Mt. Sanjō, and decided on the promotion of their subordinates and other important matters. In the sixteenth century, the membership of Tōzan Shōdaisendatsushū was about thirty-six temples, so they were known as the Tōzan Sanjūroku (thirty-six) Shōdaisendatsushū. The distribution of the main temples of these Tōzan Shōdaisendatsushū was as follows:

1. Yoshino: Sakuramotobō, which was the main temple of the *mandō* group, and became the basic temple for entering the peak by Tōzan Shōdaisendatsushū.
2. The mountain range from Mt. Kasagi, passing through the eastern hills of Nara to Hasedera. In this area are the temples Kaijusanji, Bodaisan Shoryakuji, Reizanji, Miwasan Byōdōji, Uchiyama Eikyūji, and Hasedera.
3. Ikoma Mountain range and surrounding area of Hōryūji, Matsuoji, Senkōji, and Shigisan.
4. Katsuragi Mountain range and the surrounding area of the temples of Kishōsōji, Negoroji, and Kōyasan.
5. The remaining temples of Handōji: Umemotoin and Iwamotoin of Ōmi, and Segiji of Ise. Handōji expanded its power by controlling the monks and nuns of Kumano Shingū who collected donations. Segiji controlled the Isegata Shugen who paired with female shamans.

Figure 7. Traditional view of Ozasa

For this reason, these two temples, Handōji and Segiji, joined the Tōzan Shōdaisendatsushū, in spite of the great distance between them. The Tōzan Shōdaisendatsu traveled around the countryside and attracted apprentices from these regions. In these regions, the *kesagashira* (literally "head of surplices," a sub-leader) and *chōmoto* (his subordinate officials) who were appointed by Tōzan Shōdaisendatsu controlled the apprentices. This management style was called *kesasuji* management. Each member of Tōzan Shōdaisendatsushū entered the Ōmine peak with their fellow practitioners of austerities, which was called *kesashita*. The ranks of Tōzan Shōdaisendatsushū were conferred according to the number of times a practitioner had entered Mt. Ōmine. After passing through the lower ranks and *ni no shuku* (second level), he arrived at *ōshuku*, the highest rank. These two ranks of practitioners (*ōshuku* and *ni no shuku*) gave the *buninjō* (certificate of rank) with their signature to the apprentice of each Tōzan Daisendatsu *kesashita*, who gave the *buninjō* to his apprentice.[17] In the sixteenth century, many *shugenja* entered the peaks of Mt. Kinbu and Mt. Ōmine. Therefore the doctrine and ritual of Shugendō was well established. Of greatest importance was Sokuden, who practiced at Mt. Nikkō, Mt. Ōmine, and Mt. Hiko and wrote *Shugen shūyō hiketsushū, Sanbusosho hōsoku mikki*. These are the most influential books of Shugendō. Local Shugendō mountains such as Mt. Haguro in Tōhoku, Mt. Nikkō in Kantō, and Mt. Hiko in Kyushu came to be established, and many *shugenja* practiced mountain austerities in these mountains.

Shugendō in the Edo Period (1603–1868)—the Honzan Sect and the Tōzan Sect

In the latter half of the sixteenth century, the Shōgoin *monzeki*, who was head of the Honzan sect, and the Kumano Sanzan *kengyō* were authorized to control their respective religious territory (*kasumi*) and maintained their activities with the support of Nyaku Ōji Jōjōin of Kumano Sanzan *bugyō*. As a result, there were frequent conflicts with the Tōzan Shōdaisendatsu who directly controlled apprentices throughout Japan. The Tōzan Shōdaisendatsushū could not sustain their organization through their own management, because the Shōgoin *monzeki* had strong secular power. Therefore they belonged to the Sanbōin *monzeki* that was established by their legendary founder Shōbō and tried to oppose the Honzan sect. The Edo shogunate tried to offset the Tōzan sect with the Honzan sect, in order to control the power of the latter. So the Edo shogunate supported the argument of the Tōzan sect. Then they handed down the Shugendō Hatto (the law of Shugendō) in 1613 (the eighteenth year of Keichō). By this law the Edo shogunate officially recognized two Shugen sects, the Honzan sect of Shōgoin, and the Tōzan sect of Daigo (Sanbōin); all *shugenja* in Japan were ordered to belong to either the Honzan or Tōzan sect. But Mt. Kinbu and Mt. Haguro belonged to Nikkō Rinnōji *monzeki* and Mt. Hiko became an independent sect.

The Honzan sect created the temple status of *inge*, such as the Kyoto temples of Nyaku Ōji Jōjūin, Jūshin'in and Shakuzen'in, and Gayain in Harima, which constituted the central core of this sect. It also created *sendatsu* temples in main provinces, and temples such as Nengyōji and Junnengyōji (subordinates of Nengyōji) in almost every district, as a local office. They were given a prescribed area, their *kasumi*. And they officially recognized the control of subordinates and the distribution of talismans, and the right to guide pilgrims to sacred mountains. The *monzeki* of Daigo Sanbōin, which became the head temple of the Tōzan sect for the first time, entered Ōmine peak for religious practices, and he appointed his direct subordinates who were another line of the Tōzan Shōdaisendatsushū. At that time, they decreased in number to twelve temples and were called the Tōzan Jūni (twelve) Shōdaisendatsu. Daigo Sanbōin also insisted that Shōbō open the *e'in kanjō* (wisdom seed consecration rite) at Hōkaku Temple in Torisumi, Mt. Yoshino and establish the Tōzan sect. Then Sanbōin also established this Hōkaku Temple at Edo and Hamamatsu, where there were many Tōzan Shugen subordinates. The head priest of Edo Hōkaku Temple held the office of head priest of Torisumi and Hamamatsu Hōkaku temples as an additional office and appointed the Shokokusōkesagashira (the head of the subordinates all over the country). In the seventeenth century, the Edo shogunate created the position of *furegashira*, which was in charge of messengers between the *jisha bugyō* (a magistrate of temples and shrines) and the head temple of each sect. Responding to this policy, Sanbōin appointed the Edo Hōkakuji as this *furegashira*, in addition to the position of Shokokusōkesagashira. The Honzan sect appointed Hikawa Daijoin, who was the administrator of Hikawa Shrine at Edo, to be the *furegashira* of Honzan sect.[18]

The *shugenja* who belonged to the Honzan sect, the Tōzan sect, Mt. Haguro, Mt. Hiko, and Mt. Kinbu were all settled in their local communities. They managed local shrines, practiced exorcism, and served as guides to sacred mountains. Generally they are called *sato shugen* (village *shugen*). From the latter half of the seventeenth century, many of the Japanese populace visited sacred mountains. At this time, *fuji-kō* (religious fraternities of Mt. Fuji) and *kisoontake-kō* (religious fraternities of Ontake) were formed. At the three mountains of Dewa, and at Mt. Nikkō, Mt. Tateyama, Mt. Hakusan, Mt. Ōmine, Mt. Ishizuchi, and Mt. Hiko, many religious fraternities of lay people appeared. The *oshi* (religious guide) of these sacred mountains received the members of the religious fraternities who arrived at their temple under the guidance of *sendatsu*, and after praying for them, guided them in their ascent of the mountain. In the eighteenth century, Nakayama Miki (1798–1887), who was possessed while serving as a medium for a *shugenja* of the Tōzan sect, later founded Tenrikyō; Akazawa Bunji (1814–83), who was a *shugenja* of Mt. Ishizuchi, founded Konkōkyō.

THE SHUGENDŌ OF THE MODERN PERIOD

In 1868 (the first year of Meiji), the Meiji government officially announced the separation of Shinto and Buddhism. Through this policy, the government prohibited the worship of *gongen* (avatars), which signified that a Japanese deity was the incarnation of a Buddha or bodhisattva. Also prohibited was the management of shrines by *shasō* (shrine monks) and *shugenja*. Shugendō, the typical syncretic religion of Shinto and Buddhism, was abolished by the government in 1872 (the fifth year of Meiji). The Honzan sect, the Tōzan sect, and the Shugen of other sacred mountains were ordered to become a part of either the Tendai or the Shingon sect; this was determined by the group as described by their head temples. As a result, the Honzan sect, Mt. Kinbu Temple of Yoshino, and Haguro Shugen came to join the Tendai sect, and the Tōzan sect joined the Shingon sect. However, Haguro Gongen, Kumano Gongen, and Hikosan Gongen changed to Shinto shrines, and many of the village Shugen became Shinto priests or farmers.

In the twentieth century, pilgrimages to sacred mountains such as Mt. Ōmine (Mt. Sanjō), the three mountains of Dewa, Mt. Hakusan, Mt. Tateyama, and Mt. Fuji all increased; in particular, many *kō* (religious fraternities) of the Kansai District visited Mt. Sanjō. Therefore, Shōgoin and Sanbōin, which had been the head temples of the Honzan sects and the Tōzan sects, tried to control these *kō* and to strengthen the foundation of their religious order. *Fuji-kō* were recognized officially as Fusōkyō and Jikkōkyō, *kisoontake-kō* as Ontakekyō. But after these official acts of recognition, the creation of Shugen-type new religions was not permitted. Therefore, ascetics who acquired religious experiences in mountain austerities were forced to belong to the established religious organizations in order to legitimate their activities.

At the end of World War II, the Religious Corporation Ordinance was enacted. Under this law, the establishment of a religious organization was permitted through notification of the government. This enabled many of the Shugendō sects to become independent, such as Shugenshū (now

Figure 8. Zaōdō

called Honzan Shugenshū) centered at Shōgoin as the head temple, Shin-gonshū Daigoha, which is centered at Daigo Sanbōin as the head temple, Kinbusen Shugen Honshū of Mt. Yoshino, and Hagurosan Shugen Honshū. Moreover Dewa Sanzan Shrine and Ishizuchi Shrine had many *kō* and prac-ticed mountain austerities similar to Shugendō. The Shugen-type new re-ligions such as Gedatsukai and Shinnyoen, which belonged to Shingonshū Daigoha during World War II, became independent and flourished.[19]

NOTES

1. For a more complete treatment of Japanese folk religion, see part 2.
2. *Shugenja* will be treated herein as a Japanese term that can be either singular or plural.
3. Tamura Yoshirō, *Kamakura shinbukkyō shisō no kenkyū* (A study of the thought of Kamakura new Buddhism) (Kyoto: Heirakuji Shoten, 1965).
4. Shugen is an abbreviation for Shugendō (and occasionally for the members of Shugendō known as *shugenja* or *yamabushi*).
5. Takatori Masao, *Shintō no seiritsu* (The establishment of Shinto) (Tokyo: Heibonsha, 1979).
6. For Kumano and Kumano Shugen, see Miyake Hitoshi, *Kumano Shugen*, Nihon Rekishi Sōsho 48 (Tokyo: Yoshikawa Kōbunkan, 1992).
7. For Kinbusen and Kinbu Shugen, see Shutō Yoshiki, *Kinbusen* (Yoshino: Kinbusenji, 1985).
8. *Chōkan no kanmon*, no. 463 in *Zatsunobu*, Gunsho Ruijū 26 (Tokyo: Gunsho Ruijū Kankōkai, 1952), 242–43.
9. Entry for Tennin 2 (1109) Oct. 26, *Shiryō taisei*, vol. 10, ed. Sasagawa Taneo and Yano Tarō (Tokyo: Naigai Shoseki, 1934).
10. For Kumano Shugen, see Miyake, *Kumano Shugen*.
11. Dōkō, *Kaikokuzaki*, no. 337 in *Kikōbu*, Gunsho Ruijū 18 (Tokyo: Gunsho Ruijū Kankōkai, 1977).
12. Miyake, *Kumano Shugen*, 293–302.
13. Miyake Hitoshi, *Shugendō soshiki no kenkyū* (A study of the organization of Shugendō) (Tokyo: Shunjūsha, 1999), 543–59.
14. Naraken Kyōiku Iinkai Bunkazai Hozonjimusho, ed., *Ōminesanji: hondō shūrikōji hōkokusho* (Report on the repairing of Ōmine Main Temple) (Nara: Naraken Kyōiku Iinkai, 1986).
15. Miyake, *Shugendō soshiki*, 172.
16. Shutō, *Kinbusen*.
17. See Suzuki Shōei, "Shugendō tōzanha no kyōdan soshiki to nyūbu" (The organization of the Tōzan sect and its mountain authorities), in *Yoshino Kumano shinkō no kenkyū* (Studies of Yoshino and Kumano belief), ed. Gorai Shigeru, Sangaku Shūkyōshi Kenkyū Sōsho 4 (Tokyo: Meichō Shuppan, 1975).
18. See Takano Toshihiko, *Kinsei Nihon no kokka kenryoku to shūkyō* (The national power of modern Japan and religion) (Tokyo: Tōkyō Daigaku Shuppankai, 1988), 124–212.
19. Miyake, *Shugendō soshiki*, 1076–98.

Kumano Gongen: The Idea of Deity in Shugendō

Kumano Sanzan (the three shrines of Kumano), consisting of Hongū, Shingū, and Nachi Shrines in the southern part of Kii Peninsula, had numerous worshippers from the end of the Heian period through the Middle Ages, ranking with Ise as one of Japan's most sacred shrines.

In the twelfth century, Shugendō prospered with Mt. Kinbu in Yoshino as its center, and it came to influence the worship of Kumano. Kumano became the headquarters of the ascetics who were called *yamabushi* or *shugenja*. In their ascetic practices in the mountains, they often carried small images of *dōji* (a child deity) or *ōji* (a prince deity) as their guardian deities, or sometimes they enshrined these images at the roadside. Actually, a similar prince deity, known as Komori, is enshrined at Yoshino, and the Ōmine Hachidai Kongō Dōji (the eight great Kongō child deity) is enshrined at Mt. Ōmine. These deities seem to have influenced the pattern of the Kumano pantheon.

Soon so many pilgrims came in procession to visit Kumano that there arose a saying, "*ari no Kumano mōde*" (pilgrims to Kumano are like a procession of ants). In effect, Kumano became as important a shrine as Ise Shrine. Accordingly, there were some attempts to reconcile the two sacred places. Some noticed the correspondence of the deities of Kumano with those of Ise. Some also saw the shrines of Kumano in the same light as those of Ise: Kumano's Hongū with Ise's Naikū; Shingū with Gekū; and Nachi with Aramatsuri no Miya. And some even went so far as to insist that the deities of Kumano were identical with those of Ise.[1] Kumano *shugenja* not only claimed that the twelve deities of Kumano were the manifestations of the Buddhist deities, but they also took the additional step of inventing their peculiar myth that Ketsumiko no Kami was an alien god, Jihi Daiken Ō of Makada (Skt. Magadha) Kingdom in India who had traveled to Japan. Some thought that, in accordance with esoteric Buddhist doctrine, Kumano was the *taizōkai* (womb store world) and Mt. Kinbu was the *kongōkai* (diamond world), and therefore that the twelve deities of Kumano were the manifestations of the *taizōkai* deities. Others thought that, in accordance with the doctrine of the Tendai sect, the three shrines of Kumano corresponded with the three aspects of Buddha, that is, *hosshin, hōshin*, and *ōjin*.[2]

Thus the study of the twelve manifestations of Kumano involves various problems: native deities and foreign deities, the cult of manifestations of deities, *dōji* worship, and explanations of the deities through mythology or Buddhist doctrines. Because Kumano and Ise were worshipped most widely and ardently by the Japanese, the study of these Kumano deities will throw considerable light on Japanese notions of deity. In fact, various studies have been made from the earliest times about the deities, history, and legends of the twelve manifestations of Kumano. But there have been very few studies about the worship of Kumano by *shugenja* (mountain ascetics), who contributed greatly to the development and prosperity of Kumano.[3] Therefore, in this chapter I take up Shugendō documents as the basic data for interpreting the framework of the deities, legends, rituals, and images of the Kumano Jūnisha Gongen.

DEITIES OF THE KUMANO JŪNISHA GONGEN

In the Middle Ages the character of the twelve deities of Kumano, according to the work *Shugen shinanshō* (written by a *shugenja* of the Kumano lineage, and read widely in the fourteenth century), was as follows.[4]

Ketsumiko no Kami was the chief god of Hongū and the manifestation of Amida; he was also called Shōjōden ("shrine to prove the truth") because he showed people the truth of divine salvation through praying to Amida. His appearance was that of a Buddhist priest, made manifest in Bodaisenna (Baramon Sōjō, 704–60), who came from India to Japan. His function was to eliminate poverty and bring wealth. Musubi no Kami was the chief goddess of Nachi and thought to be another name for Izanami no Mikoto and also was called Nishi no Goze (west shrine) because she was enshrined to the west of Shōjōden. Her appearance was that of a woman, and she was thought to be the manifestation of Senju Kannon (Thousand-armed Avalokiteśvara) and made manifest in Kūkai. Her function was to drive out demons and to overcome heretics. Hayatama no Kami, the chief god of Shingū, was thought to be another name for Izanagi no Mikoto and also was called Naka no Goze (middle shrine) because his shrine was between Shōjōden and Nishi no Goze. His appearance was that of a layman and was thought to be the manifestation of Yakushi Nyorai and made manifest in Saichō. His function was to cure illness and prolong life. These three deities were called Sansho Gongen (manifestations of three places). Musubi no Kami and Hayatama no Kami were called Ryōsho Gongen (manifestations of two places).

Next we take up Gosho Ōji (the five children shrines): (1) Wakamiya Nyoichi Ōji, (2) Zenji no Miya, (3) Hijiri no Miya, (4) Chigo no Miya, and (5) Komori no Miya. Wakamiya Nyoichi Ōji had the appearance of a woman and also was called Wakadono. She was a daughter of Ryōsho Gongen (who represented Izanami no Mikoto and Izanagi no Mikoto, and so by some was thought to be Amaterasu Ōmikami). She was thought to be the manifestation of Jūichimen Kannon (Eleven-headed Avalokiteśvara) and was made manifest in the priest Enchin (814–91), the founder of the temple, Onjōji, which controlled Kumano Shugendō. It was said that this shrine was the earliest "child-shrine" of the Sansho Gongen. Zenji no Miya had the appearance of a Buddhist priest and was thought to be the manifestation of Jizō; he was made manifest in the priest Genshin (942–1017), who was a pioneer of the Jōdo (Pure Land) school at Mt. Hiei. Hijiri no Miya had the appearance of a Buddhist priest and was thought to be the manifestation of Ryūju (Nāgārjuna); he was made manifest in Senkan (?–983), who studied at Onjōji and later retired to Mt. Minoo. Chigo no Miya had the appearance of a boy and was thought to be the manifestation of Nyoirin Kannon. Komori no Miya had the appearance of a woman and was thought to be the manifestation of Shō Kannon. The two deities Chigo no Miya and Komori no Miya were made manifest in Zōmyō (843–927), a disciple of the priest Enchin who became the chief abbot of Onjōji.

Next we consider the Shisho Myōjin (four subordinate shrines): (1) Ichiman and Jūman, (2) Kanjō Jūgosho, (3) Hikō Yasha, and (4) Meiji Kongō. Ichiman had the appearance of a layman and was thought to be the manifestation of Fugen Bosatsu. Jūman also had the appearance of a layman and was thought to be the manifestation or reincarnation of Monju. These two deities were made manifest in the priest Ennin (784–864) and thought to be a pair. Kanjō Jūgosho had the appearance of a layman and was thought to be the manifestation of Shaka Nyorai (Buddha); he was made manifest in Bodaisenna (Baramon Sōjō).

As will be mentioned later, this deity was the deified form of Gaken, who was a retainer of Jihi Daiken Ō who flew from India to Japan to become Shōjōden. Hikō Yasha and Meiji Kongō both appeared as Yasha (Skt. Yakṣa) and were made manifest in the priest Enchin; the former was thought to be the manifestation of Fudō Myōō and the latter of Bishamonten.

Shugen shinanshō tells us nothing about the functions of Gosho Ōji and Shisho Myōjin, but the work *Kinbusen himitsuden* gives us the following information about their functions.[5] The first of the Gosho Ōji, Wakamiya

Nyoichi Ōji, removed people's pain; Zenji no Miya saved the people who were enmeshed in vices. Hijiri no Miya revealed the light of wisdom of *bosatsu* (bodhisattva), and Chigo no Miya comforted people, while Komori no Miya reverently loved people.

This work *Kinbusen himitsuden* also provides some information about Shisho Myōjin. Ichiman expelled people's delusions, and Jūman led people to the world of peace. Kanjō Jūgosho delivered people from the dirty world, and Hikō Yasha flying in the sky sought to conquer devils. Meiji Kongō bestowed good fortune on people.

In *Shugen shinanshō*, in addition to the twelve deities of Kumano, other deities worshipped by *shugenja* at Hongū, Shingū, and Nachi are also described. At Hongū, Shūkongōjin was enshrined in Raiden (the ritual hall) where *shugenja* performed their rituals. Shūkongōjin was said to be an earlier manifestation of Kongō Zaō Gongen, the chief deity of Mt. Kinbu and was also thought to be the manifestation of Hachiji Monju (Eight-letter Monjushiri); he was made manifest in the priest Enchin. The deity at Yunomine near Hongū was thought to be the manifestation of Kokūzō and was made manifest in Bodaisenna. At Shingū information was given concerning three deities: Asuka Shrine located at the old site of the Kumano divine village, Kannokura, where *shugenja* performed ascetic practices, and Manzan Gohō who protected the entire area of the Shingū Shrine. Asuka Shrine was thought to be the manifestation of Daiitoku Myōō and was made manifest in the priest Ennin. Kannokura was thought to be the manifestation of Aizen Myōō and was made manifest in Saichō. Manzan Gohō was thought to be the manifestation of Miroku and was made manifest in the priest Ennin. Hirō Gongen, the deification of the Nachi waterfall, was thought to be the manifestation of Senju Kannon and was embodied by Ragyō Shōnin, who drifted ashore at Shingū.

In considering the deities of Kumano we must not neglect the *ōji* enshrined along the routes of the Kumano pilgrimage. According to the "Diary of Visiting Kumano" ascribed to En no Ozunu in the book *Shozan engi* (written at the end of the twelfth century), *ōji* were enshrined at some important locations to protect pilgrims—and were also called *dōji*.[6] The places where *ōji* or *dōji* were enshrined were either defiled or haunted by evil deities, so people passing there were told to hold purification ceremonies or to perform rituals for the enshrined deity. It is noteworthy that among the priests who first enshrined these *ōji* are some foreign priests, such as Fukuryō of the T'ang dynasty of China, who enshrined Hosshinmon Ōji, and Ekan (ca. 645) of Kokuryo (Korea), who enshrined Yukawa Ōji. In the book *Ryōbu mondō hishō*, written about the fifteenth century, it is recorded that *ōji* were the attending deities who protected the pilgrims traveling to Kumano by accompanying them. For example, Isonokami Ōji is dedicated to Shinra Myōjin (the manifestation of Monju Bosatsu), who attended the priest Enchin on his visit to Kumano.[7]

About the twelfth century there were only a few *ōji* shrines,[8] among them the following: at Fujishiro (Daihishin Ōji as the manifestation of Senju Kannon), at Kirume (Kongō Dōji as the manifestation of Jūichimen Kannon), at Inabane (Inari as the manifestation of Nyoirin Kannon), at Takijiri (Kōtei Dōji as the manifestation of Fukūkensaku Kannon), and at Hosshinmon (Kongō Dōji as the manifestation of Daibyakushin Bosatsu). But by the beginning of the thirteenth century nearly one hundred *ōji* were enshrined on the route from Osaka to Kumano; they were referred to generally as the "Tsukumo *ōji*." And it was generally thought that the enshrined deities of these *ōji* were the deities of Ichiman and Jūman in the set of Shisho Myōjin.[9]

Finally, we should survey the mutual relations among all these deities. In the early stages, we find the theme of "mother and child deities" in the native tree deity, i.e., Ketsumiko no Kami, and his mother Musubi no Kami. We also find interaction between these native deities and foreign deities like Hayatama no Kami. The "mother and child" theme can also apply to the group consisting of Musubi no Kami as mother, and Wakamiya Nyoichi and Komori as daughters, and Chigo no Miya as son.[10] It is also noteworthy that in this group the mother and children were all thought to be the manifestation of Kannon, and that all were made manifest in Enchin and his disciple Zōmyō (except for Musubi no Kami who was made manifest in Kūkai).

Shōjōden was thought to be the manifestation of Amida, and Taki no Miya of Nachi was thought to be the manifestation of Kannon. Shōjōden was made manifest in Bodaisenna, while Taki no Miya of Nachi was made manifest in Ragyō Shōnin—both were made manifest in priests from abroad. This may be connected to faith in Amida's otherworldly paradise, and faith in Kannon's Elysium beyond the sea (known as Fudaraku). We also notice that Zenji no Miya (as the manifestation of Jizō) was made manifest in Genshin, who was the advocate of faith in Amida's paradise. But foreign priests were connected not only with the faith of otherworlds. Kanjō Jūgosho was the deification of Gaken, who came from India and was thought to be the manifestation of Shaka (Buddha); Kanjō Jūgosho was made manifest in Bodaisenna. Moreover, the two attendant deities of Buddha, Fugen (whose manifestation was Ichiman), and Monju (whose manifestation was Jūman), were both made manifest in the priest Ennin who visited the T'ang Dynasty of China. Ryūju (Nāgārjuna), the originator of esoteric Buddhism, whose manifestation was Hijiri no Miya, was also

Table 1 Kumano Jūnisha Gongen and Related Deities

	Name of deity/manifestation	Original Buddha deity	Manifested as	Style	Function	Remarks
1	Ketsumiko/Kunitokotachi	Amida Nyorai	Bodaisenna	Buddhist priest	bring wealth	Shōjōden (Hongū); Sansho Gongen
2	Hayatama/Izanagi	Yakushi Nyorai	Saichō (Tendai)	layman	cure illness	Naka no Goze (Shingū); Ryōsho Gongen
3	Musubi/Izanami	Senju Kannon	Kūkai (Shingon)	woman	drive out demons	Nishi no Goze (Nachi); Ryōsho Gongen
4	Wakamiya/Amaterasu	Jūichimen Kannon	Enchin (Tendai)	woman	remove pain	Wakadono; Nyaku Ōji; Gosho Ōji
5	Zenji no Miya	Jizō Bosatsu	Genshin (Tendai)	Buddhist priest	save from vices	Gosho Ōji
6	Hijiri no Miya	Ryūju (Nāgārjuna)	Senkan (Tendai)	Buddhist priest	give wisdom	Gosho Ōji
7	Chigo no Miya	Nyoirin Kannon	Zōmyō (Tendai)	boy	comfort	Gosho Ōji
8	Komori no Miya	Shō Kannon	Zōmyō (Tendai)	woman	love people	Gosho Ōji
9–1	Ichiman	Fugen Bosatsu	Ennin (Tendai)	layman	expell delusion	pair; Shisho Myōjin
9–2	Jūman	Monju Bosatsu	Ennin (Tendai)	layman	give peace	pair; Shisho Myōjin
10	Kanjō Jūgosho/Gaken	Shaka Nyorai	Bodaisenna	layman	deliver from dirty world	Shisho Myōjin
11	Hikō Yasha	Fudō Myōō	Enchin (Tendai)	Yasha	conquer devils	Shisho Myōjin
12	Meiji Kongō	Bishamonten	Enchin (Tendai)	Yasha	bestow good fortune	Shisho Myōjin
13	Hirō Gongen/Taki no Miya	Senju Kannon	Ragyō Shōnin	layman		Taki no Miya of Nachi
14	Shūkongōjin	Hachiji Monju /Miroku	Enchin (Tendai)	Yasha		Raiden (Hongū)
15	Yunomine Deity	Kokūzō Bosatsu	Bodaisenna	layman		Hongū
16	Asuka Gongen	Daiitoku Myōō	Ennin (Tendai)	layman		Shingū
17	Kannokura Gongen	Aizen Myōō	Saichō (Tendai)	layman		Shingū
18	Manzan Gohō	Miroku Bosatsu	Ennin (Tendai)	layman		Shingū

Figure 9. The images of Kumano Jūnisha Gongen. Numbers correspond to table 1. A. En no Gyōja (legendary founder of Shugen), B. Daiikoku, C. Lion.

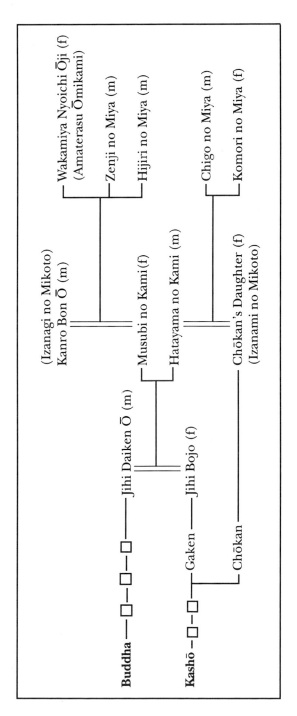

Figure 10. The lineage of Kumano Jūnisha Gongen

a priest from India. And just as Hayatama no Kami who drifted ashore was the manifestation of Yakushi Nyorai, so the deity of Yunomine (where people cured their illnesses by bathing in the hot spring) was made manifest in Bodaisenna.

All of these deities—Hikō Yasha (the manifestation of Fudō Myōō), Meiji Kongō (the manifestation of Bishamonten), Shūkongōjin (the manifestation of Hachiji Monju or Miroku), and Manzan Gohō (the manifestation of Miroku)—were directly connected with Shugendō, and they were all made manifest in the ascetic priest Enchin, who founded Onjōji (which controlled Kumano Shugendō). Among these deities, Shūkongōjin had a close relation with Kongō Zaō Gongen in Kinbu, and Manzan Gohō was also enshrined in Kinbu. This may show that Kumano and Kinbu had a close connection. Daiitoku Myōō (whose manifestation is Asuka Shrine) and Aizen Myōō (whose manifestation was Kannokura Gongen), were also deities related to Shugendō. The faith of the attending deities in the worship of ōji was also based on Shugendō.

Thus, the twelve deities of Kumano, with the contrasting pattern of native deities and foreign deities at the center, consisted of native deities of mother and son, the foreign deities of Amida and Fudaraku Kannon, and Shugendō deities who overcame demons and protected the faith by harmonizing native and foreign deities. The functions of these deities had the greatest variety, not only for assurance of the benefits in this world, such as an abundant harvest, wealth, success in life, avoiding disasters, and curing illnesses, but also in the benefits of faith in the future life. It was because Kumano deities had miraculous virtues both for this world and for the future life that Kumano attracted a great number of devotees.

TRADITIONS OF KUMANO GONGEN

In *Shugen shinanshō* we find the following story about the deities that are manifestations of Kumano Gongen. In the kingdom of Makada in middle India there lived a king named Jihi Daiken Ō and his vassal Gaken Chōja. Jihi Daiken Ō was the fifth descendant of Jōbon the Great, father of Buddha, and Gaken was the third descendant of Kashō, disciple of Buddha. Jihi Bojo, Jihi Daiken Ō's queen, was a daughter of Gaken. Gaken, by the order of Jihi Daiken Ō, went to study and train at Mt. Ryōju and Mt. Dantoku, both practice places of the Buddha. Later Jihi Daiken Ō flew to Japan to save the Japanese people and landed at Sonaezaki of Muro-gun in Kii Province, and at Yōshutsudake of Yoshino-gun in Yamato Province, becoming Kumano Gongen in Kii and becoming Zaō Gongen in Yamato. At that time Gaken, who came to Japan accompanying the king, went at once to Ise Shrine and respectfully informed Amaterasu Ōmikami that he was the messenger of Kumano and Zaō Gongen, who had flown from India, and that his master wanted to be allowed to stay at the places where he landed, to protect the king's laws and save the people.

Amaterasu Ōmikami answered that she herself was a fifth ancestor of Jihi Daiken Ō and that she would give him the sacred places of Muro-gun and Yoshino-gun, but because the head of the Japanese people was Emperor Jinmu, his permission was also needed. So Gaken went to Emperor Jinmu to ask for his permission. Thus the Jūnisha Gongen came to be enshrined at Muro-gun in Kii, and Zaō Gongen at Yoshino-gun in Yamato. And at that time Gaken became Kanjō Jūgosho, one of the twelve deities. Tradition relates that in the twelve hundred years after that event, it took Gaken seven existences in this world to complete his training at Mt. Ōmine, and that in his seventh existence he became En no Ozunu, founder of Shugendō.

Jihi Daiken Ō and his queen Jihi Bojo had a son and a daughter. The daughter was called Musubi no Kami, and the son Hayatama no Kami. Musubi no Kami married Kanro Bon Ō and gave birth to a daughter, Wakamiya Nyoichi Ōji, and two sons, Zenji no Miya and Hijiri no Miya. Hayatama no Kami married a daughter of Chōkan Chōja, Gaken's younger brother, and had a son, Chigo no Miya, and a daughter, Komori no Miya. A tradition tells that Kanro Bon Ō was Izanagi no Mikoto, his daughter Wakamiya Nyoichi Ōji was Amaterasu Ōmikami, and Chōkan Chōja's daughter was Izanami no Mikoto. Thus the deities of Gosho Ōji were all thought to be sons or daughters of Musubi no Kami and Hayatama no Kami, and also offspring of Izanagi no Mikoto and Izanami no Mikoto. (The foregoing lineage of Kumano Jūnisho Gongen is diagrammed in figure 10.) The deities of Shisho Myōjin can be regarded as the group of retainers guarding the family of Jihi Daiken Ō.

This tradition seems to have been well known to *shugenja* and is contained in the later works *Ryōbu mondō hishō* and *Kumanosan ryakki.*[11] *Kumano Gongen gosuijaku engi* (History of the Manifest Deities of Kumano), contained in the document *Chōkan no kanmon* written in the twelfth century, and *Kumano Gongen no koto*, contained in the book *Shintōshū* written in the fourteenth century—all tell us stories about Kumano Gongen flying to Japan. *Kumano Gongen gosuijaku engi* has the account that follows.

Prince Shin (son of Reio of the Chou Dynasty), a guardian deity of Mt. T'ien-t'ai in T'ang Dynasty, China, journeyed by way of Mt. Hiko in Kyushu, Mt. Ishizuchi in Shikoku, and the island of Awaji, landing at Shingū and later landing at Hongū in the form of three moons. Eight years later a hunter named Chiyosada, when he went deep into the mountains of Kumano following a wild boar, found the three moons hanging from a yew tree, and he enshrined them. This was the origin of the Kumano Sansho Gongen.[12]

The stories in *Shintōshū* give us the following scenario: First, it is written that En no Ozunu and Baramon Sōjō worshiped the deities that are manifestations of Kumano Gongen. Next comes the above mentioned story of Prince Shin, a guardian deity of Mt. T'ien-t'ai, flying to Japan to become Kumano Gongen. Then we find the story about King Zenzai of the kingdom of Makada in middle India, who repents the murder of his beloved court lady Gosuiden (having been deceived by other consorts' slander), and flew to Japan with the prince born by Gosuiden, and the priest Kiken Shōnin, who had saved the prince. And it is related that Kiken Shōnin became Shōjōden, King Zenzai became Naka no Goze, Lady Gosuiden became Nishi no Goze, and the prince became Wakamiya Nyakuichi Ōji, forming the pattern of Kumano Gongen. Thus this legend consists of the story of Lady Gosuiden, Prince Shin flying to Kumano, and the account of the hunter Chiyokane's inspired discovery of Kumano Gongen.[13] These stories seem to have been widely known. Many books in different forms were written, especially about the legends of the original deities of Kumano Gongen centered around the story of Gosuiden.[14]

In the books of Shugendō we also find stories of the origin of Kumano Sanzan. Some stories are the same as the above mentioned legends, while others take a different form. What follow are some of the chief accounts about Hongū, Shingū, and Nachi. To take up Hongū first, in *Enkun keiseiki* (Life of En no Gyōja) we read the story of the hunter Chiyokane going after a wild boar and finding the three moons hanging on a yew tree at Ōyu no Hara in Hongū, and then enshrining them. The *Ryōbu mondō hishō* recounts that Chiyosada made a *himorogi* (divine hedge) to enshrine the Sansho Gongen.[15] In *Shōbodaisan engi* it is recorded that when Chiyokane was staying in the mountain to serve the Kumano Sansho Gongen, an ascetic hearing the story from Chiyokane's wife went into the mountain to join him.[16]

For accounts of Shingū, we find in the above mentioned *Kumano Gongen gosuijaku engi* the story that Prince Shin flew to Kannokura and Asuka Shrine. There is also an account of the origin of Kannokura, a place of ascetic practices in *Kumano Gongen kongōzaō hōdenzōkō nikki*: the story relates that a hunter in pursuit of a big bear about one *jō* (three meters) tall went into the hills to the northwest of Shingū and found three mirrors, and that a foreign priest named Ragyō was there guarding the mirrors.[17] We find the following story about Ragyō in *Gyōja denki*. In the reign of Emperor Keikō (71–130), a storm forced seven fishermen ashore at Shingū, and six of them left and returned to their homes. The one who remained was Ragyō.[18] Accounts of Taki no Miya (Waterfall Shrine), the center of Nachi worship, are found in *Ryōbu mondō hishō*. Here it is told that in 243 when Ragyō was purifying himself by bathing in water at Nachi no Ura, Senju Kannon appeared and led him to the waterfall, and at this point Ragyō was inspired by a deity and built a small temple to worship Kannon: this is the origin of the Nachi Shrine.[19]

To this point we have introduced several traditions about the enshrine-ment of Kumano Gongen. We now wish to summarize these stories, focus-ing on the characters of the deities. The oldest story may be the one of the hunter Chiyosada led by a wild boar, and his finding the deities hanging on a yew tree and then enshrining them. This is the story about the hunter who through divine inspiration found the native god Ketsumiko no Kami who was a tree deity, and so can be considered a mountain deity. Such stories are also found at mountains such as Mt. Daisen in Hōki Province and Mt. Tateyama. But when Kumano came to be connected with foreign religions, its origin was sought outside Japan. So first there appeared the story of Prince Shin of Mt. T'ien-t'ai in China coming to Japan to become Kumano Gongen. Then came the story of Jihi Daiken Ō, who was closely related to the Buddha, and also the legend of the foreign priest Ragyō. These stories came to be merged with the sad story of Lady Gosuiden, which was based on the sutra *Sendaetsukokuōkyō*.[20] And even in these sto-ries there still remains the account of the hunter Chiyokane finding the deity. I think this shows that the old legend of a hunter's inspired discov-ery of the deity persisted and was widespread.

We also find some interesting points in the tales of the foreign origin of Kumano Gongen contained in *Shugen shinanshō*. One is that the kings and their vassals in India were thought to be the reincarnations of Bud-dha and his disciples. It was thought that Buddha was reborn as another person and that the person came to Japan to become a deity. Another interesting incident is that the deities coming from abroad went to seek the permission of Ise Shrine and Emperor Jinmu after they settled in Yoshino and Kumano. It seems to me that this may show the basic struc-ture of foreign deities trying to settle in Japan. It is also significant that the daughter and son of Jihi Daiken Ō coming from India married Izanagi no Mikoto and Izanami no Mikoto and had children; then they became prosperous through the service of their retainers attending them, and they all became the Kumano Jūnisha Gongen. We can conclude from this that the stories may show the necessary process by which foreign deities settle in Japan and come to be worshipped.

RITUALS OF KUMANO GONGEN

Some rituals performed during pilgrimage to Kumano, from the end of Heian times to the Middle Ages, clearly demonstrate the characteristics of Kumano deities—the main rituals are introduced here.[21] In those days pilgrims to Kumano first paid visits to the Fushimi Inari Shrine and each was given a *gohō* (guardian deity) to accompany them. The *gohō* attended the pilgrims and protected them. When they went back to Kyoto safely from Kumano, they again paid a visit to the Fushimi Inari Shrine and returned the *gohō*.[22] In *Shozan engi* we find a description of "the ceremonies of returning the *gohō*."[23] According to *Ryōbu mondō hishō*, the Fushimi Inari Shrine was dedicated to Chōkan Chōja, the younger brother of Gaken, who came to Kumano with Jihi Daiken Ō. The brothers pledged an oath to each other that the elder was to be at Kumano and protect Jihi Daiken Ō and the worshippers and that the younger was to be in Kyoto and protect the pilgrims traveling to Kumano. So the deity of Fushimi Inari Shrine kept his word and protected pilgrims by sending *gohō* to accompany them.[24]

Guided by leaders, the pilgrims made their way, requesting purification ceremonies at holy places and performing ablutions at the appointed locations. The holy places were sites haunted by demons or evil deities, and for this reason Kongō Dōji or ōji came to be enshrined there. As mentioned before, these *ōji* numbered about ninety-nine. Well known as places for ablution were seven rivers: Kinokawa, Ishidagawa, Ishikawa, Chikatsuyu, Yukawa, Otonashigawa, Kumanogawa, and two beaches, Minabe and Detachihama.[25] The Kumano Gongen whom they visited, after numerous purifications and ablutions, were thought to be deities of miraculous virtue, granting divine favors both in this life and in the next life.

The *Kumano Gongen kōshiki*, widely read among *shugenja* in the Edo period, was chanted before Kumano Gongen to honor the deities. In this sutra we find the following story of the origin of Kumano Gongen. The Kumano Gongen first arrived from India at Muro-gun in Kii and resided there in the form of moon disks. Kumano Gongen then attracted hunters to them by changing into boars, bears, or crows, so as to make their presence known to people. The sutra tells about the deities, manifestations of the twelve shrines, and their miraculous deeds. These deeds are almost the same as those described in the above mentioned *Ryōbu mondō hishō*. Toward the end of the work it is written that those who make pilgrimages to Kumano Gongen will be able to attain *bodai* (supreme enlightenment). Then prayers were offered to the Sansho Gongen, *ōji*, *kenzoku* (a retinue of deities), and Manzan Gohō.[26] Here it is quite noteworthy that such deities as *ōji*, *kenzoku*, and *gohō* had very important roles. In passages of the *Heike monogatari* we read that when people wanted to ask a favor of the Kumano Gongen, entreaties were made to these *gongen* and Kongō Dōji.[27] In short, such deities as *dōji*, *ōji*, and *gohō* were prized as the mediators of people's wishes to the *gongen*.

The Kumano Gongen were well known as deities who not only gave favors in this life and in the next life, but also provided oracles. Even the book *Gotakusen kiroku* (Records of Kumano Oracles) survives. It is said that it was *dōji* or this kind of deity that provided oracles to worshippers. Here, too, we see the importance of *dōji* or *gohō* as the mediators of the deities' intentions. We can appreciate that the Kongō Dōji in Kumano were highly valued from the fact that, in the *Kongō Dōjihō* (an ascetic rite honoring Kongō Dōji) found in the temple Onjōji, directions are given to practice this asceticism at Kumano where there are a hundred thousand Kongō Dōji.[28] Reflecting on how the *gohō* accompanied the pilgrims, how *ōji* protected them en route, and how Kongō Dōji mediated the gods' and people's wishes at Kumano, we can conclude that in the rituals related to Kumano Shugendō, such deities as *ōji* and *dōji* were highly esteemed.

IMAGES OF THE KUMANO GONGEN

The arrangement of shrine buildings in each location of the Kumano Sanzan clearly displays characteristics of the three shrines and the mutual relations of the twelve deities to one another. The disposition of the main buildings of Kumano Sanzan at the end of the thirteenth century, which we can see in the *Ippen shōnin eden* (A Pictorial Biography of Saint Ippen),[29] is sketched in figure 11.

In figure 11 we see that at Hongū, in front of the gate are Shōjōden and Nyaku Ōji (Wakamiya), and at the left Musubi no Kami and Hayatama no Kami are enshrined together, across the corridor in front of the building called Raiden. On the right of Nyaku Ōji, there is a building dedicated to the four *ōji*, i.e., Zenji no Miya, Hijiri no Miya, Chigo no Miya, and Komori no Miya. To the right we find the Shisho Myōjin enshrined together.

At Shingū we see at the left Musubi no Kami, Hayatama no Kami, Shōjōden, and Nyaku Ōji enshrined separately. To the right of these buildings four *ōji* are enshrined together, and the Shisho Myōjin are enshrined together. In front of the Musubi and Hayatama Shrines is the Raiden. In front of Shōjōden there is a large "Nagi" tree (*Podocarpus nagi*), and in front of that is the gate. In addition, it is recorded that at Shingū there were two guardian shrines of Kannokura and Asuka, and the shrines of the deities of Onmyōdō near the main shrines. At Nachi, from the left we find Nyaku Ōji, Musubi no Kami, Hayatama no Kami, Shōjōden, and Taki

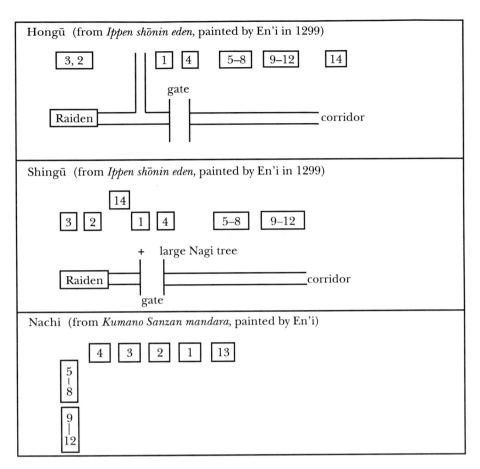

Figure 11. Schematic drawings of the main buildings of Kumano Sanzan: 1. Shōjōden, 2. Hayatama no Kami, 3. Musubi no Kami, 4. Nyaku Ōji, 5. Zenji no Miya, 6. Hijiri no Miya, 7. Chigo no Miya, 8. Komori no Miya, 9. Ichiman and Jūman, 10. Kanjō Jūgosho, 11. Hikō Yasha, 12. Meiji Kongō, 13. Taki no Miya, 14. Jinushi no Kami. Numbers correspond to table 1.

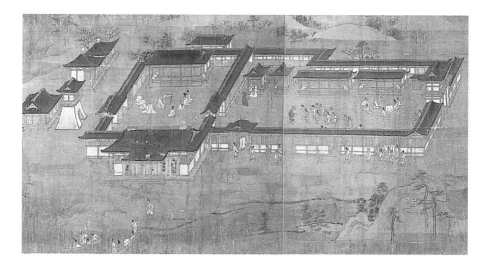

Figure 12. Hongū, from *Ippen shōnin eden*

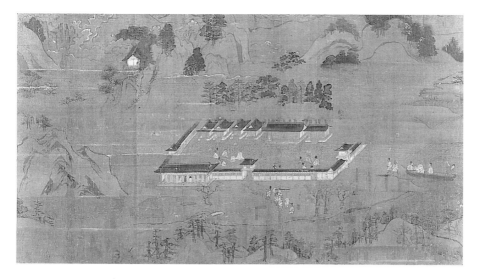

Figure 13. Shingū, from *Ippen shōnin eden*

Figure 14. Nachi, from *Ippen shōnin eden*

no Miya, each with its own shrine. To the left of these, at right angles there are two buildings for the four ōji and Shisho Myōjin enshrined therein. In addition, in the mountains of Nachi there are branch shrines of the main Kongō Dōji shrines built along the routes of Kumano pilgrimage.

In these schematized maps of shrines, what is most noteworthy is the position of Shōjōden and Nyaku Ōji at Hongū, of Musubi no Kami and Hayatama no Kami at Shingū, and of Nyaku Ōji and Taki no Miya at Nachi. Generally the Sansho Gongen are emphasized in all the shrines. It is also important to point out that Nyaku Ōji has a separate building apart from the other Gosho Ōji. This may be due to the greater popularity of Nyaku Ōji, thought to have more miraculous power than even the chief deities. But we can also consider that the emphasis on Nyaku Ōji may be due to the fact that, when the identification of Kumano with Ise was proposed, the correspondence of Shōjōden with Kunitokotachi no Kami, Hayatama no Kami with Izanagi no Kami, Musubi no Kami with Izanami no Kami, and Nyaku Ōji with Amaterasu Ōmikami had been established. Therefore the latter three shrines were venerated much more than other deities because of their close association with Ise's central deities.

The various forms of Kumano mandala, which picture either the manifested or manifesting deities, or deities within the shrine buildings, are quite interesting, for by looking at them we can recognize the mutual relations among the Kumano deities and also the general religious notions behind them.[30]

The oldest Kumano mandala is said to have been painted in the second year of Kenpō (1214) on the order of the Retired Emperor Go-Toba, in the form of the manifested deities of Kumano Sanzan, and was worshipped as an alternative to making the actual pilgrimage to Kumano. This form of the mandala came to flourish gradually from the fourteenth century onward. Afterwards the Kumano *shugenja* and *bikuni* nuns came to carry copies of this mandala to show to followers in order to spread their message and gather contributions. There were various kinds of mandala: a portrait of the twelve deities; a picture of the twelve manifesting deities (*suijaku mandara*); a picture of the manifested and manifesting deities (*honjaku mandara*); a landscape picture of the view of the shrine buildings (*miya mandara*); and other images. The manner of painting was almost the same. At the center of the *Kumano honji mandara* are the Sansho Gongen and Gosho Ōji; Kanjō Jūgosho of the Shisho Myōjin is also part of the arrangement in the central circle (similar to the Chūdai Hachiyōin of the *taizōkai mandara*). The other Shisho Myōjin are placed outside the central circle. Ichiman and Jūman are separated and located above and below the circle. (See figure 15.) At the upper part of this picture can be seen the scenery of

Mt. Yoshino and Mt. Ōmine, as well as Kongō Zaō Gongen and En no
Ozunu, while in the lower part are the manifested deities of the chief *ōji*
shrines.

In the mandala of Shingū, we see at the upper part of the picture
Fudō Myōō manifested by the Kannokura Shrine, and Daiitoku Myōō
manifested by the Asuka Shrine. In the *Nachi mandara*, we see Jūichimen
Kannon manifested by Taki no Miya. Thus, the *honji mandara* is designed
on the basis of the Shugendō idea that views Mt. Kinbu as the *kongōkai
mandara* and Kumano as the *taizōkai mandara*; this explains how the
Kumano deities are arranged in the manner of the central circle of the
taizōkai mandara. Also, in this mandala, we notice that among the Shisho
Myōjin only Kanjō Jūgosho is put in the central circle, which separates it
from its original conjunction with Ichiman and Jūman. This may be partly
explained by noting that the balance of the picture and its unity as a whole
is best achieved by separating Ichiman and Jūman. But I think this can
also be accounted for by the traditional stories. Kanjō Jūgosho, in its relationship to the twelve Kumano deities, represents Gaken (manifesting
Shaka or Buddha), who is the father of Jihi Daiken Ō's wife. And in the
mandala, Gaken is put in the central circle. In this fashion, we find a vertical arrangement of the central circle by the placement of the father of
the king's wife, the king, and his granddaughter. The horizontal arrangement is formed with the king at the center, his daughter on the left, and
his son on the right. This composition can be interpreted as showing that
Jihi Daiken Ō's family occupies the central circle of the mandala and that
his retainers are placed outside the circle to protect the family.

In the *suijaku mandara*, at the center of the picture we see a three-
tiered stand. On the top tier the Sansho Gongen are depicted: from the
left, Musubi no Kami (female), Hayatama no Kami (male), and Shōjōden
(in the form of a Buddhist priest). On the second tier are the Gosho Ōji:
Nyaku Ōji (female), Zenji no Miya and Hijiri no Miya (both in the form of
a Buddhist priest), and Chigo no Miya (in the form of a boy) and Komori
no Miya (in the form of a girl). On the third tier, we see the Shisho Myōjin:
Ichiman, Jūman, and Kanjō Jūgosho (all in the form of a layman), and
Hikō Yasha and Meiji Kongō (both in the form of Yakṣa). At the upper
part of the picture we see the landscape of the Ōmine Mountains, Kongō
Zaō Gongen, En no Ozunu, and the Ōmine Hachidai Kongō Dōji. At the
lower part of the picture are seen the chief *ōji* shrines. Only in the *Nachi
mandara* do we find, on the right side of the top tier, the deity of Hirō
Gongen (representing the waterfall), in the form of a girl.

In the *honjaku mandara* both the manifested deities and manifesting
deities are depicted in the same picture. Similar to the *suijaku mandara*,
manifested deities are painted on a three-tiered stand, and beside them

are found the manifesting deities. Therefore, we can conclude that the *suijaku mandara* and the *honjaku mandara* both show the relationship among Sansho Gongen, Gosho Ōji, and the Shisho Myōjin (subordinate deities).

As a final example, in the *miya mandara* we see the landscape of the shrine buildings described at the beginning of this section. A small image of the manifested deity is drawn above each shrine.

Thus, in the various Kumano mandala, the Kumano Jūnisha Gongen are divided into the three groups of Sansho Gongen, Gosho Ōji, and Shisho Myōjin. Sansho Gongen and Gosho Ōji are thought to be at the core of this composition. We note that, individually, in the arrangement of the shrine buildings, Nyaku Ōji and Jinushigami (the landlord deity) are highly esteemed, and that in the mandala, Kanjō Jūgosho is greatly emphasized.

CONFIGURATION OF THE KUMANO JŪNISHA GONGEN

I have been analyzing the characters of the deities of the Kumano Jūnisha Gongen from the viewpoint of the doctrines, traditions, rituals, and images of Shugendō. Therefore, in conclusion I want to clarify the general characteristics of the configuration of the Kumano Jūnisha Gongen. For this purpose I will stress the contrast of native and foreign deities in the Kumano Jūnisha Gongen.

The original deities of the Kumano Jūnisha Gongen were Ketsumiko no Kami, who was a tree deity and seems to be the landlord god of Hongū; his mother Musubi no Kami, who was a mountain deity; and Hayatama no Kami of Shingū, who is thought to be a deity that came from across the sea. At the same time, the Kumano Sanzan (Hongū, Shingū, and Nachi) all came to have the three deities of Ketsumiko no Kami, Musubi no Kami, and Hayatama no Kami as their enshrined deities. However, at Nachi, Taki no Miya (the goddess of the waterfall) was valued as highly as the three deities; thus in Kumano Sanzan, the original three deities already featured the contrast of native deities and foreign deities (or original deities and invited deities from other shrines). Later, the Gosho Ōji, who can be considered native deities because they are the children of Musubi no Kami and Hayatama no Kami, and the foreign subordinate deities (Shisho Myōjin) symbolized by Kanjō Jūgosho coming from abroad, all came to be enshrined at Kumano. In this fashion the Kumano Jūnisha Gongen came to be established. In addition to these, numerous deities of *ōji*, who are said to have been related to Ichiman and Jūman of the Shisho Myōjin, were enshrined on the routes to Kumano. In the configuration of these deities, as can be seen in figure 16, the native deities are inside, and the foreign subordinate deities are placed outside. So I think we can infer that fundamentally the Jūnisha Gongen present a configuration open to the outside.

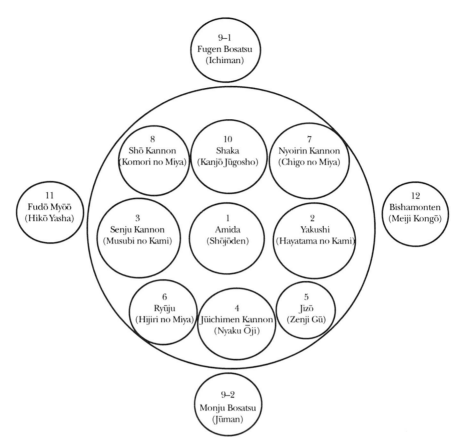

Figure 15. Composition of the *Kumano honji mandara.* Numbers correspond to table 1.

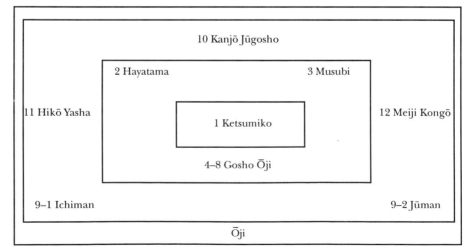

Figure 16. Constitution of the Kumano Jūnisha Gongen. Numbers correspond to table 1.

Next we note that in the manifested deities of the Kumano Jūnisha Gongen (which follow the idea of *honji suijaku* that was prominent in Japan after the eleventh century), we find deities who provide welfare in this life and deities who bless people in the paradise of the otherworld. The former deities focusing on this life include Yakushi, Kannon, and Fudō Myōō; the latter deities, focusing on the next life, include Amida and Kannon of Fudaraku. There are stories that report the deities of Kumano Gongen were originally from China or India and flew to Japan. This foreign aspect was so accentuated that even the deity found by the hunter who was guided by a wild animal (and who must therefore have originated from a native mountain god) came to be explained as having flown from China or from India before he was found. We may also surmise that this was an attempt to give the native deities more universal authority by connecting them with a foreign deity. In addition to these accounts, there were other interpretations taken from Buddhist doctrine, such as regarding the whole of Kumano as the *taizōkai mandara*, or regarding the Kumano Sanzan as the three bodies of Buddha (*hosshin*, *hōshin*, and *ōjin*).

It is also significant that in order to settle in Japan these foreign deities had to ask permission of the deity of Ise Shrine, the central shrine of Shinto, and of Emperor Jinmu, the ancestor of the imperial house. We also note that, in order to be accepted in Japan, the pantheon of deities had to be fashioned in the form of a family familiar to the Japanese people. The consorts of the son and the daughter of the foreign Jihi Daiken Ō were identified with Izanagi no Mikoto and Izanami no Mikoto, and their daughter was thought to be Amaterasu Ōmikami. In this way, Ketsumiko no Kami, who was originally a native god of Kumano, came to be connected with the Ise Shrine, which can be called the ancestral shrine of the Japanese people, and this in turn gave rise to the theory of the identification of Kumano and Ise.

The deities of Kumano, so skilled at absorbing foreign features, came to be worshipped by the people for their miraculous powers of giving both immediate and future blessing. In this process, such deities as the *ōji* and *dōji* connected with Shugendō played important roles. Originally in Kumano worship there was the aspect of faith in mother and child deities, such as Musubi no Kami and Hayatama no Kami (Ryōsho Gongen) and their children the Gosho Ōji. These child deities, with Nyaku Ōji at their center, had important roles in the offering of prayers or in the receiving of oracles. We can also deduce that the faith in the subordinate deities and *ōji* shrines originated from this faith in parent and child deities. These subordinate and *ōji* deities, located outside the above mentioned central circle of deities, had the role of leading people to the sacred site of Kumano

with Shōjōden at the center, in accordance with the will of the deities in
this pantheon, and acting as their agents to satisfy the requests of the worshippers in offering prayers and receiving oracles. It was the work of this
system of deities or pantheon, open to the outside, with the *dōji* and *ōji*
leading people from the general populace, that enabled Kumano to attract numerous worshippers in the Middle Ages.

NOTES

1. For the idea of identity of Kumano with Ise, see *Chōkan no kanmon*, no. 463 in *Zatsunobu*, Gunsho Ruijū 26 (Tokyo: Gunsho Ruijū Kankōkai, 1952), 242–43.
2. "Kumano Sansho Gongen no daiji," *Hikosan Shugendō hiketsu kanjōkan*, in *Shugendō shōso*, ed. Nakano Tatsue, Nihon Daizōkyō 47 (Tokyo: Ryūbunkan, 1919), 2:566.
3. For the origin and development of Kumano Jūnisho Gongen, and the influence of Shugendō, see Kondō Yoshihiro, "Kumano Sanzan no Seiritsu" (The formation of the three mountains at Kumano), in *Kumano*, ed. Takigawa Masajirō (Tokyo: Chihōshi Kenkyūsho, 1957).
4. *Shugen shinanshō*, annotated by Murayama Shūichi, in *Shugendō*, ed. Murayama Shūichi, Shintō Taikei 75 (Tokyo: Shintō Taikei Hensankai, 1988): 213–39.
5. *Kinbusen himitsuden*, in *Shugendō shōso*, ed. Nakano Tatsue, Nihon Daizōkyō 46 (Tokyo: Ryūbunkan, 1916), 1:447–48.
6. *En no Gyōja no Kumano sankei no nikki* and *Shōzan engi*, in *Jisha engi*, ed. Sakurai Tokutarō, Hagiwara Tatsuo, and Miyata Noboru, Nihon Shisō Taikei 20 (Tokyo: Iwanami Shoten, 1975), 104–8.
7. *Ryōbu mondō hishō*, in *Shugendō shōso* 2:607. See notes 14, 18, 22, 27.
8. *Shozan engi*, in *Jisha engi*, 107–8.
9. Tsukumo means ninety-nine. For the ninety-nine *ōji*, see Nishida Nagao, "Kumano tsukumo ōji kō," in *Shintōshi no kenkyū* (Tokyo: Risōsha, 1957), 2:268–324.
10. For the mother and child deity, see Ishida Eiichirō, "Mother and Son Deities," *History of Religions* 4.1 (1964): 30–52.
11. See *Ryōbu mondō hishō*, in *Shugendō shōso* 2:600–2; *Kumanosan ryakki*, in *Kumano*, 417–20.
12. *Kumano Gongen gosuijaku engi*, in *Chōkan no kanmon*, no. 463 in *Zatsunobu*.
13. *Kumano Gongen no koto*, in *Shintōshū*, ed. Kondō Yoshihiro (Tokyo: Kadokawa Shoten, 1959). In this story, the name of the hunter changed to Chiyokane from Chiyosada.
14. For many books in different forms of "Kumano no Honchi" (Original deity of Kumano), see Matsumoto Ryūshin, *Chūsei ni okeru honjimono no kenkyū* (A study of the account of the original deity's story in the Middle Ages) (Tokyo: Kyūko Shoin, 1967), 19–87.
15. *Ryōbu mondō hishō*, in *Shugendō shōso* 2:603. In this story, the name of the hunter is Chiyokane. According to this book also he is called Asuga Myōjin and his original Buddhist deity is Daiitoku Myōō.
16. *Shōbodaisan engi*, in *Shugendō shōso* 3:372.
17. *Kumano Gongen kongōzaō hōdenzōkō nikki*, in *Shugendō shiryōshū*, ed. Gorai Shigeru, Sangaku Shūkyōshi Kenkyū Sōsho 18 (Tokyo: Meicho Shuppan, 1984), 2:208.
18. Gakuhō, *Gyōja denki* 1 (Kyoto: Mizuta Jinzaemon, 1691).
19. *Ryōbu mondō hishō*, in *Shugendō shōso* 2:606–7.
20. *Sendaetsukokuōkyō*, no. 518 in *Kyoshūbu*, ed. Takakusu Junjirō, Taishō Shinshū Daizōkyō 14 (Tokyo: Taishō Issaikyō Kankōkai, 1924), 1:791–92; Matsumoto Ryūshin, *Chūsei ni okeru honjimono no kenkyū* (Tokyo: Kyūko Shoin, 1996), 29–35.
21. For details of Kumano pilgrimage, see Miyake Hitoshi, *Kumano shugen* (Tokyo: Yoshikawa Kōbunkan, 1992), 73–88.

22. Kondō Yoshihiro, *Kodai shinkō kenkyū* (A study of ancient belief) (Tokyo: Kadokawa Shoten, 1963), 211–88.
23. *Kumano sankei genko no shidai, Shozan engi*, in *Jisha engi*, 108–9.
24. *Ryōbu mondō hishō*, in *Shugendō shōso* 2:611.
25. *Shōbodaisan engi*, in *Shugendō shōso* 3:377.
26. Ryūju Endō, *Kumano Gongen kōshiki*, manuscript copy owned by Seigantoji, Nachi, Kumano.
27. "Yasuyori Notto," in *Heike monogatari*, ed. Takagi Ichinosuke et al., Nihon Koten Bungaku Taikei 32 (Tokyo: Iwanami Shoten, 1959), 2:198–201; "Koremori Kumano sankei," in *Heikei monogatari*, ed. Takagi Ichinosuke et al., Nihon Koten Bungaku Taikei 33 (Tokyo: Iwanami Shoten, 1960), 10:277–80; "Kumawakadono no koto," in *Taiheiki*, ed. Gotō Tanji and Kamada Kisaburō, Nihon Koten Bungaku Taikei 34 (Tokyo: Iwanami Shoten, 1960), 2:72–79; "Daitōnomiyakumanoochi no koto," in *Taiheki*, ed. Gotō Tanji and Kamada Kisaburō, Nihon Koten Bungaku Taikei 34 (Tokyo: Iwanami Shoten, 1960), 5:165–79.
28. Shochō, "Kongō Dōjihō," no. 133 in *Asabashō*, Dainihon Bukkyō Zensho 30 (Tokyo: Bussho Kankōkai, 1913), 396–407.
29. *Ippen shōnin eden* (A pictorial biography of Saint Ippen), ed. Komatsu Shigemi, Nihon no Emaki 20 (Chūō Kōronsha, 1988), 66–74.
30. See Miyake Hitoshi, "Kumano mandara no sekai—Kumano Shugen denraibon o chūshin ni" (The world of Kumano Mandala—as seen in the books transmitted with Kumano Shugen), in *Seinaru kūkan* (Sacred space), ed. Miyake Hitoshi and Ogawa Hideo (Tokyo: Lithon, 1993).

Religious Rituals in Shugendō[1]

THE SUBJECT AND METHODOLOGY

Shugenja traveled widely throughout the mountains and plains of Japan during the medieval period, but in later times, in part because of the restrictive policies of the Tokugawa government, they settled down and became a regular part of local communities. By this time local communities in Japan already had shrines dedicated to the local guardian deities, and temples that took care of funerary rites. The role undertaken by *shugenja* who settled in these communities was to respond to the various mundane needs of the common people in the areas of disease and problems of daily life, offering religious services such as fortune-telling and divination (*bokusen*), obtaining oracles through mediums (*fujutsu*), prayers or ritual incantations (*kitō*), and exorcism (*chōbuku*). Thus, in the Edo period the *shugenja* were responsible for offering "worldly benefits" within the context of the religious activities of the common people and played a major role in these religious activities.[2] It can also be said that Shugendō provided the central model for the religious activities of many of the new religions (e.g., sectarian Shinto) that proliferated from the latter part of the nineteenth century and continue to this day.

The importance of research on Shugendō is not limited to religious studies but is also imperative for the areas of historical and folk studies. However, Shugendō studies so far have, with few exceptions, concentrated on such limited aspects of Shugendō as sectarian history or mountain practices. There have been no comprehensive studies of the religious rituals of Shugendō, which include festivals, fortune-telling, divination, prayers and incantations, exorcism, spells, charms, and so forth. These are religious rituals that are performed by *shugenja* in response to the daily needs and requirements of the people. They are the key to understanding Shugendō as a popular religion. In order to study Shugendō as a single religious system, it is important to grasp the aggregate relationships among these religious rituals. However, much of the information concerning these rituals is hidden behind the veil of oral and secret transmissions. Thus these activities have been inaccessible to academic research through normal research methods.

In my own studies I have examined the written documents concerning these religious rituals that are available, analyzed and clarified them further through on-the-spot observation of the practices of various Shugendō organizations, and have thus attempted to grasp the symbolic meaning of Shugendō rituals as a whole; in this chapter I will attempt to summarize my conclusions.[3] I have identified thirteen categories of religious rituals that have an organic relationship within the entire system of Shugendō religious rituals.

1. Practices in the Mountains (nyūbu shugyō)

There are three types of *nyūbu*. The first is entering the mountain to make offerings of flowers, read or bury sutras, and so forth, in honor of various buddhas or other deities, based on the belief that the mountain is a sacred area like a mandala. Examples of this type of *nyūbu* are the offerings of flowers at Kinbusen, Hongū, and Shingū of Kumano; the *higan* ceremonies at Nachi in Kumano; the *nyūbu* by the Honzanha at Mt. Katsuragi for the purpose of praying at sutra mounds; and the summer *nyūbu* (*natsu no mine*) at Mt. Haguro. This first type of *nyūbu* eventually developed into ceremonies performed in preparation for the second type of *nyūbu*, i.e., entering the mountains for a certain period of time. Examples of this second type include the *nyūbu* of *yamabushi* from around the country at Kinbusen, the summer ascetic practices at Nachi in Kumano, and the fall *nyūbu* (*aki no mineiri*) of the Honzanha, Tōzanha, and at Mt. Haguro. All of those retreats in the mountains occur for a set period of time during which various ascetic practices are cultivated, culminating in the transmission of secret lore (*hihō*) or performance of initiations. This kind of *nyūbu* is an essential experience for any serious *shugenja*. At present, however, there are few transmissions of secrets or initiations during *nyūbu*, and there is increasing participation by lay people.[4] This type of *nyūbu* was and remains the central and most popular practice of *shugenja* at major Shugendō centers throughout Japan.

The third type of *nyūbu* is the most severe, consisting of a difficult ascetic retreat in the mountains during the wintertime. Examples include the *nyūbu* of the *misoka* ("New Year" or winter peak) *yamabushi* of Kinbusen, Hongū, and Shingū; the practices of *toshigomori* ("retreat over New Year's day") at Nachi; and the winter *nyūbu* (*fuyu no mine*) of Mt. Haguro. At Mt. Haguro only the most advanced *yamabushi* participated in this *nyūbu*. The purpose of this kind of *nyūbu* was to acquire special spiritual powers.

Figure 17. *Nyūbu shugyō* of Shugendō

2. Consecration Ceremonies (shōkanjō)

Shugendō, as a movement very much influenced by esoteric (Mikkyō) Buddhism,[5] involves a great variety of consecration ceremonies (*kanjō*). The central and most important consecration, however, is the *shōkanjō* performed at the end of a *nyūbu*. *Shōkanjō* is a distinctly Shugendō consecration and is performed at Jinzen[6] towards the end of the Ōmine *nyūbu*. It is performed on the assumption that the *shugenja* has passed through the "ten realms" from hell to buddhahood during practice in the mountains, and it symbolizes one's final attainment of "buddhahood in this body" (*sokushin sokubutsu*).

3. Demonstration of Magico-Religious Powers (genjutsu)

The spectacular demonstration of spiritual powers attained through the cultivation of ascetic practices in the mountains is perhaps the most well-known aspect of Shugendō in present-day Japan. These demonstrations once included flying through the air, walking on swords, walking on fire, symbolically "hiding" one's body, and immersion in boiling water.[7] The details concerning some of these powers, such as flying through the air and hiding one's body, are unknown, with only scant information concerning them available in the surviving Shugendō records. Other demonstrations such as walking on fire are still performed today, often with much fanfare, in places such as Mt. Takao outside of Tokyo, Mt. Ishizuchi in Ehime, and by the *ontake-kō*.

4. Commemoration Rites (kuyōhō)

By *kuyōhō* I refer to rites of worship whereby the *shugenja* expresses his reverence toward certain deities through the chanting of sutras or other offerings. Ui Hakuju classifies *kuyō* into three types: offerings of respect (*kei kuyō*), such as the decoration and cleaning of the worship hall; offerings of action (*gyō kuyō*), such as the chanting of *sutra*s and performance of worship; and offerings of "benefit" (*ri kuyō*), such as the offerings of food and water.[8] The *kuyō* offerings in Shugendō follow the same pattern. The central Shugendō *kuyō* is that performed for Fudō Myōō (*Fudō hō*), in which the presence of Fudō is solicited, offerings are made, and the *shugenja* becomes symbolically identified with him.

5. Participation in matsuri for the kami, for the Sun, Moon, and Stars (hitsuki-hoshi no matsuri), and for Small Shrines (shōshi no matsuri)

Shugenja have always been involved in "Shinto" *matsuri* (festivals) for the *kami*. These activities include chanting sutras in front of the *kami*, "calling"

Figure 18. Jinzen (on the right) and Zenki (on the left), the sacred site for *shōkanjō*

Figure 19. *Hiwatari* (walking on burning coals)

Figure 20. *Hawatari* (climbing a ladder of swords)

on the *kami* and making offerings, visiting shrines and participating in worship, performing rites of purification, and so forth.

One type of *matsuri* in which *shugenja* were particularly active were those connected with the sun, moon, and stars. The *matsuri* for the sun include rituals whereby *shugenja* and other believers gather together to worship the sun for the purpose of averting disasters or promoting prosperity. This ritual involves undergoing purification and then staying awake all night, making offerings, reading sutras, and performing other rites until the sun rises in the morning. *Matsuri* that involve worship of the moon include gatherings of *shugenja* and believers at certain phases of the monthly cycle to eat and drink together, watch for the rising of the moon, and pray for the realization of certain requests. Festivals for the stars include worship of the North Star and performance of various forms of divination based on the calendar and astrology.

Other *matsuri* in which *shugenja* are often involved are *matsuri* for small shrines. In Japan there are innumerable small shrines throughout the country dedicated to, for example, the *kami* of the hearth, family deities, and especially Kōjin ("fierce deity" of the kitchen). *Shugenja* were often called upon to participate in *matsuri* or rituals connected to these small shrines.[9]

6. Fortune-telling and Divination (bokusen)

Shugenja were and are involved in many types of fortune-telling and divination, from the analysis of good and bad days of the calendar, *yin-yang* divination, the determination of lucky and unlucky directions, divination of a person's fate through astrological signs or guardian deities on the basis of a person's birth date, and so forth.

7. The Art of Obtaining Oracles Through Mediums (fujutsu)

In addition to the aforementioned methods of divination, some *shugenja* obtain oracles by acting as mediums, calling on the spirits of the *kami* or buddhas to possess them and give oracles. However, I believe that the *shugenja* as medium is a marginal role within Shugendō because there are various mediums outside Shugendō. But it is often difficult to draw the line between mediums who are affiliated with Shugendō and those who are not.[10] Nevertheless, the art of obtaining oracles through mediums is not an uncommon occurrence within the framework of Shugendō.

8. Prayers of Possession (yorigitō)

Yorigitō is a form of obtaining oracles peculiar to Shugendō. In this ritual a *shugenja* uses a medium as a vehicle for possession by a deity, which

Figure 21. *Yorigitō*

is then asked to reply to various queries or requests concerning the next harvest or one's personal fortune.[11]

9. Fire Ceremonies for Averting Misfortunes (sokusai goma)

The *goma* fire ritual is a form of Shugendō prayer. A certain liturgy is performed, including various chants, before and while the fire is burnt. Offerings are burnt in the fire for the object of worship, usually Fudō Myōō, and prayers are offered for the realization of certain requests. These ceremonies are much the same in content as the *Fudō hō* discussed earlier.

The *saitō goma* is a fire ceremony unique to Shugendō. This ceremony often forms the central part of major Shugendō ritual performances, especially before, during, or after a *nyūbu*.[12]

10. Rituals Centered on Various Deities (shosonbō)

In addition to fire ceremonies, Shugendō rituals include many ceremonies (*shūhō*) utilizing *mudrās* (*inzō*) and spells (*shingon*; Skt. *dhāraṇī*) for the purpose of realizing the attainment of one's prayers. These ceremonies address certain deities: buddhas such as Yakushi and Amida, bodhisattvas such as Monju and Kokūzō, various forms of Kannon, various Myōō such as Fudō, Indian deities such as Benzaiten, Japanese *kami* such as Kōjin, Inari, and Daikoku. An examination of the ceremonies listed in Shugendō manuals shows that these ceremonies are most often addressed to the Myōō or the Indian deities and their retinue, with Fudō Myōō the most common figure.

11. Incantations (kaji)

The word *kaji* is often combined with *kitō* ("prayers" or ritual incantations) to form the compound *kajikitō*, and in the popular mind this is believed to be the most common activity or function of a *shugenja*. However, *kaji* and *kitō* are not the same. *Kitō* refers to the prayers or ritual incantations offered to a deity as a form of request in ceremonies such as the *Fudō hō*, *sokusai goma*, and *shosonbō*. *Kaji*, however, refers to the identification (*ka*) of the *shugenja* with the deity in order to realize (*ji*) a certain purpose.[13] Therefore *kaji* is a religious ritual wherein the *shugenja* achieves identification with the deity and manipulates the power thus obtained in order to gain certain benefits.

12. Exorcism (tsukimono otoshi, chōbuku)

Shugenja also perform rites of healing by determining the cause of a disease (such as the spirit of an evil deity, the dead, or an animal) and then perform ceremonies to exorcize these spirits. *Shugenja* were known as figures who could control or manipulate such spirits of possession (*tsukimono*).

There are some cases of possession, however, that cannot be resolved through ceremonies of *tsukimono otoshi* and require the more demanding ritual of exorcism called *chōbuku* ("subduing" of spirits).[14] An example of this ritual is the *kuji* ("nine letters") practice that utilizes nine *mudrās* and nine formulas to draw on the power of supernatural deities.[15] This ceremony is based on a Taoist practice but is one of the most fundamental practices of Shugendō.

13. Spells and Charms (fuju, majinai)

Finally, *shugenja* utilize various forms of charms and spells in response to simple requests by people for healing, safe childbirth, protection from theft, and so forth. These spells are simpler than the aforementioned prayers and incantations, often consisting of a short phrase (the gist of a sutra, an esoteric formula, or the name of a deity) written on a small amulet. These amulets are carried by people in their pockets or around their necks, or placed somewhere such as on the oven in a house, in order to divert misfortune or solicit good fortune.[16]

On the basis of the concrete examples outlined above, I understand the structure and function of Shugendō religious rituals as follows: each of these individual religious rituals assumes a symbol system that reflects a specific religious worldview. In other words, the activity undertaken in each of those rituals is symbolic action, and the various devices used in the rituals are symbols. These numerous symbolic actions and symbols combine to form a symbolic system that reflects a certain religious worldview.

The symbol system of the religious rituals, and the religious worldview of Shugendō, is revealed through the activities of the *shugenja* themselves. The rituals as a symbol system must have a motif, which is based on the religious worldview of Shugendō. By analyzing and clarifying this religious worldview in light of the concrete religious rituals, we can avoid the pitfall of an overly abstract or inconsistent analysis.

Each of the individual rituals, in order to symbolize a religious worldview, fulfills a proper ritualistic function within that religious worldview and forms a symbol system centered on a motif that is close to the daily lives and concerns of the *shugenja* and the faithful. Numerous symbolic actions or symbols are the elements that form this symbol system. The elements of each religious ritual have a nucleus–a central motif–from among these elements. The elements are bound together and mutually related, and thus form a single, ordered mechanism. My study of these individual Shugendō rituals involves analyzing this mechanism and clarifying

Figure 22. *Kaji* at Mt. Takaita

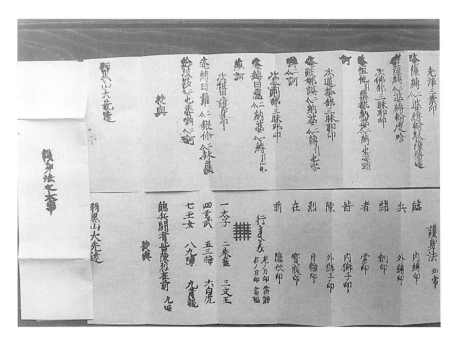

Figure 23. *Kuji* and *goshinpō* of Haguro Shugendō

the central motifs. In the other direction, the religious worldview of Shugendō is reinterpreted through the motifs from the perspective of the religious rituals.[17]

THE STRUCTURE OF SHUGENDŌ RITUALS

Let us first concentrate on the structure and the central nucleus–the motif–of the elements in these individual Shugendō rituals and clarify them in light of the religious worldview of Shugendō.

First, practices in the mountains (*nyūbu shugyō*) and consecrations (*shōkanjō*) involve spiritual identification with the central deity Fudō Myōō through reception of a secret transmission while the *shugenja* is in the mountains. These rituals signify the rebirth of the ascetic as a Buddha who has acquired the ability to control or utilize the power of Fudō Myōō. Therefore the central element of both of these rituals is the symbolic action exhibited in a state of identification with the central deity Fudō Myōō. The performance of various practices and rituals in the mountains assumes that the mountains are a supernatural spiritual realm, the dwelling of deities and objects of worship such as Fudō Myōō, separate from the realm of our daily lives. This belief is based on a religious worldview that considers the mountains to be symbols of the universe.

The demonstration of magico-religious powers (*genjutsu*) involves rituals in which the *shugenja* who has achieved symbolic identification with Fudō Myōō then demonstrates this identification by entering the spiritual realm. Identification is the central element of these activities. An underlying assumption of these activities is the shamanistic idea that the *shugenja* who has become identified with the figure of Fudō Myōō can in fact enter the spiritual realm.

Next, commemorative rituals (*kuyōhō*) and services for *kami*, for the sun, moon, and stars (*hi-tsuki-hoshi no matsuri*), and for small shrines (*shōshi no matsuri*), are rituals often performed by *shugenja*. A typical example of *kuyōhō* is the service for Fudō Myōō, a ritual in which Fudō Myōō is invited by the *shugenja* as a guest to the altar (*shuhōdōjō*) for the purpose of achieving identification with the deity. The "object of worship" is welcomed and favored with the chanting of scriptures (*dokyō*) or performance of *matsuri* for the *kami*. Thus the structure of this ritual consists of the elements of communication and identification between the *shugenja* and the object of worship.

Rites in honor of the sun, moon, and stars consist of bringing down these heavenly bodies and achieving their identification with Fudō Myōō, for the purpose of "extinguishing the seven kinds of adversities" (*shichinan sokumetsu*) and "arousing the seven kinds of blessings" (*shichifuku sokushō*).[18] The festivals of small shrines, which celebrate local kitchen gods (*kōjin*), deities of the earth (*chijin*), and so forth consist of the *shugenja* achieving identification with Fudō Myōō, and then removing evil influences by exorcising evil deities or evil spirits (which are causing misfortune) and inviting good spirits to take their place. In a broad sense those two rituals both have prayers for the removal of evil influences as their central structural element. Both rituals are based on a religious worldview that accepts as normal the possibility that the *shugenja*, through identification with Fudō Myōō, can remove misfortunes by exorcising evil spirits or modifying the unfortunate influences of heavenly bodies.

Various forms of divination and fortune-telling are used to discover the causes of misfortune and the fates of human beings. Fortune-telling methods such as *kikkyō* and *unsei* use the motif of analyzing the smaller realm of human beings within the larger universe through the structure of the five forces of *yin* and *yang*, and through the ten calendar signs and twelve signs of the zodiac. In this case the religious worldview involved is one in which daily fortunes depend on the power of various deities or vengeful spirits, or the fates of human beings depend on the astrological influences of the stars. There are also rituals for determining the cause of disease, and so forth, through *bokusen*, *kikkyō*, or *unsei*. These rituals are based on the assumption that disease is caused by angry spirits or spirits of the living or dead that hamper the proper and normal course of the universe.

The practice of obtaining oracles through mediums (*fujutsu*) involves rituals by which a *shugenja* makes his guardian spirit possess the medium in order to obtain an oracle. In the case of *kuchiyose* oracles by *itako*-type mediums, the mediums achieve identification with their own guardian spirits and use the power thus acquired to call forth the requested spirit (of the living or the dead), which then takes possession of the medium. "Prayers of possession" (*yorigitō*) are one specifically Shugendō-type practice that consists of a *shugenja* achieving identification with Fudō Myōō in order to manipulate deities (usually tutelary deities) so that the medium is possessed by them and grants an oracle.

Fire ceremonies for averting misfortune (*sokusai goma*) are rituals wherein a *shugenja* achieves identification with Fudō Myōō in order to manipulate the deity of fire (*katen*) and the stars governing fates (*yōshuku*) for the purpose of removing evil influences. This activity is based on the religious worldview that it is possible to obtain good fortune by determining the cause of misfortune through divination, and that one can then "burn away" misfortune. *Shosonbō* involves a *shugenja* attaining identification with a certain object of worship and then performing certain actions that symbolize salvific activity. The central structural element of both these rituals is prayer. *Kaji* prayers or incantations, on the other hand, are rituals that utilize the power of the object of worship in order to remove or exorcize evil influences, or that seek the protection of the object of worship by transferring its power into a tool, weapon, clothing, and so forth.

Another type of religious ritual that *shugenja* often perform is exorcism (*tsukimono otoshi* and *chōbuku*). *Tsukimono otoshi* is a ritual of exorcism wherein a *shugenja* drives out a possessing spirit by teaching it the error of its ways or by threatening it. *Chōbuku*, on the other hand, involves identification of the *shugenja* with Fudō Myōō so that the *shugenja* can control Fudō Myōō's retinue of servants and have them bind, kick, beat, or otherwise subdue evil deities or evil spirits. Both of these rituals are based on the religious worldview that evil deities or evil spirits are the cause of misfortune and that the *shugenja* through identification with Fudō Myōō can directly utilize his supernatural power, or can manipulate Fudō Myōō's retinue, in order to control and defeat these evil deities and spirits.

On a simpler level is the use of various charms (*fuju*) and spells (*majinai*). The motif here is the removal of evil influences by using charms onto which the *shugenja* has transferred the supernatural power of a deity, or by manipulating magical instruments. Thus the last four types of rituals, i.e., incantations, exorcism, charms, and spells, all have the removal (or exorcism) of evil influences as their central motif.

THE LOGIC OF RELIGIOUS RITUALS IN SHUGENDŌ

The individual religious rituals of Shugendō outlined above have the following interrelationship within the total structure of Shugendō rituals. The primary Shugendō rituals are those associated with *nyūbu* and consecration, through which *shugenja* achieve identification with a deity and gain the ability to control the power thus attained. Next, these powers are manifested to the *shugenja*'s followers through rituals such as *genjutsu*, the demonstration of magico-religious powers. The identification and communication with deities continue in rituals such as *kuyōhō* and various activities connected with *matsuri*. On the basis of these preparations, *shugenja* respond to the requests of their followers by performing divination and the art of obtaining oracles through mediums to avert misfortune by clarifying the causes of these misfortunes, whether evil deities, evil spirits, or unlucky stars. Evil influences are removed and blessings solicited through the performance of *goma* fire ceremonies, rituals centered on various deities, and services for the heavenly bodies and small shrines. At other times evil deities or evil spirits are exorcized. Other accessible means for averting misfortune or soliciting blessings include *kaji* incantations, charms, and spells.

I have attempted to grasp the whole of the Shugendō ritual system as one which is structured from central elements found in these individual rituals. I have concluded that Shugendō rituals as a whole are made up of seven major elements:

> 1. Rituals for the purpose of achieving identification with the object of worship (*nyūbu*, consecration, the demonstration of magical powers, rites for Fudō Myōō).
> 2. Rituals for the purpose of communication with the object of worship (chanting of sutras, *matsuri* for deities).
> 3. Rituals as means of achieving identification with the object of worship (divination, obtaining oracles through mediums, prayers of possession, *goma* fire ceremonies, rites for deities, *kaji* incantations, exorcism).
> 4. Rituals to achieve the power to manipulate these deities (prayers of possession, *goma* fire ceremonies, *kaji* incantations, exorcism, charms, spells).
> 5. Rituals to receive oracles (divination, oracles through mediums, prayers of possession).
> 6. Rituals of prayer (services for the sun, moon, and stars, and small shrines, *goma* fire ceremony for averting misfortunes, rites for various deities).
> 7. Rituals of exorcism or removing evil influences (*kaji* incantations, removing a possessing spirit, "defeating" spirits, charms, spells).

When considering the interrelationship among these elements, we can reach the following conclusions concerning the structure of Shugendō rituals as a whole.

Shugendō rituals begin with the *shugenja* attaining a spiritual identification with Fudō Myōō, the main deity, thereby gaining the ability to control this spiritual power. When a *shugenja* receives a request from a follower, he must first determine the cause of the misfortune through divination. There are many possible causes for misfortune: the spirits of animals, the spirits of the living or the dead, evil deities, and so forth. In general, the most common means for putting an end to this evil activity is to pray to a deity. In Shugendō the more common approach is to have the *shugenja* experience identity with Fudō Myōō and have the evil activity cease through manipulating the supernatural power of Fudō Myōō or his retinue.

Thus it can be said that the structure of the Shugendō ritual system is as follows. First, the *shugenja* identifies himself with a deity in order to learn, through an oracle, which evil deity or evil spirit is causing misfortune. He then wields the supernatural power of the deity or its retinue, and finally exorcizes or removes the evil influences. Within this structure one can see that the three elements of identification, manipulation, and exorcism are the three central motifs of the Shugendō ritual system.

These three motifs are particularly suitable to the function of Shugendō rituals from the perspective of the religious worldview of Shugendō. The explicit function of the religious rituals of Shugendō, especially the people's appeal for worldly benefits, is to remove evil influences and misfortunes from their daily lives. The implicit functions of these rituals for the believers, in contrast, include the transmission of the teachings and supernatural revelations possessed by the *shugenja*, and integration with already-existing forms of folk religion.

The fact that an explicit function of Shugendō rituals is to remove the cause of misfortunes is a reflection of the "exorcism" motif. The implicit functions such as the revelation of the *shugenja*'s supernatural power to the believers and the dissemination of teachings reflect the "identification" motif, i.e., that the *shugenja* is identified with Fudō Myōō and his activity. A particularly graphic illustration of this motif is *genjutsu*, the demonstration of magical powers, where the *shugenja* symbolically enters the spiritual realm after identification with Fudō Myōō. These teachings of Shugendō (the religious worldview that has been authorized by its organization) are also expressed in manifestations or clearly expounded in the course of various rituals.

The idea that Shugendō rituals have served to integrate Shugendō with previously existing forms of folk religion is reflected in the role *shugenja* play at shrines or at *matsuri* such as those for small shrines. An interesting aspect of this idea, in connection with the "manipulation" motif of Shugendō rituals, is that the retinue of powers manipulated by the *shugenja* after identification with the deity often turn out to be the tutelary deities of the local society wherein the ritual is being performed. By controlling these powers the *shugenja* could succeed in having his religious activity accepted by the local community, and the rituals could eventually achieve a more prestigious status than the religious activities that existed previously within the local society.

In this way the motifs of identification, manipulation, and exorcism are intimately related to the function of the religious rituals of Shugendō. It must be noted, however, that these motifs are ways to symbolize the religious worldview of Shugendō through the form of religious rituals. With this in mind let us take another look at the motifs of identification, manipulation, and exorcism from the perspective of the religious worldview of Shugendō and as revealed in Shugendō rituals.

THE RELIGIOUS WORLDVIEW OF SHUGENDŌ AND SHUGENDŌ RITUALS

The religious worldview that underlies Shugendō rituals assumes there are at least two realms of existence, that of the daily lives of human beings, and a separate, supernatural spiritual realm behind (and controlling) that of the daily lives of human beings. The mountains are seen as a sacred space that either is part of both of these worlds or is a part of the spiritual world. The altar space during the fire ceremony, or the area of a *matsuri*, is also considered to be this kind of sacred space.

The supernatural spiritual world of Shugendō contains a large syncretistic pantheon of various *kami*, deities, buddhas, spirits, and so forth that are believed to control the daily lives of human beings. Fudō Myōō plays a central role in this pantheon. The residents of this spiritual realm, with Fudō Myōō in the center, can be classified into three types of entities.

First are various buddhas and other Buddhist Mikkyō-type figures, such as Fudō Myōō and Dainichi Nyorai (Mahāvairocana). These include as well specifically Shugendō objects of worship such as Zaō Gongen, and *kami* that are honored by many shrines all around Japan or that have a universal character. These *kami* often serve to symbolize the universe as a whole.

The second type of spiritual entities are the *kami* with a more individual or local character, such as tutelary deities, guardian deities, the retinue of more powerful figures, and so forth. The members of this second group often serve as the retinue of those in the first group. Zaō Gongen and some of the *kami* honored in many shrines around Japan were originally local figures like those in the second category, but they later took on a more universal character.

Third, there are evil deities and evil spirits that are the actual causes of various misfortunes. When these evil deities and spirits are brought under control by the *shugenja* and "enshrined" in a small shrine, they take on the character of those in the second category.

Shugendō teaches that a human being is a product of the universe and is himself or herself a "small" universe. Thus all things, including human beings, are thought to have the same nature or character as the divine, the primary and original form of all things. Therefore it is possible for a human being to become a divine being. A *shugenja*, by cultivating ascetic practices in the mountains (a symbol of the supernatural spiritual world or of the universe itself) and by receiving secret transmissions (i.e., *kanjō*), can become spiritually identified with Fudō Myōō, who already possesses a universalistic character. If you recall the structure of Shugendō ritual as outlined above, *shugenja* first enter the mountains and receive consecration in order to achieve identification with Fudō Myōō and gain the ability to control Fudō Myōō's spiritual power. The *shugenja* who have obtained this spiritual power can communicate with the more local and individual spiritual entities who are believed to have a more intimate relationship with the daily lives of the people, and can thus discover the causes of people's misfortunes, and identify which evil deities or spirits are to blame.

On this basis the *shugenja* use their universal spiritual power to manipulate the individual deities (category 2) and control the evil deities and evil spirits (category 3) and thus exorcize or remove evil influences. (In chapter 5 exorcism is treated more fully.)

NOTES

1. This is a translation of the concluding summary chapter of Miyake Hitoshi, *Shugendō girei no kenkyū* (A study of religious rituals in Shugendō), 2d ed., rev. (Tokyo: Shunjūsha, 1985), 686–95.

2. Usually the *shugenja* who lived in local community are called *sato-shugen* (village Shugen). See Miyamoto Kesao, *Sato Shugen no kenkyū* (Study of local community *shugenja*) (Tokyo: Yoshikawa Kōbunkan, 1984).

3. For details concerning the argument in this chapter, and concrete examples of Shugendō rituals, see Miyake, *Shugendō girei no kenkyū.*

4. For *nyūbu* at present, see Paul L. Swanson, "Shugendō and the Yoshino-Kumano Pilgrimage: An Example of Mountain Pilgrimage," *Monumenta Nipponica* 36.1 (1981): 55–79.

5. For esoteric Buddhism, see Minoru Kiyota, *Shingon Buddhism: Theory and Practice* (Los Angeles-Tokyo: Buddhist Books International, 1978).

6. "Jinzen" means deep mountains. It is located at the foot of Mt. Shaka, which is the central peak of Mt. Ōmine.

7. Such performances can be seen in the shaman's practices in northeast Asia. Mircea Eliade, *Shamanism: Archaic Techniques of Ecstasy,* trans. W. T. Trask, rev. ed. Bollingen Series 76 (New York: Pantheon 1964), 412, 415, 485. For the case of Shugendō, see Carmen Blacker, *The Catalpa Bow: A Study of Shamanistic Practices in Japan* (London: George Allen and Unwin Ltd., 1975), 247–51.

8. Hakuju Ui, *Konsaisu bukkyō jiten* (Concise Buddhist dictionary) (Tokyo: Daitō Shuppansha, 1938), 206.

9. See Iwasaki Toshio, *Honpō shōshi no kenkyū* (Study of small shrines in Japan) (Fukushima: Iwasakihakase Gakuironbun Shuppan Kōenkai, 1963; Tokyo: Meicho Shuppan, 1977).

10. See Sakurai Tokutarō, *Nihon no shamanizumu* (Shamanism in Japan), 2 vols. (Tokyo: Yoshikawa Kōbunkan, 1974–77).

11. Blacker, *The Catalpa Bow,* 252–97.

12. For the *saitō goma,* see plates 18–22 in Blacker, *The Catalpa Bow.*

13. Nevertheless, one must admit that in practice there is a mixture of these concepts. For example, various forms of *kaji* are incorporated into ceremonies of "prayer" such as the *sokusai goma.*

14. For details concerning exorcism, see chapter 5, "The Structure of Exorcism in Shugendō."

15. The practitioner treats nine *mudrās* one by one; then using the *mudrā* that symbolizes a sword, cuts the air vertically and horizontally nine times and recites nine letters in succession, that is, *zin pyō tō sha kai gin retsu zai zen.*

16. For amulets, see H. Byron Earhart, "Mechanisms and Process in the Study of Japanese Amulets," in *Nihon shūkyō e no shikaku* (Approaches to Japanese religions), ed. Okada Shigekiyo (Osaka: Tōhō Shuppan, 1994), 611–20.

17. For details of these methods see Miyake, *Shugendō girei no kenkyū,* 42–61.

18. This phrase is found in a passage from the *Jen-wang ching* (*Ninnōgoku hannya haramitsukyō* Z), no. 246 in *Hannyabu,* ed. Takakusu Junjirō, Taishō Shinshū Daizōkyō 8 (Tokyo: Issaikyō Kankōkai, 1924), 843. The "seven kinds of adversities" are calamities connected with the sun and moon, astrological calamities: fire, heavy rain, high wind, draught, and theft. The "seven kinds of blessings" are not listed. It is best to understand these in a general sense of gaining relief from all adversities and welcoming all blessings.

Mountain Austerities in Shugendō

Shugendō and Mountain Austerities

One of the best ways to introduce Shugendō is to focus on mountain austerities, which are the most important rituals in Shugendō. However, this is a large theme, so in this brief treatment I will discuss only the mountain austerities at Mt. Ōmine and Mt. Haguro. These two Shugendō centers developed during the Middle Ages in Japan. My approach is as follows: I will take mountain austerities as a symbolic action system, and I will interpret the symbolic meaning of everything in the austerities and the religious worldview that sustains mountain austerities. First it is necessary to outline the mountain austerities and to explain the rituals at each of the mountains.

According to the doctrine of Shugendō, the object of mountain austerities is to become a Buddha in one's human body (*sokushin jōbutsu*). In other words, the purpose of mountain austerities is to transform a profane man into a sacred man by mystic training at a sacred mountain.

We can divide mountain austerities into three elements: the first is the mountain as a sacred place; the second is the *shugenja* who has the ability to become a sacred being; and the third is the process of mystic training at the mountain that transforms the practitioner into a sacred being.

First I will discuss briefly the religious meanings of the mountain and *shugenja*, and then treat in detail the ritual process of mountain austerities. Finally, I want to make clear what kind of sacred being the *shugenja* becomes as a result of mystic training in the mountain.

The Religious Significance of the Mountain

Not only in Shugendō but also in Japanese religion as a whole, mountains are considered to be sacred places. There are several rationales for

78

the sacred character of mountains. In order to grasp the meaning of mountain austerities in Shugendō in a wider perspective, I will consider the religious meanings of mountains in Japanese folk religion in general, including Shugendō.[1]

First, mountains are viewed as the dwelling place of spirits of the dead and ancestor spirits. Tombs are built on mountains. The procession to the place of burial is called "going to the mountain" (*yamayuki*). In ancient times, the tombs of emperors were called mountains. These customs are evidence that Japanese people perceive mountains as a dwelling place of spirits of the dead. In particular, caves and valleys are feared as dwelling places of these spirits. Accordingly, mountains are believed to be the otherworld.[2] A spirit of the dead that has been worshipped by his descendants for thirty-three years becomes a deity (*kami*). The deity remains on the mountain during the winter, but at the beginning of spring it descends from the mountain to the village and protects the rice fields. After the ceremony of harvest in the autumn, it returns to the mountain. This deity is called a deity of the mountain (*yama no kami*)[3] during the winter, and a deity of the rice field (*ta no kami*) from spring to autumn.

Second, mountains are regarded as liminal space between this world and the otherworld. The mountain is an avenue to heaven; a mountain cave is an entrance to the otherworld.[4] Therefore, the living beings on a mountain also have a liminal character. To be more exact, they have both a sacred and a profane character. A long-nosed demon (*tengu*),[5] a demon (*oni*), and also a *yamabushi*—all of which reside on the mountain—share this liminal character.[6]

Third, mountains possess the same character as the cosmos. The mountain is viewed as the axis connecting heaven and earth, and also as the cosmos itself and as the deity itself, which in turn symbolizes the cosmos.[7] For example, Mt. Kinbu, which is the most famous Shugendō mountain in Japan, is also called "Mountain of the Axis in Japan" (Kokujikusan), and also "Gold Mountain." It is well known that gold is a characteristic of a cosmic mountain. So Mt. Kinbu is seen as a cosmic mountain. In the doctrine of Shugendō, the mountain is seen as a womb-and-diamond mandala (cosmos), as Mahāvairocana (Dainichi Nyorai), which is the symbol of the cosmos, and as a deity itself.

Shugendō has a close relationship with Japanese folk religion, so we can find the same notions of mountain within Shugendō. But in the doctrine of Shugendō, the mountain is considered more as a cosmic mountain, and the believers of Shugendō view the mountain as the otherworld and/or a liminal place between this world and the other world.

THE RELIGIOUS SIGNIFICANCE OF *SHUGENJA*

In Japanese folk religion, it is believed that ascetics such as *shugenja* who have undergone rigorous and mysterious austerities and obtained supernatural power become deities in their lifetime. The *shugenja* is feared as a liminal man who is half man and half deity. The doctrine of Shugendō explains the religious character of *shugenja* as follows: He has the same nature as a Buddha but unfortunately is not aware of this; if he awakens to this through mountain austerities, he will be a Buddha in his own body.

The key to understanding the religious character of *shugenja* is in the costume and religious equipment of mountain austerities. Each of these items has interesting symbolic significance, but generally we can identify three connotations: first, a womb-and-diamond mandala (cosmos); second, Dainichi Nyorai (Mahāvairocana) and/or Fudō Myōō (Acala); and third, the doctrine of becoming a Buddha in this body. Each of these items is explained briefly.[8]

1. *Tokin*: a small black skullcap worn on the head. It is a symbol of Mahāvairocana.

2. *Ayaigasa*: a straw hat that serves to ward off sun and rain, and that symbolizes the growth of the *shugenja* in the mother's womb.

3. *Suzukake*: the formal robe of a *shugenja*; it consists of an upper garment and Japanese trousers (*hakama*). The upper garment symbolizes the diamond mandala and the trousers symbolize the womb mandala. There is also a more informal robe, a white robe with a symbolic Sanskrit character for Acala (i.e., Kanman). This robe is called *kanmangi* (robe of Acala), and symbolizes Acala.

4. *Yuigesa*: surplice; the *yuigesa* is a special kind of surplice that is used only in Shugendō. It has six colored tassels and is a symbol of the womb-and-diamond mandala.

5. *Hora*: a conch shell; it is blown as a signal and is used for setting a rhythm in sutra readings. Blowing the *hora* symbolizes the preaching of Mahāvairocana. *Kai no o* is a rope, originally a cord attached to the *hora*. Now it is wound around the waist of *shugenja* and is something like a rope for rock climbing and other uses. The *kai no o* is a symbol of the umbilical cord.

6. *Irataka no juzu*: a rosary composed of 108 wooden beads; rubbing this rosary symbolizes the transformation from a profane state to a sacred state.

7. *Shakujō*: a priest's staff; it serves both as a walking staff and as a magical tool for protection from evil spirits and exorcism and symbolizes the purification of man's sins and becoming a Buddha.

8. *Oi*: a portable wooden box; the *oi* is carried on the back and contains the objects of worship, scriptures of Shugendō, and ritual tools used in the mountains. It is a symbol of a womb-store mandala or a womb, so,

shugenja who carry an *oi* are symbols of an embryo growing in the mother's womb.

9. *Katabako*: a shoulder box; a small box that is placed over the *oi*. The *katabako* is the counterpart or "mate" of the *oi*, symbolizing a diamond mandala or father. Placing the *katabako* over the *oi* symbolizes the communion of a diamond mandala and a womb mandala, or intercourse between father and mother.

10. *Kongōzue*: a "diamond" (*vajra*) cane; it is used for climbing mountains and symbolizes becoming a Buddha.

11. *Hisshiki*: a sitting mat; ideally, it should be made from a lion's pelt. It hangs at the back from the waist and is used for resting during mountain travel and symbolizes purification of sin.

12. *Kyahan*: leggings; they serve the practical purpose of protecting the skin during mountain trips and symbolize becoming a Buddha.

13. *Hiōgi*: a cypress fan; it is used in fanning the fire in the rite of *goma*, and symbolizes becoming a Buddha.

14. *Shiba-uchi*: wood-cutter; it is a short sword used to cut wood for the fire rite and a symbol of Fudō Myōō's activity as the destroyer of evil.

15. *Hashiri nawa*: a rope; this rope is used during mountain austerities and also is a symbol of Fudō Myōō's activity.

16. *Waraji*: a type of straw sandals that are used as the pilgrim's foot gear and symbolize a lotus, a seat of the Buddha.[9]

The robe of Haguro Shugendō has a picture of a lion, and ideally the sitting mat is made from a lion's pelt. These items show that the *shugenja* is a ruler of the animal world. In Japanese folk religion animals are believed to be mediators between the spiritual world (the world of deities) and the world of men.[10] Therefore, the *shugenja* becomes a mediator between the spiritual world and the human world.

Another important feature is the hair style of the *shugenja*. Usually Buddhist priests shave their heads, but the *shugenja* has cropped hair. This hair style shows that the *shugenja* is a liminal man between the priests and the common people. Dressing in this costume, the *shugenja* changes symbolically to a lion, that is, a ruler of animals, or Mahāvairocana, or the microcosmos, which has the same character as the macrocosmos.

THE TYPES OF MOUNTAIN AUSTERITIES

Originally the period of mountain austerities in Shugendō lasted from fall until the beginning of spring. The ascetics went into the mountains in early fall, passed the cold winter in the mountains, and came back early in spring. Most of the austerities that were practiced during the early period of the Shugen sect (from the tenth century to the thirteenth century) took the form of winter confinement in the mountains. But it is impossible to

Figure 24. *Shugenja* costume: 1. *Tokin*, 2. *Ayaigasa*, 3. *Suzukake* (back and front), 4. *Yuigesa*, 5. *Hora*, 6. *Irataka no juzu*, 7. *Shakujō*, 8. *Oi*. Facing Page: 9. *Katabako*, 10. *Kongōzue*, 11. *Hisshiki*, 12. *Kyahan*, 13. *Hiōgi*, 14. *Shiba-uchi*, 15. *Hashiri nawa*, 16. *Waraji*.

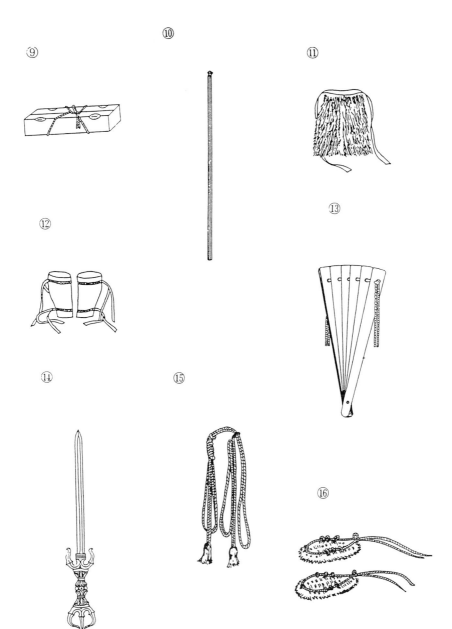

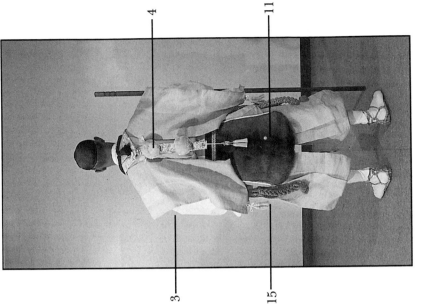

Figure 26. *Shugenja* costume (back). Numbers correspond to figure 24.

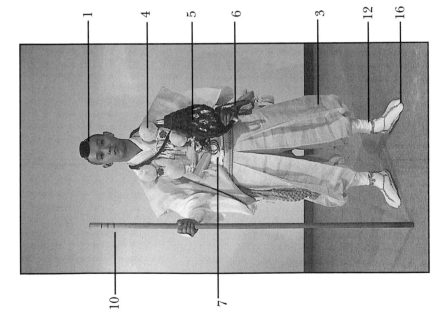

Figure 25. *Shugenja* costume (front). Numbers correspond to figure 24.

know what kind of mystic training was practiced by these mountain ascetics during the winter. We can only infer the form of mountain austerities at that time from fragmentary materials and the remains of ascetics. This evidence leads us to the following scenario.

The ascetics confined themselves in mountain caves during winter. Even today, these caves can be seen near the valleys on the mountainside. The larger ones are stalactite grottos in which there are small ponds, rivers, and deity-like rock formations. The smaller ones are something like small shelters surrounded by rocks. In ancient times, dead bodies were placed in these caves, so these caves were called *tamaya*, the house of souls. Also, the caves were believed to be entrances to the otherworld.

In the mountains the ascetics collected twigs for the fire rite (*goma*) and drew water for purification. They poured cold water over themselves and fasted for many days. During winter they spent almost all day in the caves. For many hours they prayed to the deity-like rock formations in order to gain their power. In these lonely practices they sometimes saw visions of supernatural beings. These visions were perceived by the mountain ascetics as evidence that they had gained supernatural powers of deities.[11] The ascetics who were convinced that they had obtained supernatural power then descended from the mountain with twigs of evergreen on April 8.

In Japanese folk religion the day of April 8 is believed to be the day when the deity of the mountain (*yama no kami*) descends to the rice fields, so on this day maidens ascend the hills and come back with twigs or flowers.[12] Therefore, we can consider that the ascetics who descended from the mountains with evergreens were believed by villagers to be religious men with the power of the deity of the mountain.

The winter austerities of the Haguro sect, called the winter peak,[13] is an interesting example that still survives as a vestige of ancient confinement austerities during winter. Two senior *shugenja* (*matsu hijiri*)[14] practice the winter peak austerities in their temple for a span of 100 days. There are several kinds of practices that begin on September 30 and go to the end of the year. The main practices are purification, praying at a miniature hut (*kōya hijiri*) that contains grain, worshipping an undefiled fire in order to control fire, and religious mendicancy. On the last day of these hundred-day austerities, December 31, there is a very interesting festival called Shōreisai (the Festival of Souls). In this festival there are contests between the two senior *shugenja* of magico-religious powers (*genkurabe*) that they have acquired by rigorous and mysterious training. Actually, these contests are held between the followers of the two *matsu hijiri*, who are manipulated by the *matsu hijiri's* supernatural power. One of the most interesting

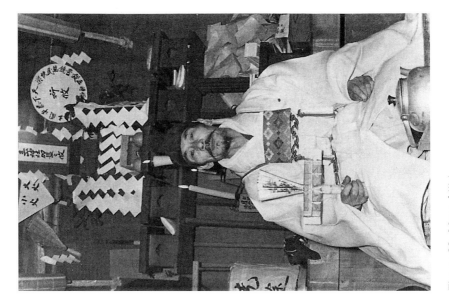

Figure 28. *Matsu hijiri*

Figure 27. *Kōya hijiri* (a miniature hut containing grain)

contests is the crow-leap in the shrine hall: two *kohijiri* (followers of the *matsu hijiri*) who symbolize the crow, the messenger of the Haguro deity, compete in leaping power. Another interesting contest involves extinguishing the old fire of the present year and lighting a new fire for the coming year. Although these contests are performed by *kohijiri*, the two *matsu hijiri* are manipulating them with their supernatural powers. After these contests the grain of the miniature hut of the winning side is used as seed for that year. The grain of the defeated side is scattered on the floor. Also as part of this festival, a dramatic ceremony that acts out the origin of Haguro sect is performed.[15] From the contents of these contests we can see that the supernatural powers that the *matsu hijiri* obtained as a result of winter austerities are as follow:

> 1. The ability to manipulate his spiritual followers (*kohijiri*) using his spiritual power; or, more simply, the power to manipulate spirits.
> 2. The ability to manipulate fire as a shaman—who can fly to heaven.
> 3. The ability to offer seed for agriculture as the guardian of agriculture.

We can conclude from the above observations that the object of the winter peak austerities, in general, is to acquire the ability to manipulate spirits and the power of a shaman.

By the end of the Middle Ages (about the sixteenth century), Shugendō had become completely institutionalized, and mountain austerities were systematized as a form of group training. That is, the confinement austerities from fall to early spring (winter peak) were differentiated into fall peak, winter peak, and spring peak austerities. In addition to these three, the summer peak, which was mainly practiced by lay believers during the summer, appeared as a new form. Thus, every season came to have its own mountain austerities.

Of these four types of mountain austerities, the most systematic austerity was the fall peak, which was practiced by Shugendō practitioners, and even today is considered by the Shugendō practitioner as the most important. (This austerity will be described in detail later.)

In recent times the winter peak is rarely seen, except at Mt. Haguro. It is rather a specific austerity for the individual. The spring peak is called *hanaku no mine* (the practice of offering flowers). This is the ceremony of the *shugenja's* going into the mountain at spring, descending with evergreens, and putting them in the rice fields. This, then, is a ceremony of inviting the deities of the rice field through the supernatural power of *shugenja*.

In the practice of the summer peak, common believers climb the mountain mainly at the time of Bon (the Festival of the Dead), so the object of this practice is to go into the mountain that is the living place of their ancestors in order to worship them. During the Tokugawa period, many believers of Shugendō practiced the summer peak, and even at present in the summer many believers of Shugendō visit mountains for this practice.

Out of these four mountain austerities, I will focus mainly on the fall peak, which is the most important practice for the Shugendō practitioner.

REBIRTH AND THE TRAINING OF THE TEN WORLDS

The fall peak, which is practiced from the end of summer to the beginning of fall, has the character of an initiation rite for the practitioner of Shugendō. The fall peak of Mt. Ōmine during the Middle Ages observed ten kinds of special rites called the training of ten worlds (*jikkai shugyō*).[16] The ten worlds (*jikkai*) are the ten stages through which the initiate must pass before he achieves the state of a Buddha in his own body: hell (*jigoku*), hungry ghost (*gaki*), beasts (*chikushō*), asuras (*shura*), human (*ningen*), heaven (*ten*), disciple (*shōmon*), self-enlightened one (*enkaku*), enlightened being (*bosatsu*), and Buddha (*butsu*). Each of these ten stages has its own prescribed practices, which will be discussed later. We can also recognize the motif of death and rebirth in the mountain practices of the fall peak.

At present, the training of ten worlds at Mt. Ōmine has changed to a kind of ethical teaching and is little practiced. Also, the motif of death and rebirth is not so noticeable. But the fall peak of Haguro still retains that motif, as well as the first six practices of the training of ten worlds. Therefore, I will take up the fall peak of Haguro and present it in outline.[17]

The fall peak of Haguro is practiced at Kōtaku Temple on Mt. Haguro from August 24 to 31. The sequence of practices during this period is presented below.

On the evening of the 24th, the rite of the celebration of the *oi*, which is the object of worship during the fall peak, is practiced by the leaders of this training at the temple called Shōzenin at the foot of Mt. Haguro. This ceremony, called *oikaragaki*, means the funeral ceremony of the initiates.

On the morning of the 25th, the procession of the *shugenja*, starting from Shōzenin goes to the nearby Koganedō. Here the main leader (*daisendatsu*) turns around three times a long pole with paper streamers (*bonten*) and throws it up the steps of the temple (Koganedō). This action symbolizes conception. After this ceremony the procession begins, stopping to pray at shrines of Mt. Haguro and other prescribed sacred places. Then, going deeper into the mountain, they arrive at the training place,

Kōtaku Temple. This temple symbolizes a womb. At this place the initiates pass through three stages of mystic training (*ichi no shuku, ni no shuku, san no shuku*).

Ichi no shuku (the first division) lasts from the 25th to the 27th. On the evening of the 25th, the positions of every initiate in the training room are decided by the staff leaders (*sendatsu*). After they sit down at their prescribed seats, two round wooden sticks are hit together above each member's head by the staff leaders. This signifies the purification of each initiate. They then pray to the *oi* (which is covered with a straw hat) by reading sutras (*gongyō*).

In the midst of the *gongyō*, there is heard a loud pounding on the wooden doors (*amado*) around the temple. This frightening noise resounds three times. The purpose of this action—which is called *shirabe*—is to awaken the initiates from the slumber of illusion (and to awaken their Buddha nature).

As the *gongyō* ends, three charcoal braziers are ordered into the room. Three leaders throw spices on the red hot coals and fan the coals vigorously so that the fumes immediately fill the room. This is repeated several times. This ceremony, which is held to exorcize the bad spirits in the initiates, is called *nanban-ibushi*.

After these exercises, the initiates present water and twigs to the staff leaders. These exercises in the room are held at the beginning of night (*shoya*) and about midnight (*goya*) each day until the 27th.

On the 26th the initiates are prohibited from eating anything or drinking or using water. And in the daytime, they walk for long distances.

On the 27th day the leaders perform a memorial service for the dead.

On the 28th, the staff leaders hold the ceremony for entering into the second division (*ni no shuku iri*) on the road to Kōtaku Temple. In this ceremony two staff leaders hold two torches together. This action signifies conception.

Ni no shuku (second division) takes place on the days of the 28th and the 29th. During this division, *gongyō* is conducted without the frightening noises and rites of exorcism. In place of these activities, there are *toko-sanjō* and confession of sins to the main leader. The *toko-sanjō* is a distinctive rite, in which the staff leader takes two sticks, waves them before him three times in a circular motion, and strikes the altar with the sticks. The purpose of this rite is to bind souls.

On the afternoon of the 28th, the initiates engage in sumo wrestling, and in the evening they are taught mysterious rites by the main leader. At midnight, the leaders have a specific fire ritual called *saitō goma*. The *goma* is a unique Shugendō rite in which a large fire is built near the temple. The sequence of this rite is as follows:

Figure 30. *Toko-sanjō* at Hagurō Shugendō

Figure 29. *Bonten taoshi* (throwing the *bonten* up the steps of Koganedō)

At first, two staff leaders put together two torches. This is a rite similar to the entrance rite for the second division. One of the staff leaders uses a torch to set fire to a mound of logs and leaves, which burns brightly. Around the fire, the initiates read sutras. One of the staff leaders moves around the fire with a long stick. The purpose of this action is said to be to bind the souls of the initiates.

After the fire rite, the leaders and initiates go to the entrance of Kōtaku Temple, where the head leader moves a fan up and down. At that moment white and red cloth streamers descend from the temple ceiling almost to the floor. This is a sign of the beginning of the third division and also symbolizes the communion of heaven and earth. The initiates sing songs of celebration and drink rice wine together.

The third division lasts until the 31st. In the third division they pray to the founders of the Haguro sect instead of the *oi* covered with a straw hat, and they pray for the well-being of the believers. During the daytime they make pilgrimages to sacred places where ancestors live.

On the 31st they descend from the mountain. Starting from Kōtaku Temple in ranks, they arrive at Haguro Shrine. After worshipping at the shrine, they crouch down and rise up giving a "birth-cry" (*ubugoe*), and then the initiates leave the shrine and jump over a fire that is burning in front of Koganedō. This fire is the same style as the ancestor-welcoming fire of Bon. Therefore, these rituals symbolize the rebirth of initiates as buddhas. That night the main leader gives a certificate for participation in the fall peak and a new religious name to the initiate. After this ceremony they have a feast in celebration of becoming a Buddha.

In this fall peak we can also find the first six practices of the training of the ten worlds, that is, hell's *nanban-ibushi*, hungry ghost's fasting, beast's prohibiting water, *asura's* sumo wrestling, human's confession of sin, heaven's singing songs of celebration. These six practices are usually called the practices of "six worlds" (*rokudō*).[18]

Thus, we can find such interesting elements in this fall peak as a funeral rite (celebration of *oi*), sexual intercourse and conception (throwing the *bonten* upon the steps of Koganedō, putting together two torches), exorcism (*nanban-ibushi*), growth in the womb (Kōtaku Temple, *oi*, and straw hat), binding of a new soul (*toko-sanjō*, and walking with a stick at the fire rite), and rebirth (the first cry of a newborn baby at Haguro Shrine). That is to say, in this fall peak the initiates first die symbolically, become embryos through sexual intercourse, and then they exorcize bad spirits from their bodies and bind new spirits. Thus, they become sacred men and are reborn.

These sacred men also have obtained the status of a Buddha because they have gone through the practices of the "six worlds" that are required for becoming a Buddha. Furthermore, another important motif can be seen in the fall peak: communion and separation between earth and heaven (the origin of cosmos).

What, then, are the steps necessary for a mountain ascetic to become a Buddha? This can be illustrated in the training of the ten worlds, which is the process of becoming a Buddha through mountain austerities. The training of the ten worlds at Mt. Ōmine in the latter half of the Middle Ages (fourteenth century to sixteenth century) consisted of the following practices[19]:

1. The practice of hell is *tokogatame*. This is a rite that is held on the first night in the mountain austerities. The initiate strikes himself with a small round wooden stick and convinces himself of his ability to achieve the state of being a Buddha in his own body.

2. The practice of hungry ghosts is a confession. The initiate confesses his sins to the main leader in a secret room.

3. The practice of beasts is the practice of *gō no hakari* (weighing his sin). The leaders tie up the hands of the initiate, and lift him up to weigh his sin.

4. The practice of devils is the abstention from water.

5. The practice of humans is a rite using water. The main leader pours drops of water on the head of initiates using a thin stick (*sanjō*).

6. The practice of heaven is the sumo of initiates. In this case, sumo has the same meaning as dance.

7. The practice of disciples is a dance celebrating longevity (*ennen*).

8. The practice of a self-enlightened Buddha is the rite of *kogi*. The initiates collect twigs (*kogi*) and present them to the main leader. After that all the members participate in a fire ritual using these twigs.

9. The practice of an enlightened human being is abstention from grains for seven days until the day of the consecration rite.

10. The practice of Buddha is the consecration or status bestowal rite (*kanjō*). In this rite the initiates who have undergone severe training until this day are taught the *mudrā* (gesture of esoteric Buddhism) of Dainichi Nyorai and the *hashiramoto goma*, i.e., the pillar erection ritual (the most important mysterious rite in Shugendō).[20] They are taught this at Jinzen, in the heart of the Ōmine Mountains. Completing this consecration rite, the person who has been initiated into mountain austerities now completely becomes a Buddha in his own body.

Therefore, we can say that the initiate can be a Buddha in his own body by completing the process of the mysterious training of ten worlds. At first the initiate convinces himself of his ability to be a Buddha in his very body. Then his sins are weighed by the leader and he confesses his sins. Thus he can cancel his sins. After these preparations the austerities begin. The initiates recognize the importance of water by abstaining from water. Then they use water in order to become reborn as a Buddha. Sumo and dancing are carried out as a celebration for this rebirth.

Once more the initiate burns off his sinful desires in the fire ritual. He changes his body physiologically by abstaining from grains for seven days. And at last he receives a *mudrā* of the cosmos itself and/or its incarnation (Dainichi Nyorai or Fudō Myōō) from the main leader. Thus he accomplishes becoming a Buddha in this body. To summarize, the initiate purifies himself and practices mysterious training using symbols of water and fire. Then he becomes a Buddha in his own body.

The initiate becomes a Buddha in his own body or ascends to heaven by practicing the training of ten worlds. The initiate dies symbolically, then undergoes conception as a Buddha, and is reborn as a Buddha. In this way, the initiate's transformation into a Buddha is intensified by the motif of death and rebirth. So the initiate who has practiced such mysterious training is strongly convinced of his transformation into a Buddha in his own body.

THE CONSECRATION RITE AND *HASHIRAMOTO GOMA* (PILLAR ERECTION RITUAL)

Finally, I shall describe the consecration or status bestowal rite[21] and the *hashiramoto goma,* which are the most important and mysterious rites in mountain austerities. In recent times these two rites have not been practiced often. But fortunately I was able to study the consecration rite at Mt. Katsuragi in September 1968, and the *hashiramoto goma* at Shōgoin in Kyoto in September 1969. I shall discuss these two rites in order to illustrate what kind of sacred being the initiate changes into by means of mountain austerities.[22]

The consecration rite at Mt. Katsuragi consists of three parts. First are preliminary mountain austerities for the consecration rite. Until the Middle Ages, fasting for seven days was practiced as a preliminary austerity. Second is the consecration rite itself. Third is the fire ritual for celebration of the consecration and new status. I shall only explain the second part, which is the most important rite.

The consecration rite consists of four parts: the preliminary rite, the purification rite, the rite of gaining a guardian deity, and the bestowal of a *mudrā*. At the preliminary rite, the leaders present the main leader with twigs (*kogi*) and water (*aka*). This symbolizes fostering the initiate's Buddha nature by fire and water. Then the main leader preaches that the purpose of this consecration rite is for the initiate to become a Buddha in his very body, by himself.

At the purification rite, the initiate confesses his sins and removes them by purification. Then he enters into the stage of a Buddha. At the rite of gaining a guardian deity, the leader blindfolds the initiate. Then he guides the initiate to a picture of many deities that has been placed on an altar. The deity onto which a twig drops is considered his guardian deity.

In the last stage, the head leader pours drops of water on the head of the initiate using a slender stick. Then he teaches the initiate the *mudrā* that symbolizes becoming a Buddha in his own body and tells the initiate that from now on whenever he forms this *mudrā* he becomes a Buddha in his own body. In his usual religious activity, the *shugenja* makes this *mudrā* first, and then performs a rite of exorcism.

One more important thing to understand is the fasting for seven days that was done in ancient times. By fasting for a long time, the initiate changed his body physiologically. Thus he reached a spiritual state of self-lessness through a state of semistupor. While in this state, he often had a vision of a guardian deity or unconsciously made a *mudrā* of this deity. Therefore, in earlier times, the consecration rite in Shugendō was not a regular ceremony but a mysterious ritual similar to a vision quest.[23]

This same ritual can be seen in the mysterious initiation rite of ascetics (*gyōnin*) and female shamans (*miko*). They perform fasting and ablution for several weeks. Then they wear a white robe, take a ritual symbol (*gohei*), and sit down in front of their leader. The leader performs a rite of inviting a deity to possess an initiate. Many of the initiate's religious companions loudly read sutras around him or her. Suddenly the initiate shakes his or her hands up and down violently and cries out. This is the sign he or she has a guardian spirit. Thus the initiate has received the guardian spirit in a state of trance. I believe the consecration rite in Shugendō originally was the same process as these initiation rites.[24]

Hashiramoto goma is a rite that dramatizes the origin of the cosmos and the rebirth of the *shugenja* as a sacred man.[25] This rite is practiced in a temple with the use of a small platform for the fire ritual. The instruments used in this rite are many and quite complicated, so I will mention only the most important items. A board is placed on the platform of the *goma*. On this board there is one cylindrical water pot and offerings (water, flowers, grain, etc., which are put in the small bowl). All of these materials are of a golden color. Three small pillars are erected in the water pot. The central one is a little larger, and the other two black pillars a little smaller. These instruments have interesting symbolic meanings. The board indicates the undifferentiation of heaven and earth, and the cylindrical water pot symbolizes the union of heaven and earth. The central pillar is the initiate himself, and the other two pillars are father and mother.

This rite consists of five parts, that is, introduction, *tokogatame*, *hashiramoto*, *goma*, and conclusion. In the introduction, the initiate undergoes the rite of extinguishing his sinful desires. In the *tokogatame*,[26] he convinces himself

Figure 31. The rite of receiving a guardian spirit

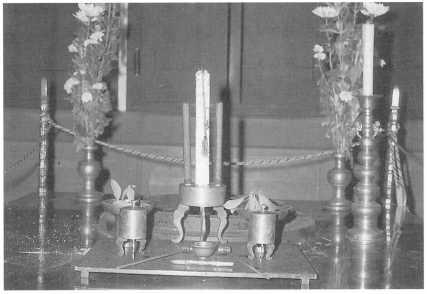

Figure 32. Instruments of the *hashiramoto goma*

of his ability to become a Buddha in his own body. The *hashiramoto*, the central part of this rite, features the following ritual process. At first, the initiate pours water into the cylindrical water pot. This action symbolizes that the water of heaven and earth are mixed to bring forth father and mother. Then he picks up two black pillars and puts them together. This action symbolizes sexual intercourse and the creation of an embryo. This embryo is the initiate himself and the symbol of this is the central pillar. So the initiate presents to this central pillar the offerings of water, flower, grains, etc., and prays for its growth.

The part of *goma* symbolizes the rebirth of the initiate as Mahāvairocana (symbol of the cosmos) through the fire of *goma*. At the conclusion, the initiate puts the central pillar between his clasped hands and confirms that he has become the same being with Mahāvairocana.

If we consider the central part (that is, *hashiramoto*) of the *hashiramoto goma* of Shugendō, we can perceive the following drama. At first, heaven and earth are created from chaos. Then, father and mother are created by the communion of heaven and earth. Finally, the embryo, that is, the initiate himself, is created by intercourse between father and mother and is born. Thus the *hashiramoto goma* portrays the motif of rebirth of the cosmos and the initiate.

In this rite of the small pillar, therefore, we can see that the initiate is reborn, and transforms himself into the central pillar. According to the doctrine of Shugendō, this pillar links heaven and earth and is the place where a person emerges when he is born, and where he returns when he dies. That is to say, the central pillar in the cylindrical water pot has the character of *axis mundi* or cosmic mountain that links heaven and earth. So, at the base of this rite of the small pillar, we find the worldview that the initiate who has practiced this mysterious rite is transformed into the *axis mundi* or cosmos itself. As a matter of fact, the initiate who has been transformed into the *axis mundi* becomes an excellent religious practitioner who knows and controls all things in the cosmos. Such a mediator or manipulator is called a shaman.

Therefore, the purpose of the mountain austerities in Shugendō—which are concluded by the consecration rite and/or the erection pillar—is to give the initiate the same supernatural powers as a shaman. So, when the initiates complete their mountain austerities, they compete with their shamanistic supernatural power, that is, the power to manipulate spirits and deities, the power to control fire, and the power to fly to heaven. To state this conversely, these mysterious demonstrations of the *shugenja* show that he has become transformed into the *axis mundi* and the cosmos itself.

NOTES

1. Ikegami Hiromasa, "The Significance of Mountains in the Popular Belief in Japan," in *Religious Studies in Japan*, ed. Japanese Association for Religious Studies (Tokyo: Maruzen, 1959), 152–60.
2. Hori Ichirō, "Mountains and Their Importance for the Idea of the Other World in Japanese Folk Religion," *History of Religions* 6.1 (1966): 1–23.
3. For further information on *yama no kami*, see Nelly Naumann, "Yama no Kami—die japanische Berggottheit," *Asian Folklore Studies* 22 (1963): 133–366; (1964): 48–199; also Kurata Ichirō, "Yama-no-kami," *Contemporary Japan* 9 (1940): 1304–12.
4. For the liminal character of mountains and hills, see Yanagita Kunio, *The Legend of Tōno (Tōno monogatari)*, trans. Ronald A. Morse (Tokyo: The Japan Foundation, 1975).
5. For further information on *tengu*, see M. W. de Visser, "The Tengu," *Transactions of the Asiatic Society of Japan* 36 (1908): 25–99; also, Miyamoto Kesao, *Tengu to shugenja (Tengu and shugenja)* (Kyoto: Jinmon Shoin, 1989).
6. Yoshida Teigo, "The Stranger as God: The Place of the Outsider in Japanese Folk Religion," *Ethnology* 20.2 (1981): 87–99.
7. The idea of the cosmic mountain can be seen in many religions. For example, see Richard J. Clifford, *The Cosmic Mountain in Canaan and the Old Testament* (Cambridge: Harvard University Press, 1972).
8. Miyake Hitoshi, *Shugendō shisō no kenkyū* (Tokyo: Shunjūsha, 1985), 614–58.
9. These sixteen items of costume and equipment are called *yamabushi jūroku dōgu*, the "*yamabushi's* sixteen tools."
10. For the character of animals in Japanese folk religion, see Emiko Ohnuki-Tierney, *The Monkey as Mirror: Symbolic Transformation in Japanese History and Ritual* (Princeton: Princeton University Press, 1987).
11. Yanagita Kunio, "Kebōzukō" (On ascetics with cropped hair), *Teihon Yanagita Kunio shū* 9 (Tokyo: Chikuma Shobō, 1962), 403–9.
12. April 8 is also the birthday of the Buddha, and the date for the ceremony for the rite commemorating it at Buddhist temples.
13. The four "peaks" of Haguro Shugendō are comparable to the *nyūbu shugyō* ("practice in the mountains" or *mineiri*—mountain entry) of other Shugendō groups. See H. Byron Earhart, "Four Ritual Periods of Haguro Shugendō in Northeastern Japan," *History of Religions* 5.1 (1965): 93–113.
14. *Matsu hijiri* means literally "pine saint." For *hijiri* see Hori Ichirō, "On the Concept of Hijiri (Holy-Man)," *Numen* 5 (1958): 128–60, 199–232.
15. See H. Byron Earhart, *A Religious Study of the Mount Haguro Sect of Shugendō. An Example of Japanese Mountain Religion* (Tokyo: Sophia University, 1970), 89–99.
16. Carmen Blacker, "Initiation in Shugendō: The Passage Through the Ten States of Existence," in *Initiation*, ed. C. J. Bleeker (Leiden: E. J. Brill, 1965), 96–111.
17. See Earhart, *A Religious Study*, 111–46; also Togawa Anshō, *Shugendō to minzoku* (Shugendō and folklore) (Tokyo: Iwasaki Bijutsu Shuppan, 1972), 94–154.
18. *Rokudō* means the six worlds through which the souls of living beings transmigrate.
19. Miyake, *Shugendō shisō no kenkyū*, 714–37.
20. The *hashiramoto goma* (pillar erection ritual) will be described in the next section.
21. See Miyake Hitoshi, *Shugendō girei no kenkyū* (A study of religious rituals in Shugendō), 2d ed., rev. (Tokyo: Shunjūsha, 1985), 93–108. "Status bestowal rite" (*kanjō*) is a complex form of consecration ceremonies.
22. Miyagi Taimen, ed., *Katsuragi kanjō*, Special issue of *Honzan shugen* 23 (1968): 16–22.
23. Hori Ichirō, *Nihon no shamanizumu* (Shamanism in Japan) (Tokyo: Kōdansha, 1971), 79–112.
24. Sakurai Tokutarō, *Nihon no shamanizumu* (Shamanism in Japan), 2 vols. (Tokyo: Yoshikawa Kōbunkan, 1974–77).

25. See Miyake, *Shugendō shisō no kenkyū,* 213–35; also Nakayama Seiden, "Tendai hongaku shisō to shinbutsu konkō shisō—toku ni hashiramoto goma o chūshin to shite" (Tendai *hongaku* thought and Shinto-Buddhist amalgamation thought—with special emphasis on the pillar erection rite), *Indogaku bukkyō kenkyū* 23 (1975): 368–71.

26. The practitioner strikes together two small sticks (*udekora*) and puts one on each side of his waist. Then he convinces himself of his ability to become a Buddha in his own body.

The Structure of Exorcism in Shugendō

SHUGENDŌ AND EXORCISM

Shugendō has two major goals: the first is to acquire supernatural power through mountain austerities, and the second is to practice magico-religious activities using this power in the local community. Of these two goals, religious activities in the local community are more closely related to the religious life of the Japanese people. In this chapter I will focus on this second aspect.

During the Edo period (1603–1868), the religious life of the local community was supported mainly by shrines, priests of temples, and religious specialists such as *shugenja*. Shrines "contain" or "enshrine" guardian deities of the community. The priests of temples hold funeral rites and memorials for ancestors. Religious specialists such as *shugenja*, however, perform various activities in response to the common people's requests for immediate assistance and concrete benefits. Usually these *shugenja* are called *sato shugen* (village *shugen*).[1]

These activities of *shugenja* include a variety of practices. First, the *shugenja* is a leader of mountain austerities and pilgrimages to shrines and temples. Second, he leads the observances at small shrines. Third, he performs divination. Fourth, he serves as a magico-religious specialist. Usually the same *shugenja* carries out all four of these religious activities by himself. But at times, these activities are handled by different *shugenja*. In modern times, some of the *shugenja* and other religious specialists who practiced similar activities became the founders of new religions.[2] Therefore, Shugendō can be considered a fountainhead of the history of Japanese popular religions.

Of the above four aspects, I will select magico-religious activities, specifically, exorcism, for special attention; but of course I shall also take up the other three aspects in so far as they have some relationship to exorcism. This magico-religious aspect is widely known as the religious activities of a *shugenja* that he practices in response to the requests of the immediate material needs of the common people.[3] Many new religions that have appeared in modern times practice similar religious activities.

The *shugenja* uses a piece of secret practice paper (*kirigami*) on which the procedures of the rites are written to perform each rite.[4] The procedures of a rite differ according to its purpose. The various types of papers show the kinds of practices that the *shugenja* carries out in response to the petitions of the common people. At the beginning of this century, *Shugen jinpi gyōhō fujushū*, a textbook of magico-religious practices in Shugendō, was compiled from many of these papers possessed by *shugenja* all over Japan. This textbook forms the basic material of the present chapter.[5]

We can see the kinds of requests the *shugenja* responds to by noting the purposes of rites written on these secret practice papers. The total number of rites, i.e., papers that are contained in this text, is 587. Grouped by their purpose, they consist of: illness, 134; birth and child rearing, 51; agriculture, 22; daily life (food, clothing, and housing), 54; human relations, 88; war, 23; removal of misfortune, 121; and general prayers, 61. From this numerical count we see that the actual number for illness and removal of misfortunes is much greater than for others. We also note that the number for rites of exorcism is much higher than the number of prayers for good luck in daily life. Therefore we can conclude that an important part of a *shugenja's* religious activities is removal of misfortunes such as illness, strife in human relations, and accidents in daily life and/or birth and child rearing, and that *shugenja* practice exorcism more than prayer to deities in order to respond to these requests. In this analysis, I will trace the procedures a *shugenja* uses in order to remove the misfortune of his believer, and then interpret the worldview sustaining such religious activities.

My point of view is as follows. I take the magico-religious activities such as exorcism as a symbolic action system, and interpret the symbolic meanings of every action and situation in them. By using this method, I try to uncover the general meaning of these activities and the religious worldview that supports them. For the purpose of clarity I will first discuss the religious worldview that sustains the *shugenja's* magico-religious activities. Then I will examine the procedures of magico-religious activities that are intended to remove misfortune.

THE WORLDVIEW OF EXORCISM

Not only Shugendō but also all folk religion in Japan depends on a basically animistic worldview. Moreover, for the Japanese people who live

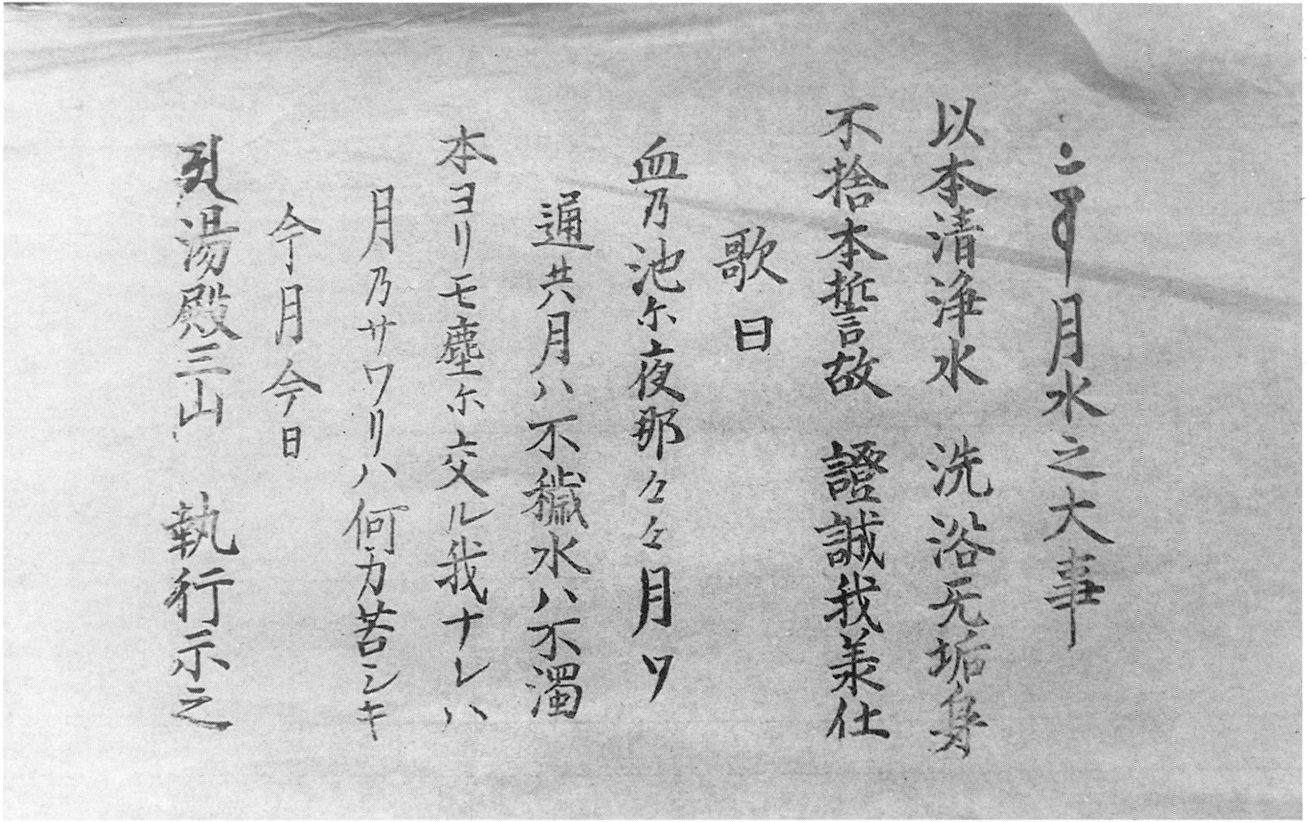

口ア月水ノ大事

以冬清浄水　洗浴先婦

不痊本性故　鬱誠救末仕

歌曰

血乃汍不夜郱ルヲ月ヤ

通其月八不穢水八不濁

本ヨリモ塵モ文ヒ敦トヽ

月乃サワリハ何カ苦シキ

今月今日

五逆物咒言山　執行立之

Figure 33. *Kirigami* for menstruation

permanently in a certain locale and are engaged in agriculture, nature is conceived as coexisting with humans. They consider both nature and humans as situated in the order of the cosmos.

A person begins life by receiving a soul and the person grows up according to the maturation of this soul. He or she marries and produces children. The individual dies when this soul has left the body. The detached soul grows in the otherworld in a cycle similar to the living soul by receiving the worship of its descendants, and after thirty-three years it becomes a deity. This worshipped soul and deity protects the lives of its descendants. A living person must not struggle with others or injure others and should follow the rules of society. He or she worships the spirits and/or deities of nature and farms the family fields diligently according to the law of nature. Daily life is sustained by the actual food this person has produced. This is the normal lifestyle of the Japanese people; this lifestyle is not only "the way" (*michi*) that Japanese people must obey, but it is also a law of the cosmos that humans must obey. And they feel happy if they can pass each day in this lifestyle.[6]

However, even if people have lived rightly according to "the way," they will encounter various accidents and misfortunes, such as illness, accidental death, a long drought, and so on. In such situations they want a religious explanation for these misfortunes. They are convinced that if they had obeyed the right "way" of the Japanese people, such an accident or misfortune would not have happened. Conversely, they may suppose that such accidents or misfortunes happened because they or someone else went against the "way." With these considerations in mind, we can interpret the rationale for accidents and misfortunes as follows.

It is believed that a person has been punished by an accident for the following bad conduct: first, quarreling with others about trifling things; second, not worshipping the deities of nature and/or ancestors; third, disturbing the law of the cosmos. When misfortune is due to these bad actions, people can correct the misfortune by repentance, worshipping the ancestors and/or nature deities, and obeying the law of the cosmos. But actual life is not so simple.

In some cases, even after a person has carried out these religious activities, he or she still cannot remove the misfortunes and regain happiness. In such cases misfortune is believed to have been caused by other reasons. The following four kinds of reasons are considered to be the specific causes of misfortune: first, people who are envious of a person may cause one misfortune; second, unworshipped souls of the dead and one's ancestors' souls may be responsible; third, the anger of unworshipped deities of nature can cause trouble; fourth, violation of the law of the cosmos can bring about misfortune. Each of the four reasons can be understood as follows.

First, accidents and misfortunes are due to other people's ill will that originates from the strife between men and women, political strife, and other conflict. Above all, a woman's jealousy is dreadfully feared.

Second, accidents and misfortunes are brought about by the souls of the dead, ancestor souls, and deities. In this case not all of these souls and deities are dangerous beings. Those that cause accidents and misfortunes are the souls of those who died accidentally (*onryō* or *goryō*), souls of dead persons not worshipped by their descendants (*yūrei*), and deities not worshipped by a local community (*jashin*).

Third, the deities of nature are considered to be the cause of accidents and misfortunes. These include mountains, water, trees, stones, wind, and so on, and animals such as snakes, foxes, birds, and so on, which are believed to be the messengers of deities.

Fourth, violation of the laws of the cosmos, such as proscribed ("taboo") days and directions, are feared. In the third and fourth cases, accidents and misfortunes are due to the violation of taboos of the deities of nature, the messengers of deities, or the laws of the cosmos.[7]

What worldview has made it possible for these persons, spirits of the dead, deities, and violations of the law of the cosmos to be considered the cause of accidents and misfortunes? Exploring this worldview is essential for comprehending the rationale of misfortune and exorcism.

First of all, we must remember that in essence, nature, humans, and all other things are granted their lives and their daily existence by these spirits. These spirits are benevolent beings that make all things work in conformity with the law of the cosmos. According to the doctrine of Shugendō, all things have Buddha nature; therefore, to the extent that they realize this and use their Buddha nature, the order of the cosmos is sustained and people are happy. But sometimes these spirits and Buddha nature become defiled, and therefore disturb themselves and other people.

Disturbances are of two major types. First is a curse, which is called *tatari* or *sawari* in Japanese. In this magico-religious phenomenon, living souls, the souls of the dead, ancestor deities, deities of nature, and the deities that symbolize the law of the cosmos, can use their special power to disturb or inflict suffering upon other persons and society. That is to say, they curse and harm specific people or society. Particularly in the case of strife between living persons, a sorcerer manipulates evil spirits and/or deities and injures the person designated by his client.

Second is the phenomenon of possession. In this case, the evil spirits and/or deities disturb a person by possessing his or her body. In traditional

Japan, illness, particularly mental diseases, were thought to be due to possession by these evil spirits and/or deities. In the case of possession, it is believed that a sorcerer (*gyōja*) manipulates his evil spirits and causes other people to be possessed by these spirits as a way of harming them.[8]

The magico-religious activities of *shugenja* or exorcists depend on this folk religious worldview. The *shugenja* who has practiced mountain austerities is worshipped by many people as a special magico-religious performer of prayer and ritual who can identify himself with Fudō Myōō (Acala, destroyer of evil) and thereby manipulate spirits and deities in the cosmos at his will. That is to say, they believe that the *shugenja* manipulates at his will the spirits and/or deities who are the agents of curses and possessing spirits, and makes their disturbance stop.

On the basis of the foregoing general treatment of *shugenja* and the worldview of exorcism within the larger folk religious worldview of Japan, we can proceed to an interpretation of the actual methods of magico-religious activities performed by *shugenja* in response to the requests of their believers.

METHODS OF EXORCISM

As previously mentioned, a *shugenja* practices various activities such as leading mountain austerities, serving as priest of the observance of small shrines, divination, and magico-religious prayer. But all of these activities are closely related to the requests of their believers to remove misfortunes. For example, in mountain austerities there are practices in which the participants confess their sins, repent, communicate with a Buddha, and finally become a Buddha in their own bodies. So in this case, through ascetic training in the mountain, a man purges himself of his sin that is the cause of his misfortune. At small shrines in which deities of the sun, moon, stars, and so on are enshrined, the *shugenja's* observances have a similar religious meaning. In these observances the *shugenja* symbolically identifies himself with Fudō Myōō, then restores harmony with the cosmic order of the sun, moon, and earth, or exorcizes evil deities.

Many people who suffer misfortunes such as illness, accident, and so on, call on the *shugenja* for magico-religious prayers. They want to know the causes of their misfortunes, and they want them eliminated with the *shugenja's* magico-religious methods. In response to these requests, the *shugenja* utilizes the following three kinds of magico-religious practices. First, he performs a fire rite to burn off their sins, or prays to his guardian deities for exorcism. Second, he ascertains the cause of misfortune through divination; then he practices the rites of exorcism (*chōbuku*) and/or the rite of eliminating possession. Third, he exorcizes evil spirits or deities by using magical charms. Each of these methods is treated in detail in the following paragraphs.

The fire rite is the most frequently used rite by which the *shugenja* undertakes exorcism.[9] A description of this rite follows. Initially the *shugenja* invites the deity of fire (*katen*) who is a messenger of deities. Then he asks the deities of stars, who control the fate of humans, about the cause of the bad luck of the believer. After these preparations, he invites Fudō Myōō and identifies with this deity. Then he burns up the cause of the believer's misfortunes and asks the believer's guardian spirit for the protection of the believer's life from that point on. Whenever a *shugenja* prays to his guardian deity—even without performing the fire rite—a similar process is followed. At first the *shugenja* identifies himself with these guardian deities, and then he performs the symbolic action that repels the evil spirits and/or deities.

The second method, divination-exorcism, is a uniquely Shugendō ritual process.[10] In earlier times, *shugenja* were particularly fond of this ritual procedure. Initially the *shugenja* ascertains the cause of his believer's misfortunes through divination. Two forms of divination are used by *shugenja* for this purpose. One form is an objective divination technique such as *yin-yang* philosophy and fortune telling (*eki*). He determines the cause of his believer's misfortune by examining the signs that show a deviation in the normal cycle of the cosmos. Another form is subjective or inspirational divination, which is practiced by shamans. The *shugenja* becomes possessed by his guardian spirit and makes the spirit tell the cause of his believer's misfortunes; or he receives a revelation from his guardian spirit about the cause of the misfortune.

Originally in Shugendō the *shugenja* used a female shaman (*miko*) and induced her possession by spirits, making her an oracle rather than the *shugenja* himself. So in earlier times the *shugenja* married a female shaman. The *shugenja* identified himself with Fudō Myōō and caused the female shaman to be possessed by the guardian deities of society at large, or by the evil spirits that possessed the particular sick person. He then made the deities or evil spirits tell the causes of misfortunes or the reason why they possessed the sick person. This is the specific practice in Shugendō called "prayer of possession" (*yorigitō*).[11] The causes of misfortune were usually the sin of the believer, the ill feelings of other people, dead people's spirits, unworshipped deities, violation of the law of nature, and the like. In more recent times, female shamans do not marry *shugenja*; instead, on their own they become possessed by deities and/or spirits and give oracles in response to the requests of their own clients.

Figure 34. *Tsukimono otoshi*

The *shugenja,* having found the source of the misfortune through divination, must then perform acts to remove it. The methods of exorcism vary depending on the kinds of evil spirits or deities, but basically they have the same structure. This is seen both in the rite of eliminating possession and in the rite of exorcism (in the case of a curse).

The rite of eliminating possession follows this sequence. The *shugenja* identifies with Fudō Myōō and then makes the possessing spirit repent its wickedness by enlightening it and/or expelling it by intimidation with weapons such as fire, sword, or bow. In this case, the methods of enlightenment and intimidation vary according to the kinds of possessing spirits.

The rite of exorcism is practiced as follows. The *shugenja* identifies himself with Fudō Myōō. Then he makes the subordinate deities bind, cut, beat, and finally cause the surrender of the wicked spirits and/or deities.[12] In this case the methods of attack differ according to the kinds of wicked spirits and/or deities. In summary, all exorcism in Shugendō basically follows the same process. The *shugenja* identifies himself with Fudō Myōō; then he controls the wicked spirits that are the causes of misfortunes by using Fudō Myōō's supernatural power directly or by manipulating Fudō Myōō's subordinate deities.

The third method of exorcism, i.e., incantation (*kaji*) and magical charms, is simple. At the incantation the *shugenja* who obtains Fudō Myōō's power directly exorcizes the wicked deities and/or spirits. Also, the *shugenja* exorcizes the wicked spirits using magical charms that contain supernatural power.[13]

Shugendō's uniqueness is seen in its ability to adopt the power of foreign traditions such as Buddhist deities and Chinese notions of *yin-yang* and to adapt them to the native Japanese worldview. This uniqueness is clearly shown in the patterns of exorcism within Shugendō. Such notions of misfortune, possession, and exorcism are generally found throughout Japanese religion, and the fact that Shugendō expresses and acts them out so effectively is another demonstration of how central Shugendō is to Japanese religious history.[14]

NOTES

1. See Miyamoto Kesao, *Sato Shugen no kenkyū* (Study of local community *shugenja*) (Tokyo: Yoshikawa Kōbunkan, 1984).
2. For example, Nakayama Miki (1798–1887), the founder of Tenrikyō, had a mystical experience when assisting in the practice of a *shugenja.* Also, Akazawa Bunji, the founder of Konkōkyō, was an ascetic of Mt. Ishizuchi.
3. See chapter 11, "Japanese Religion and Worldly Benefits."
4. Usually this *kirigami* was transmitted secretly from a master to his disciple.

5. See Miyake Hitoshi, "Shugendō to shomin seikatsu—Shugen jinpi gyōhō fujushū o chūshin to shite" (Shugendō in the life of common people), in *Sangakushūkyō to minkan shinkō no kenkyū*, ed. Sakurai Tokutarō, Sangaku Shūkyōshi Kenkyū Sōsho 6 (Tokyo: Meicho Shuppan, 1976).

6. See Miyake Hitoshi, *Seikatsu no naka no shūkyō* (Religion in everyday life) (Tokyo: Nihon Hōsō Shuppan Kyōkai, 1980), 78–126.

7. Ibid., 156–63.

8. Ishizuka Takatoshi, *Nihon no tsukimono* (Possessed spirits in Japan) (Tokyo: Miraisha, 1950).

9. Miyake Hitoshi, *Shugendō girei no kenkyū* (A study of religious rituals in Shugendō), 2d ed., rev. (Tokyo: Shunjūsha, 1985), 275–391.

10. Tamamuro Taijō, "Edo jidai yamabushi no kenkyū josetsu" (An introduction to the study of yamabushi in the Edo period), in *Bukkyōgaku no shomondai*, ed. Buttan Nisengohyakunen Kinengakkai (Tokyo: Iwanami Shoten, 1935), 1035–47.

11. Carmen Blacker, *The Catalpa Bow: A Study of Shamanistic Practices in Japan* (London: George Allen and Unwin, 1975), 131, 252.

12. Ibid., 298–314. Also Miyake, *Shugendō girei no kenkyū*, 445–510.

13. Ian Reader, "Actions, Amulets and the Expression of Meaning—Reflection of Need and Statements of Desire," in *Religion in Contemporary Japan* (Honolulu: University of Hawaii Press, 1991), 168–93. See also Miyake, *Shugendō girei no kenkyū*, 515–45.

14. See Miyake Hitoshi, *Shugendō to Nihon shūkyō* (Shugendō and Japanese religion) (Tokyo: Shunjūsha, 1996).

The Foundation of Shugendō Religious Thought[1]

SUBJECT AND METHODOLOGY

Subject

In Shugendō, religious practitioners called *shugenja* or *yamabushi* acquire magico-religious powers through the cultivation of ascetic practices in the mountains and utilize these powers through magico-religious activities in response to the worldly needs of the common people. In this chapter, I take up the religious thought of Shugendō that is the representation of these beliefs and actions in a systematic fashion.

Religious thought is a logically arranged and systematized thinking that is based on religious experience. Generally it means the written materials of a founder's teaching and, later, religious leaders' books. But in this chapter I would like to treat the meaning more widely, and so I include in religious thought all that is logically arranged and systematized by the researcher out of the myths, traditions, rituals, and icons of a specific religion. This is necessary because the religious thought of Shugendō originates from folk religion and does not depend on a founder's teaching, so it cannot be completely comprehended without the scholar's reconstruction.[2]

I use the term "religious thought" as a kind of religious worldview that is interpreted and systematized by the scholar from the expression (in words, rituals, and images) of religious experience and its practical dimension in everyday life and society. If we separate this broader religious thought into its various levels, we can identify four strata: doctrine and dogma, worldview, rituals and images, and religious ethics. From the standpoint of dissemination of religious thought, the order of importance starts with doctrine and then proceeds to religious ethics. But in the formation of religious thought, the order is exactly the opposite, i.e., beginning with ethics and then moving to doctrine.

The religious thought that I take up in this chapter is the second stratum, i.e., religious worldview. I define religious worldview as the sacred

109

order that consists of deities, humans and the cosmos, and the system of explanations for phenomena by this sacred order.[3]

When we approach religious thought in this fashion, the religious thought of Shugendō—which has as its principle the acquisition of supernatural power at sacred mountains and the utilization of this power—can be considered as the entire system of religious meaning found in the mountains, deities, human beings and their relationships, and also the ascetic practices and magical powers. More concretely, the principal part of Shugendō religious thought is the comprehensive teaching of the cosmos: it embraces this world, i.e., the village, and the otherworld, i.e., mountain and sea; it concerns the idea of the origin and formation of the cosmos; it treats the notion of the objects of worship, i.e., gods and buddhas, their subordinates, and the legendary founders; and it teaches the view of a human, becoming a Buddha, the cause of misfortune, and the means to salvation. In this chapter I take up the topic of cosmology, the idea of the otherworld, the notion of the object of worship, the worship of founders, and the view of human beings, becoming buddhas and achieving salvation, as the principal elements that constitute Shugendō religious thought. I will discuss these topics one by one and interpret their significance as a unified whole.

Methodology

Previous studies of Shugendō have been conducted from the viewpoints of history and folklore.[4] These studies, even when they consider Shugendō thought, focus on a specific belief of the Japanese people within Shugendō religious thought, or identify a foreign religion's elements, such as esoteric Buddhism or Taoism. Rarely has there been any attempt to grasp Shugendō religious thought as a whole. Therefore in this chapter I will examine the main elements of Shugendō (i.e., cosmology, the idea of otherworld, the notion of objects of worship, founder worship, the view of humans, becoming a Buddha and salvation), first one by one, and then as a whole. In this fashion, I try to clarify the sacred inner logic that is contained within Shugendō itself. My method is to approach the Shugendō manuscripts, rituals, and images as symbols, then to decipher their meanings using symbolic analysis and specify the religious worldview, in other words, the religious thought contained in these materials. Specifically, my analysis has the following seven goals.

1. To develop a hypothetical framework of Shugendō's religious thought and single out its constituent elements on the basis of typical Shugendō texts.

2. To collect the related materials for each element, gathering together as much as we can. Such materials comprise written materials including

legends, doctrines, sutras and their interpretations, and instruction books; ritual activities such as esoteric rituals, festivals, performing arts, and their texts; artistic forms such as images of deities, buddhas, sacred pictures, sacred costumes, sacred instruments, temples, and shrines featuring these things; and also miraculous oral traditions, legends, and sacred tales.

3. To compare the materials for each element and classify them according to their characters, times, and regions, and then to separate the materials. These define the basic "text" for describing systematically each element.

4. To decipher the meanings of these "texts" selected by the above procedure. Before beginning the deciphering, we must acquire sufficient historical knowledge about each element. Then we identify the constituent elements of that text: i.e., words if it is a sentence, actions in the instance of ritual, form and color for images as symbols. We decipher their meaning by using dictionaries, other books, the ritual manuals, iconography, and we also listen to the explanations of practitioners and informants.

But when we cannot discover their meaning by this method, we must decipher the elements by comparison with similar symbols in the "text" of another constituent element. Alternatively, we must use an analogical argument for similar forms in other elements, then situate these symbols in the context of the whole system. For this decoding it is desirable that believers and scholars should share the same sensibilities based on shared experience. After decoding all the symbols constituting the text, we arrange these meanings in syntagmatic order, and comprehend the whole system. At that time we also reflect on the paradigmatic character of the dominant symbol (for example, the object of worship and the practitioners), which is essential in that "text," and through this procedure we can grasp the meaning of the text more dynamically.[5]

It goes without saying that in these cases we consider the essential structure of religious thought, namely the polarity of the sacred and the profane. We also consider breaking through that polarity, and viewing the *shugenja* as mediator between the sacred and profane worlds. By following this approach the total meaning of the text is justified.

5. To supplement by treatment of similar texts the meaning of a typical text that is decoded by the above procedures. The meaning of a dogmatic "text" must be grasped dynamically by using the "text" of rituals, images, and miracle tales.

6. To trace the transition and diffusion of that thought by comparing the meanings of the "texts" that belong to the same element but differ in period and region. Thus we can find the structure of meaning and also its transition and diffusion of elements as a whole. And we can grasp the meaning more precisely by considering the preceding thought and the contemporary thought in Shugendō; and we can also interpret the development of that thought within the historical background and the formative process for each Shugendō sect.

7. Lastly, to examine comprehensively the religious thought of each element within the hypothetical framework. By so doing, we can comprehend the whole structure of Shugendō religious thought.

DEVELOPMENT OF SHUGENDŌ RELIGIOUS THOUGHT

Shugendō thought is centered around the significance of mountains (i.e., the place of ascetic training of *shugenja*), objects of worship, ascetic practice, mystical experience, and the supernatural power that *shugenja* acquire through this experience. As the Shugendō sects became established, the dogmatic books, ritual materials, and images became more and more sophisticated. I will now trace the formation of Shugendō religious thought through the investigation of the main Shugendō doctrinal books.[6]

At the middle of the Heian period (794–1185), when Shugendō arose, *engi* (historical accounts of a temple image or act of piety) were compiled. The typical example is *Kumano Gongen gosuijaku engi* (in *Chōkan no kanmon*) and *Ōmine engi*. The former tells the story of a hunter who found the Kumano Gongen (the avatar of Kumano), which appeared on the top of an *ichi* (yew) tree, and enshrined it in a temple. In the account of *Ōmine engi*, *shugenja* considered each peak of the Ōmine Mountain range as the abode of the Buddha in the *taizōkai mandara* (the womb store world mandala) and *kongōkai mandara* (the diamond world mandala), then placed on these peaks specific Buddha images and/or scriptures that related to that peak and wrote of these matters in this *engi*.[7]

During the Kamakura period (1185–1333), to this *Ōmine engi* were added the *engi* of Mt. Katsuragi, Mt. Kumano, Mt. Kasagi, and the names of Ōmine sacred places and the biography of En no Ozunu as well as the oral tradition of the Ōmine ascetics. This became the *Shozan engi*. The myth of Katsuragi Shugendō also appeared, i.e., *Yamato Katsuragi hōzanki*.

During the time from the end of the Kamakura period to the beginning of the Nanbokuchō period (1332–92), *Kinbusen sōsōki, Kinbusen zakki,* and *Kinbusen himitsuden* were written. *Shintōshū*, which was the collection of famous shrines' *engi* compiled about the fourteenth century, includes *Kumano Gongen no koto* (The Story of Kumano Avatar) and other *engi* of Shugen sacred mountains.

In the Muromachi period (1393–1537), when the Shugendō sect was being organized, many *kirigami* (sacred notes handed down, master to disciple) of mountain asceticism were gathered together. At this time there appeared such dogmatic books as *Aozasa hiyōroku, Ozasa hiyōroku buchū kanjō hongi* of Ōmine Shugen, and *Shugen sanjūsan tsūki* of Mt. Hiko. At the beginning of the sixteenth century, a wandering *shugenja* called Sokuden, who was staying on Mt. Hiko, compiled many *kirigami* into other dogmatic books, such as *Shugen shūyō hiketsushū, Sanbu sōshō hōsokumikki,* and *Shugen tonkaku sokushōshū*. At the same time *Shugen shinanshō* and *Ryōbu mondō hishō* of Kumano Shugen, which combined the *engi* of Kumano and Kinbu, were compiled.

Appearing about the same time was *En no Gyōja hongi,* which is the typical biography of En no Ozunu or En no Gyōja, the legendary founder of Shugendō. Thus by the end of the Muromachi period, Japan saw the completion of the *engi* of sacred mountains and Shugen temples, dogmatic books that are the collections of *kirigami,* and biographies of founders. With these accomplishments, the doctrine of Shugendō was almost established.

Early in the Edo period (1603–1868), the commentaries of *Shugen sanjūsan tsūki* and *Shugen shūyō hiketsushū* were written, as well as several biographies of En no Ozunu. In addition to these there appeared a new type of dogmatic book that gathered together accounts of the significance of the term *yamabushi,* the *yamabushi* costume, and the ten ascetic practices corresponding to the ten realms of living beings (the *jikkai shugyō*). In the middle of the Edo period, when the Honzan sect and the Tōzan sect clashed, the dogmatic texts of each sect argued its superiority over the other. Also created at this time were the commentary books of popular festivals and the *shugenja's* religious activities (for example, *Shugen koji benran*), and the instruction books, *Ryaku engi* (concise *engi*) of Shugen mountain shrines and temples. At the end of the Edo period, Gyōchi of the Tōzan sect wrote several research works, including *Konohagoromo* and *Tōunrokuji.*

In 1872 Shugendō was abolished by the policy of the Meiji government, which prohibited the mixture of Shinto and Buddhism. In spite of this prohibition, the texts *Umiura gikan, Ushikubo kozen,* and others were collected secretly as classical Shugendō books. And early in the twentieth century, *Shugendō shōso* was published. This was Shugendō's complete collection of dogmatic books—the ritual materials, *engi,* and historical documents.

Moreover, Shōgoin, the former head temple of the Honzan sect, published the journal *Shugen*; Sanbōin, the former head temple of the Tōzan sect published the journal *Jinben* and sought to disseminate Shugendō. The modern doctrine of Shugendō, which we can see in such journals, has the flavor of a lay-Buddhist movement. So the teaching of Shugendō was explained in familiar expressions—such as we can see in the explanation of *jikkai shugyō* as the ethics of everyday life.

THE DIMENSIONS OF SHUGENDŌ THOUGHT

Cosmology

The religious thought of Shugendō recognizes the existence of the cosmos, which includes this world and the otherworld, as well as humans, deities, spirits, mountains, rivers, grasses, trees, and all things in nature, and also has elaborate ideas about its creation and construction. Concerning the origin of the cosmos, of divinities, and of humans, this belief teaches that first heaven and earth separated, and then there appeared one after another a sprout of reed, a *vajra*-pounder (*kongōsho*), Jihi Shin Ō (Merciful Divine King), and *bonten* (a long pole with a paper streamer[8]). Alternatively, this belief explains that the seeds (*shūji*[9]) of Dainichi Nyorai were transformed into a mountain. The *vajra*-pounder that appeared on that mountain becomes the principal image, and then the ascetic (*shugenja*) himself.[10] Also in the *hashiramoto goma* (pillar erection ritual), its ritual manual showed that water created heaven and earth, and *yin* and *yang*. Then by means of the intercourse of *yin* and *yang*, there appeared a *shugenja*, who is an *axis mundi*. *Shikimai* (ceremonial dances) of *yamabushi kagura* (sacred dances of *yamabushi*) express that the unseparated heaven and earth (like a chicken egg) separated into heaven and earth, and then united with each other. Thus everything was created from this performance.[11]

As is well known, in esoteric Buddhism (Mikkyō), it is said that the cosmos consists of the diamond world and the womb store world. In Shugendō's cosmology, the northern half of Ōmine Mountain range, i.e., the Yoshino side, is considered the diamond world and the southern half, i.e., the Kumano side, the womb store world. Then the names of the buddhas and bodhisattvas in the mandala are assigned to each peak of the Ōmine Mountain range. Both mandalas were used during the *kanjō* (*abhiṣeka*) consecration rite. However, in the Tōzan sect's consecration rite called *e'in kanjō* (wisdom seed consecration rite), the *e'in mandara* is used; this mandala describes the seeds of the sacred character of the buddhas (*shūji*) corresponding to the deities in the Ōmine Mountain ranges.[12] The *Kumano mandara* was created depicting the images of the *honji* (original ground of avatar) and *suijaku* (the manifestation of the original Buddhist deities) of the Kumano twelve avatars (Kumano Jūnisho Gongen). The *Yoshino mandara* created at Yoshino relates the story of how En no Ozunu received his guardian deity, i.e., Kongō Zaō Gongen,[13] and describes the deities of Mt. Yoshino. In addition to these, various other mandalas appeared—for example, the mountain mandalas depicting the sacred mountains, temples, shrines, and landscape of Nachi of Kumano, and the mountains of Hakusan, Tateyama, and Fuji. Also developed at Kumano were preaching mandalas (i.e., *Kumano kanjin mandara*, the discernment of mind mandala) that show that the fortunes of everyday life and the attainment of buddhahood depend on the human mind.

The Idea of the Otherworld

In Japan from ancient times, mountains and the sea have been considered the otherworld where ancestor spirits, deities, and evil spirits dwell.

Figure 35. Kongō Zaō Gongen

This belief carried over into Shugendō. The idea of mountains as an otherworld especially can be seen at almost all the sacred mountains of Shugendō, such as Mt. Ōmine, Mt. Katsuragi, the three sacred mountains of Dewa (Dewa Sanzan, i.e., Mt. Haguro, Mt. Gassan, and Mt. Yudono).[14] The idea of the sea as otherworld can be seen at Potalaka Temple (Fudarakusenji) of Nachi, and Tomogashima of Kata Wakayama City. There were many instances when this otherworld of the mountains—consisting of beautiful forests, hills, and lakes—and also the otherworld of the sea—were likened to islands. Water, hills, and forests are considered the key elements constituting that otherworld.

However, the idea of the otherworld in Shugendō was elaborated more completely through the acceptance of Buddhist thought. That is, it was believed that lakes in the mountains and the seaside are Potalaka (Fudaraku), the pure land of Kannon. Further, the steep mountains that are the site of ascetic training are believed to be the pure land of the Vulture Peak (Ryōzen Jōdo) of the *Lotus Sutra* (*Hokekyō*), and also the mandala of esoteric Buddhism, Mt. Sumeru, and the *axis mundi*. The otherworld of the deceased is connected with the worship of Amida, Jizō, Kokūzō, hell, and the pure land. Moreover, a sacred mountain was considered as the place where the cosmos was renewed by Miroku who would descend from heaven at the end of *mappō;* sacred mountains are also considered the place of eternal youth and longevity, as seen in Hōraisan (the mountain of eternal youth) of Taoism. The ascetic training of entering the peak in Shugendō—wandering and seclusion in the mountains—has the character of a spiritual journey to the otherworld.

The Object of Worship

From its origin, Shugendō recognized the existence of spirits in natural objects, such as trees, rocks, and water, and in both the mountains and islands viewed as otherworlds. Shugendō practitioners offered prayers to them on occasions, such as during ascetic training while entering the peak. When Shugendō was established, Kongō Zaō Gongen became its characteristic deity. According to the tale of En no Gyōja's spiritual revelation, this deity is considered the raging deity that transformed the beliefs in water deity (i.e., Benzaiten) and ancestor spirits, (Jizō Bosatsu) and is seen as the embodiment of the Shaka past, Senju Kannon present, and Miroku future. From the standpoint of iconography, earlier incarnations of Kongō Zaō Gongen were Kongō Dōji (a deity in the form of a furious looking youth) or Shūkongōjin.[15] In addition, Hokki Bosatsu, as the original Buddhist manifestation of En no Gyōja, was also a characteristic deity of Shugendō.

Other deities worshipped in Shugendō are the deities with the title of Myōō (*vidyārāja*) such as Fudō Myōō (Acala) and also Kannon, Yakushi, Amida, Benzaiten, Bishamonten, Jizō, and Kokūzō. Of all these deities, Acala held the position as the main object of worship of Shugendō. Also worshipped were the Godai Myōō (the five *vidyārājas*) and Kurikara Fudō, who holds the deified sword and rope of Fudō Myōō.

At Kumano there were enshrined the twelve avatars (*gongen*) that were considered the original source of these buddhas and bodhisattvas.[16] Also, within Shugendō great importance was attached to the deity called Protector of Buddhist Dharma (Gohō), which both guided the *shugenja* into the mountains as a messenger of the main deity and was also treated by the *shugenja* as subordinate to the main deity. (See chapter 2.) The objects of worship in Shugendō thus essentially have the character of Gohō.[17]

The Worship of the Legendary Founders

Many of the founders of Shugendō's sacred mountains were the religious leaders who went to these mountains through the guidance of animals, hunters, and *dōji* (*kumāra*) who served as messengers of the mountain's female deity. After coming into contact with the female deity and worshipping her, they opened up the mountain for religious practice. They then acquired supernatural powers by practicing asceticism in the mountains and added to their supernatural powers through such practices as incantation and prayer (*kajikitō*). Later they themselves were worshipped as deities. Thus, at most of the sacred mountains of Shugendō, three kinds of deities are worshipped: a mountain goddess (female style), the *kumāra* or deified hunters who as the subordinates of the mountain goddess guided the founder to her abode (layman style), and the founder (priestly style).

The legendary founder En no Ozunu was a magician of Katsuragi at the end of the Asuka period (500–710), who was exiled to Izu island due to the false accusations of Karakuni no Muragi Hirotari.[18] During the Kamakura period, when Shugendō took the form of a religious system, En no Ozunu became the legendary founder of Shugendō and was called either En no Gyōja or Jinben Daibosatsu. (This name and title were granted by Emperor Kōkaku in 1799.) A biography suitable for a founder was then created for him. According to this biography, he is an incarnation of Acala and his original Buddhist form is Hokki Bosatsu. His mother conceived him in a dream, when she swallowed a *vajra*-pounder (*dokko*). After growing up, he practiced asceticism at such places as Mt. Katsuragi and Mt. Ōmine and received the esoteric *dharma* practices from Ryūju (Nāgārjuna) at Mt. Minoo (Osaka). After that, he was slandered by the deity Hitokotonushi no

Figure 36. Fudō Myōō and *shugenja*

Mikoto, who did not obey En no Gyōja's command to build a stone bridge between Mt. Katsuragi and Mt. Ōmine and as a result was bound by En no Gyōja's spell. Then he was exiled to Izu but was permitted to return home. Later, in an act of magical flight, he "flew" to China (Tō, Ch. T'ang), together with his mother, whom he placed in a Buddhist alms-bowl.[19]

The legendary founder of the Tōzan sect was Shōbō (832–909) who founded Daigo Temple. Shōbō is also called Rigen Daishi. He received this name from Emperor Higashiyama on the eight hundredth anniversary of his death in 1707. For Shōbō the Tōzan sect created the legend that his original Buddhist deity is Nyoirin Kannon. At Mt. Ōmine he destroyed the dragon that after the time of En no Gyōja had blocked those entering the mountains for asceticism; and he refounded the mountain asceticism there. Later he received the secret *dharma* of Nāgārjuna under the guidance of En no Gyōja. Then he created the wisdom seed consecration rite (*e'in kanjō*)[20] at the Hōkaku Temple of Yoshino. Thus within Shugendō, *shugenja* created legends deifying the founders of the various mountains, founders of Shugendō itself, and those of its sects. The founders themselves were enshrined as objects of worship.

The View of Human Beings

In the religious thought of Shugendō, human beings have fundamentally the same character as both Dainichi Nyorai, the deification of the cosmos, and as the various Buddhist deities treated as the manifestation of Dainichi Nyorai; accordingly, if human beings become aware of this, and practice asceticism, they can attain buddhahood. This thought is expressed through the meaning of Sino-Japanese characters (i.e., the character for "*yamabushi*") and the peculiar forms of dress and instruments of the *yamabushi* that adhere to the thought of esoteric Buddhism and Tendai *hongakuron* (thought of innate Buddha nature in T'ien-t'ai).

Generally, the meaning of *yamabushi* is expressed in such terms as *musa sanshin no kakutai* (the three bodies of the Buddha in the awakened essence); *jishin soku ichinen hokkai* (one's own body is the *dharma* realm in a single thought); and *shikishin soku buttai* (the identity of the material body with the Buddha). There are four forms of expression for this figure: *yamabushi, sanga, shugen, kyakusō*. *Yamabushi* means *shikaku* (realizing one's Buddha nature by undergoing religious practices). *Sanga* means *hongaku* (innate Buddha nature or original buddhahood). In the case of *shugen*, "*shu*" is *shikaku* and "*gen*" is *hongaku*, so *shugen* means to learn both *hongaku* and *shikaku*. And *kyakusō* (guest monk) is a wandering monk without permanent abode who has no attachment to life. So, *kyakusō* means *shihon funi* (nonduality of *shikaku* and *hongaku*).

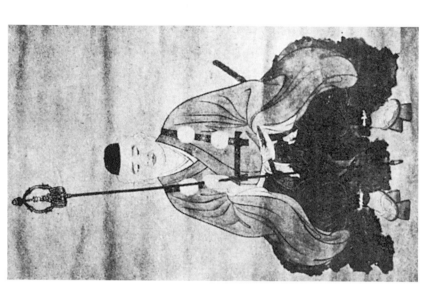

Figure 38. Shōbō, legendary founder of the Tōzan sect

Figure 37. En no Ozunu, legendary founder of Shugendō

To understand the two Sino-Japanese characters for *yamabushi*, note that the first character *yama* (山), links three vertical lines with a horizontal line; this means that the *yamabushi* is or expresses the truth of *sanshin sokuichi* (the three bodies of the Buddha are one). In other words, this is an expression of *sanbu ittai* (unity of three divisions, womb store, diamond, and the two); *santai ichinen* (the three truths—of *kū* emptiness, *ke* provisional, and *chū* the middle way—are in one thought); and *sangaku heishu* (to master all of the three types of learning *kai* [*śīla*—morality], *jō* [*samādhi*—meditation], and *e* [*prajñā*—wisdom]). Also, for the Sino-Japanese character *fushi* or *bushi*, the left side or (⼈) means *bodai* (*bodhi*, wisdom), sacred; the right side or (犬) means *bonnō* (*kleśa*, attachment), profane. So, joining the two sides together in one character means that the *yamabushi* is the being who unites wisdom and attachment and also the sacred and the profane, in his own body.[21]

The dress and the instruments of the *yamabushi* symbolize such overall meanings as *taikon ryōbu no jikitai* (the womb store world and the diamond world in one's body), *jikkai hongū no naisho* (the inner realization of the realms of living beings by one's own nature), *sokushin sokubutsu no geyū* (outward functioning of the identity of one's own body and Buddha), and Acala himself. More concretely, *suzukake* (robes), *oi* (portable wooden box), *katabako* (shoulder box), and *kai no o* (the two threads or strings that hang down from the conch shell) symbolize the unity of the diamond and the womb store world. The *yuigesa* (*yamabushi* surplice) symbolizes the ten realms of living beings. *Shakujō* (*khakkhara*, ritual staff with metal rings) and *kongōzue* (diamond cane) symbolize a pagoda. The *hora* (conch shell) symbolizes the change of the profane to the sacred. *Nenju* (rosary) symbolizes the abolition of attachment. Then *shiba-uchi* (woodcutter, sword), *hiōgi* (cypress fan), and *hashiri nawa* (rope) symbolize Acala; and individual items of the *yamabushi* dress and instruments symbolize the cosmos, attainment of buddhahood, and the object of worship. Moreover, I would like to point out that the *yamabushi* who wears this dress is conceived of as a being who transcends dualistic oppositions such as profane and sacred, the diamond world and the womb store world, *jō* (*samādhi*, meditation) and *e* (*prajñā*, wisdom), male and female, *jōku bodai* (to seek for enlightenment) and *geke shujō* (to save sentient beings from suffering).[22]

The *yamabushi* who live on the sacred mountain are called *sennin* (hermit), *tengu* (a long-nosed goblin), and *oni* (demon) by village people and are feared as strange beings. When we consider legends about strange beings in relation to *yamabushi*, then *yamabushi* and hermits are the boundary beings in between deity and human, and goblins and demons are the boundary beings between human and animal. Also, hermits and goblins live in trees and by their orientation towards heaven are related to birds. *Yamabushi* and demons live on earth or in caves next to water and are related to snakes. At any rate the *yamabushi* are viewed by village people as boundary figures who mediate between deities and animals in the otherworld of mountain, and human beings.[23]

The Idea of Attaining Buddhahood

The *yamabushi*, who inherently possess Buddha nature, can attain buddhahood by awaking to this truth and practicing mountain asceticism. Mountain asceticism consists of preparatory exercises, rituals of entry into the mountain and the training hall, the three regular daily religious services, the *jikkai shugyō* (the practices corresponding to the ten realms of living beings) in the sacred mountain, and the ritual of departure from the training hall and mountains. Of all of these, the central ritual is the *jikkai shugyō* (see chapter 4, pp. 88–92).[24] Ascetics can attain buddhahood by performing the ten ritual practices as described in the texts *Shugen sanjūsan tsūki* and *Shugen shūyō hiketsushū*. In the ten realms of living beings, the first six are called *rokudō* (the six states of existence) and the latter four, *shishō* (the four kinds of sages). Those practices that correspond to *rokudō* are considered practices of *ji* (the relative), and those of *shishō* as practices of *ri* (the absolute). So by performing both of these, ascetics reach a stage of *jiri funi* (nonduality of relative and absolute). However, within mountain asceticism, there are other kinds of combinations of practices oriented around self-enlightenment, i.e., *tokogatame* (the practice for conceiving Buddha nature), *aka* (drawing water for the purification rite), *kogi* (collecting firewood for *goma*), and *shōkanjō* (consecration). Another combination of practices, focused on compassion, which destroys the sins of other people, allocates ten practices to *rokudō*, i.e., *tokogatame* and repentance (human world), weighing of karma (hell), abstaining from water (animal world), *aka* and wrestling (*ashura*), ritual dance of pleasure (heaven), *kogi* and prohibition against eating grain (hungry spirit world), and *shōkanjō*. Then the *shugenja* attains buddhahood by performing these *jishu no shugyō* (ten practices). (This combination of practices is found in *Sanbusōshō hōsoku mikki*.) This order of ten exercises is designed to heighten the mystical experience in mountain asceticism.

In the Kamakura period, when these systematic stages of mountain asceticism had not yet appeared, *yamabushi* entered the mountain at the end of autumn, passed the year engaged in ascetic training in the mountain caves, and then descended at the beginning of spring. These exercises are called the ascetic training of *misoka yamabushi* (the *yamabushi* who spent the last day of the year in the mountains). We can see the traces of

Figure 39. *Gō no hakari* (weighing of karma)

this *misoka yamabushi* in the contest of two senior *matsu hijiri* (literally, "pine saints") at the Shōreisai of Mt. Haguro after a period of a hundred days' ascetic training. In this festival, they compete with each other's supernatural power by manipulating their subordinate deities (*gohō*) to start a sacred fire, and in the ability to bring about fertility.[25] Thus we can see that in former times *yamabushi* sought to acquire such supernatural power by confining themselves in sacred mountains.

The texts of Shugendō point out three stages in the attainment of Buddha nature. The first is *sokushin jōbutsu* (*shikaku*), in which the ascetic conceives that he possesses Buddha nature himself. The second is *sokushin sokubutsu*, in which the *sangō* (*trini karmāṇi*, i.e., deeds, words, and thoughts of ascetics) identify with the *sanmitsu* (the three secrets of the Buddha). The third is *sokushin sokushin*, which is the nonduality transcending the differences between human and Buddha (*shihon funi* nonduality of human and Buddha); the best stage is *sokushin sokushin*, in which the ascetic obtains the *jishō shōjōshin* (the innately pure mind).

The Idea of Salvation

The *shugenja* who has obtained supernatural power in his mystical experience uses this power positively in performing salvation rites. One such example is the fertility rite. It is an interesting fact that the *shugenja* who confined himself to the mountains during winter—which is the original Shugendō mountain asceticism—leaves the mountains on April 8, the day when the villagers believe the mountain deity descends from the mountain to the village and becomes the deity of rice paddies in order to protect agriculture. Therefore, it appears that *yamabushi* who descend from the mountain are thought to be the same as the mountain deity who brings fertility.

The most important salvation rite of Shugendō is the ritual to remove suffering (such as illness). *Yamabushi* explain the cause of such misfortunes as follows: the persons suffering these misfortunes had disturbed the social order (for example, by breaching common law) and/or the supernatural order (by violating taboos or neglecting rites for ancestors), and therefore, the souls of humans, the spirits of the deceased, and deities became angry and either possessed them or brought a curse on them. The *yamabushi* performs exorcism (*tsukimono otoshi*) and pronounces curses (*chōbuku*) (see chapter 5, pp. 104–7). In this fashion the *shugenja* determines the causes of misfortune and then exorcizes them using shamanistic practices.[26]

THE STRUCTURE OF SHUGENDŌ RELIGIOUS THOUGHT

Cosmos, Divinities, and Human Beings

As noted above, Shugendō created the idea of a mountain mandala that views the Ōmine Mountain range as the mandala of the diamond world and the womb store world, by adding the cosmology of esoteric Buddhism to the ancient Japanese idea of a mountain otherworld as the abode of deities. We can also see in the religious thought of Shugendō the idea of perceiving the mountain as an *axis mundi*. For example, the peak of the Ōmine Mountain range (i.e., Misen) is thought to be Mt. Sumeru and Mt. Kinbu (the northern part of Mt. Ōmine), and Mt. Zenki (near the center of Mt. Ōmine) is called Mt. Kokujiku ("Mountain of the Axis in Japan"). This designation shows us that Shugendō considers a mountain to be a sacred cosmos.

In esoteric Buddhism, Dainichi Nyorai is the deified sacred cosmos and is worshipped as the principal deity. Then all components that constitute Dainichi Nyorai's body are the universal principles that are seen in everything from buddhas and bodhisattvas to human beings and all things in nature. These universal principles that fill the entire world are, in essence (*tai*), the six elements (*rokudai, ṣaḍ dhātavaḥ*) consisting of earth, water, fire, wind, space, and consciousness; in form (*so, lakṣaṇa,* things' character), they are the four types of mandalas (*shishu mandara*), namely the *dai mandara* (images of various deities), *sanmaya mandara* (objects held in the hand of deities), *hō mandara* (*bīja*, seeds of deities), and *katsuma mandara* (postures of deities); and, in function (*yu*), they are the three mystic practices (*sanmitsu*), consisting of deeds (*shin*), words (*ku*), and thoughts (*i*). The attainment of Buddha nature should be pursued with the realization that all buddhas and humans originate from these universals.[27]

Furthermore, Shugendō accepts the belief of T'ien-t'ai doctrine that regards the previously mentioned principles of cosmos (*dharma*) as truth, and explains three kinds of truth (*santai*): *kūtai* (emptiness), *ketai* (provisional), *chūtai* (the middle way). These three kinds of truth are found in the single instance of thought (*santai ichinen*). Shugendō also accepts the principle of T'ien t'ai belief that divides the cosmos into the ten realms (which consist of six stages of existence and four kinds of sages) and considers that all things from Buddha and bodhisattvas to *shugenja* possess the ten realms of living beings and are one in thusness (*jikkai ichinyo*).[28] As was explained above, the worldview of Shugendō thought is that the cosmos, divinities, and *shugenja* in essence have the same existence; accordingly, the *shugenja* enters the mountain that is considered the cosmos itself, then becomes aware of his Buddha nature and his character as a microcosm, practices mountain asceticism, and in this fashion can attain buddhahood.

Mystical Experience and Thought

The *shugenja* obtains through mountain asceticism the mystical experience of the identity of the object of worship with the deified cosmos, which in turn enables him to arrive at the stage of *sokushin sokushin*. He then expresses this experience in religious thought. The stages of ascetic training can be divided into the *sangaku* or three types of learning, i.e., *kai* (morality), *jō* (meditation), and *e* (wisdom), according to the general plan of Buddhist ascetic exercises. Generally, the first of the three, *kai* (*sīla*) is the exercise that regulates body and mind; a more distinctly Shugendō type of regulation for *kai* is a *buchū sekai*, which states the rules for group life in the mountain.[29] The next type, *jō*, is the training that concentrates and purifies the mind. In the case of Shugendō this corresponds to *jikkai shugyō* and *zenjō (dhyāna*, i.e., meditation in a mountain cave). The third type, *e*, is the set of exercises that result in acquisition of the wisdom of enlightenment. In the case of Shugendō, this corresponds to *e'in kanjō* and to obtaining the *gochi*, the five wisdoms.

Incidentally, it is thought that the time needed for the attainment of buddhahood, by accomplishing the three types of learning (*sangaku*), is the *sandai asōgigō* (three great innumerable *kalpas*), which is a long span of time that can approach infinity. However, within Shugendō, the ascetic can attain buddhahood by repeating three times the mountain asceticism—once in spring (*junbu*, the ordinary peak, walking from Kumano to Yoshino at Mt. Ōmine), again in autumn (*gyakubu*, reverse peak; walking from Yoshino to Kumano),[30] and the third time in summer (*jungyaku funi no mineiri*, the peak of nonduality, transcending the ordinary and reverse peaks, *hanaku no mine*). Concretely, this last peak, *hanaku no mine*, includes the climb to Mt. Sanjō in order to offer flowers at the sacred sites of the mountain as a memorial service for En no Gyōja. At Mt. Sanjō we also find four gates, i.e., Hosshin (Resolving to Attain Supreme Enlightenment), Shugyō (Ascetic Exercise), Tōkaku (Equal Enlightenment), and Myōkaku (Marvelous Enlightenment). The ascetics can attain buddhahood by passing through these four gates and arriving at the summit of the mountain. In this fashion, Shugendō thought elucidates the attainment of buddhahood in this world using concrete examples.

The identification with a deity and Buddha (*funi zettai no kyōchi*, stage of absolute nonduality) attained through the three types of learning demonstrates concretely the doctrinal explanation of the Sino-Japanese character "*yamabushi*" and the *yamabushi* dress. According to the doctrinal explanations, the sense of identification with Buddha indicates the stage of such notions as: recognizing the three bodies of the Buddha are originally our own body (*musa sanshin*), realizing the ten realms of living beings are in the one thusness (*jikkai ichinyo*), and understanding the formlessness of the three mystic practices (*musō no sanmitsu*). The stage of absolute nonduality (*funi zettai*) is expressed in such terms as the nonduality of ordinary beings and holy men (*bonshō funi*), nonduality of delusion and enlightenment (*meigo funi*), nonduality of the favorable and the adverse (*jungyaku funi*), and nonduality of the ultimate principle and the transcendental wisdom (*richi funi*).

Underlying this experience of nonduality is the sense of complete purification. Thus, based on this sense of purification, the Buddhist rule of moral conduct (*kai*) is equivalent to the innate pure mind (*jishō honrai shōjō*); the notion of nondefiled and nondying (*muku musen*) meditation (*jō*) is the innate calm mind (*jishō honrai jakushō*), and motionlessness (*mudōran*); and wisdom (*e*) is the innate clarity (*jishō honrai akiraka*) and lack of suspicion (*mugishin*). Indeed, the three types of learning are grasped as the expression of the purified mind.

Supernatural Power and Thought

The supernatural power of ascetics is based on the original mountain asceticism undertaken by *shugenja*, and on the power of the main deity. But the followers of Shugendō believe that the tools used by *shugenja* in festivals and/or rites of exorcism—like the magic wand of fairy tales— have supernatural power. So we will explain the character of the festivals and rites of exorcism in Shugendō, and also the tools manipulated by *shugenja* in these instances.

The festivals and arts of Shugendō demonstrate its sacred order and origin through the performances in which the *shugenja* invites deities to the ritual site and induces possession in the medium, and then performs divination. In these rituals he uses as instruments the priest's staff (*shakujō*), a sword, a stick, and rope. Rites of affliction utilize exorcism and curse. These rites are performed in order to restore the sacred order of the cosmos that was disturbed by the evil spirits and demons that brought misfortune. In these rites of affliction, the *vajra*-pounder, sword, priest's staff, and rope are used. Thus, in these rituals two kinds of instruments are used for the manipulation of supernatural power: instruments like a stick— the *vajra*-pounder, sword, and priest's staff—and rope.

Incidentally, this pattern of stick and rope is imitative of Acala's sword and rope; Acala is the incarnation of Mahāvairocana and the main deity of Shugendō. Moreover, in Shugendō, Kurikara Fudō[31] is worshipped as Acala's deified sword and rope. And the *shugenja*, who identifies with Acala, and then performs the ritual (*shūhō*), thinks of himself as being transformed into an *axis mundi* by means of the pillar erection *goma* ritual; the

Figure 40. Kurikara Fudō

shugenja drapes around his waist the conch rope, which symbolizes the diamond and womb store worlds. The *vajra*-pounder is the source of the cosmos from which emerge Acala, En no Ozunu, and the *shugenja* himself; and the priest's staff stands for Mt. Sumeru.

The instruments such as the stick and rope bring into existence a sacred order. They also have the power to repair the sacred order, because they are Acala's instruments and they are thought to correspond to the sources of the cosmos as expressed in the form of Mt. Sumeru and the diamond and womb store worlds. As mentioned above, the supernatural power of Shugendō is connected to the source of the cosmos that pervades Acala, ascetics, and sacred instruments.

NOTES

1. This is a translation of the concluding summary chapter of Miyake Hitoshi, *Shugendō shisō no kenkyū* (A study of Shugendō thought) (Tokyo: Shunjūsha, 1985), 957–70. For details concerning the argument in this chapter and contents of Shugendō thought, see *Shugendō shisō no kenkyū*.
2. For my viewpoint, see Miyake Hitoshi, *Shūkyō minzokugaku* (A study of folk religion) (Tokyo: Tōkyō Daigaku Shuppankai, 1989).
3. For the religious worldview, see Robert Redfield, "The Primitive World View," in *Human Nature & Study of Society: The Papers of Robert Redfield*, ed. Margaret Park Redfield (Chicago: University of Chicago Press, 1963), 1:270.
4. For such studies, see "Bunken shiryō mokuroku" (A bibliography of literature and materials), in *Shugendō jiten* (Dictionary of Shugendō), ed. Miyake Hitoshi (Tokyo: Tōkyōdō Shuppan, 1986), 409–30. For a bibliography in Western languages, see Regina Hubner, "Seiyō bunken ni okeru Shugendō kenkyū no kanten" (Studies of Shugendō in Western literature), *Hikaku minzoku kenkyū* 7 (1993): 234–39.
5. See Miyake, *Shūkyō minzokugaku*, 36–59, 103–26.
6. See Miyake Hitoshi, ed., *Shugendō shōso kaidai* (An explanatory bibliography of the Shugendō texts), Nihon Daizōkyō 99, 100 (Tokyo: Suzuki Gakujutsu Zaidan, Kōdansha, 1977).
7. See Miyake Hitoshi, "Ōmine engi kō" (A study of *Ōmine engi*), in *Ōmine Shugendō no kenkyū* (A study of Ōmine Shugendō) (Tokyo: Kōsei Shuppansha, 1988), 275–305.
8. *Yamato Katsuragi hōzanki*, in *Shugendō shōso*, ed. Nakano Tatsue, Nihon Daizōkyō 48 (Tokyo: Ryūbunkan, 1979), 3:378.
9. This term can also be pronounced *shuji* or *shushi*.
10. This thought can be seen in the meditation of *Ōmine kai'e mangyō jizaihō* (one of the mystical practices of the Tōzan sect) at a holy site where the Buddha is worshipped. See *Ōmine kai'e mangyō jizaihō*, in *Shugendō shōso* 1:94. See also Miyake, *Shugendō shisō no kenkyū*, 194–98.
11. Miyake, *Shugendō shisō no kenkyū*, 198–200; Irit Averbuch, *The Gods Come Dancing: A Study of the Japanese Ritual Dance of Yamabushi Kagura*, Cornell East Asian Series 79 (Ithaca, NY: Cornell University Press, 1995), 128–58.
12. Miyake, *Shugendō shisō no kenkyū*, 244–49.
13. For Kongō Zaō Gongen, see "The Object of Worship" in this chapter.
14. See Hori Ichirō, "Mountains and Their Importance for the Idea of the Other World," in *Folk Religion in Japan: Continuity and Change* (Chicago: University of Chicago Press, 1968), 141–79.

15. Shūkongōjin (Vajra-dhara) is a Yasha who guards Buddha and gods with a *vajra* in his hand.

16. For Kumano's twelve avatars, see chapter 2, "Kumano Gongen: The Idea of Deity in Shugendō."

17. For Gohō, see Yanagita Kunio, "Gohō dōji," in *Teihon Yanagita Kunio shū* (Tokyo: Chikuma Shobō, 1969), 9:407–16; see also Miyaji Naoichi, "Gohō," in *Shintōshi* (History of Shinto) (Tokyo: Risōsha, 1959), 2:246–49.

18. *Shokunihongi*, Emperor Monmu 3 (699) May 24. This is a historical fact, but in later tradition (for example, in the *Nihon ryōiki*) the accuser changed to Hitokoto Nushi no Mikoto, who was a mountain deity of Katsuragi.

19. For the tradition of En no Gyōja, see H. Byron Earhart, "Shugendō, the Tradition of En no Gyōja and Mikkyo Influence," in *Study of Esoteric Buddhism and Tantrism*, ed. Kōyasan University (Kōyasan: Kōyasan University, 1965), 297–317. Also, Hartmut O. Rotermund, "Die Legende des En no Gyōja," *Oriens Extremus* 12 (1965): 221–41.

20. Saeki Arikiyo, *Shōbō* (Tokyo: Yoshikawa Kōbunkan, 1991).

21. Yūban, *Yamabushi nijigi* (The meaning of the two characters of *yamabushi*), in *Shugendō shōso* 2:28–41.

22. For the forms of dress and instruments, see the figure in chapter 4.

23. Miyake, *Shugendō shisō no kenkyū*, 657–87.

24. For *jikkai shugyō*, see Miyake, *Shugendō shisō no kenkyū*, 714–77; also Carmen Blacker, "Initiation in Shugendō: The Passage Through the Ten States of Existence," in *Initiation*, ed. C. J. Bleeker (Leiden: E. J. Brill, 1965), 96–111.

25. H. Byron Earhart, *A Religious Study of the Mount Haguro Sect of Shugendō: An Example of Japanese Mountain Religion* (Tokyo: Sophia University, 1970), 89–99; also plates 1–9.

26. Miyake, *Shugendō shisō no kenkyū*, 796–821.

27. Minoru Kiyota, *Shingon Buddhism: Theory and Practice* (Los Angeles-Tokyo: Buddhist Books International, 1978).

28. Tamura Yoshirō, *Hongaku shisōron* (A consideration of innate Buddha nature thought) (Tokyo: Shunjūsha, 1990).

29. For *buchū sekai*, see *Ōmine shugyō kanjōshiki*, in *Shugendō shōso* 2:56–58.

30. Paul L. Swanson, "Shugendō and the Yoshino-Kumano Pilgrimage: An Example of Mountain Pilgrimage," *Monumenta Nipponica* 36.1 (1981): 55–79.

31. Kurikara Fudō also is called Kurikara Ryūō (Kurikara dragon). See Carmen Blacker, *The Catalpa Bow: A Study of Shamanistic Practices in Japan* (London: Allen and Unwin, 1975), 178–79.

The Cosmology of Shugendō:
Shamanism and Shugendō Thought

The early stage of the study of Japanese shamanism was promoted by scholars like Yanagita Kunio, Nakayama Tarō, and others, who focused their attention on *miko*[1] (female shamans). Emphasis was placed on the so-called "possession type" of shamans who induce tutelary spirits and spirits of the living and the dead to enter their bodies and speak through their mouths. Hori Ichirō, under the influence of Mircea Eliade, saw the essence of shamanism instead in the state of ecstasy or "out of body experience," and he pointed out that, in the austere experience of the practitioners of esoteric Buddhism and of mountain asceticism, there were many accounts of ecstasy and wandering in the otherworld.[2] Furthermore, Saigō Nobutsuna showed how the experience of wandering in the otherworld was featured in the dreams of people of ancient times, and he saw in this the influence of shamanism.[3] I myself have also written about how we can discover vestiges of rituals that act out a wandering in the otherworld.[4] Such acting out is seen in the practices of Shugendō *mineiri* (entering the peak), walking on swords, the *hashiramatsu* (erecting of a sacred pillar), and fire-walking.

According to Sakurai Tokutarō and others who have systematically investigated and elucidated the religious activities of shamanesses in present-day Japan, almost all of them belong to the possession type, and there are only a few cases in which the spirit of the shamaness leaves the body and travels to the otherworld.[5] However, the idea of *chinkon* (repose of soul), for example, that is the basis for festivals and folk arts in Japan, presupposes the separation of the soul from the body. There are many tales about children and other ordinary people who, after being taken away by *tengu* (goblins) and *sennin* (mountain wizards), ascend to the sky; and tales about ascetics who, after having entered a cave, wander about in the subterranean otherworld. All these traditions show how, in former times, the ecstatic

131

type of shamanism certainly did exist. Therefore, I think that in the study of Japanese shamanism, we have to acknowledge a mixture of both the possession and ecstatic types, and we should investigate and analyze the cosmology and rituals that can explain this coexistence.

If we take this standpoint, Shugendō is an extremely appropriate object of study in dealing with Japanese shamanism, since Shugendō aims at intensifying ascetic practices in the sacred mountains that are considered the sacred otherworld, and at acquiring the power to manipulate the spirits and divinities living there.[6] Moreover, Shugendō was developed into a religious system at the end of the Heian period (782–1191) through an amalgamation of Japan's native mountain beliefs with elements of esoteric Buddhism and Taoism. It was, until the end of the Edo period (1603–1868), together with Shinto and Buddhism, one of the main pillars sustaining Japan's popular religions. It is also considered one of the sources of the new religious movements that appeared in more recent times. I would like, therefore, to focus in this chapter primarily on Shugendō and to have a new look at Japanese shamanism from the standpoint mentioned above, through an investigation of the cosmology and the rituals of Shugendō.

The word "cosmos" generally refers to the totality of all things, manifesting a certain order and unity, while "cosmology" refers to the metaphysical ideas concerning the cosmos. In cosmology, moreover, we can distinguish between the theories that discuss the structure of the cosmos (heaven, earth, and the like), and those that discuss the origin and development of heaven and earth, and of divinities and humans.[7] In this chapter, then, I will first deal with concepts concerning the structure of the cosmos in Shugendō, and particularly with the structure of the otherworld as distinct from this world. Also, I will present some myths of Shugendō in connection with the origin of the cosmos and analyze the sacred place where ascetic practices are performed, namely, altar meditation that represents these myths, and the structure of the esoteric ritual called *hashiramoto goma* (pillar erection ritual), which is a dramatic reenactment of the myths. Finally, I will explore the religious worldview that explains the coexistence of both the possession and ecstatic types of shamanism in the cosmology and rituals of Shugendō.

MOUNTAINS AS THE SACRED PLACE OF SHAMANISM

Shugendō, which is centered on ascetic practice in the mountains, considers the mountains sacred places, and this has led to the idea that these locations are the otherworld and the cosmos itself. Especially widely known as representative of the cosmology of Shugendō is the "mountain mandala," which considers the Ōmine Mountain range stretching from Yoshino to Kumano as the mandala of the diamond world (*kongōkai*) and the womb store world (*taizōkai*). However, at the core of this cosmology are concepts originating in the ascetic practices of the *shugenja* and these practices are related to the natural scenery of the mountains regarded as sacred places. Therefore, I would like to look at the scenery of these sacred mountains that constitute the archetype of the mountain mandala as it is reflected in the eyes of the *shugenja*.

If we assume an aerial viewpoint at Sanjōgatake, the entrance to the Ōmine Mountain range (and even at present the mecca of Shugendō), we see how the whole landscape is a slightly elevated plateau. Close to two-thirds of the plateau is occupied by grassland (flower gardens) and, with the Ōminesan Temple and its lodgings as a border, a rock landscape stretches out in the background. The plateau is surrounded by deep cliffs and only one road leads out to the south. This road, which at times is completely hidden in the clouds and fog, is the road leading to Kumano and is said to be the safest way for the *shugenja*. In contrast to this, the valleys and cliffs are dreadful places suggesting death and hell, and there are, for example, places called Shashindani, literally "the Valley of Self-abandonment," and Akoya, "the Abode of the Dead Spirits." There are, moreover, caves in the mountainside that, in addition to being sites for ascetic practices, are feared as entrances to the otherworld.

In Kumano, the forty-eight waterfalls of Nachi are worthy of attention. They seem to fall from heaven and, until the Edo period, flourished as places for austere practices for the *shugenja* of Nachi. According to the research done by Nikō Ryōei, these forty-eight waterfalls are thought to be the abode of *kami*, such as Ten no Nijūhasshuku (the *kami* or deities of twenty-eight solar stages along the zodiac), Shitennō, i.e., the Four Quarter Kings (who protect the eastern, southern, western, and northern continents respectively), *chigi* (earthly *kami* or deities), Amatsukami (the heavenly *kami* or deities), and of buddhas such as Kannon, Benzaiten, and others; in a word, of all *kami*, buddhas, and stars of the heavenly world.[8] This whole plateau above the great Nachi Waterfall is modeled after the heavenly dwelling place of the *kami*, and it is in this sense that in Shugendō the mountains were considered to be the heavenly world and that the heavenly world and the nether world were believed to coexist there.

Another feature of the mountains is the contrast between the green stretches of land and the rock fields. Moreover, in the sacred mountain sites, water is highly prized. In close relationship to these things, an interesting point is that Sanjōgatake and Kumano and other sacred places, or

Figure 41. Aerial view of Sanjōgatake

the strangely shaped rocks there, are often linked to turtles, dragons, and the like. For example, the former site of Kumano Hongū[9] is, as a whole, considered a supernatural turtle, as is also the case for the worship of Gotobiki Rock of the Kannokura Shrine (on Mt. Gongen) of Kumano Shingū. On the other hand, Mt. Nachi is said to have the shape of a sacred dragon lying down. The same is also said about Sanjōgatake, while the sacred turtle stones on the mountains are believed to appear all along the way to distant Kumano. As is well known, turtles and dragons are traditionally viewed as animals supporting the cosmos. In this sense, the tradition of linking the mountains to dragons and turtles can be interpreted as being based upon the belief that these sacred places symbolize cosmic mountains, i.e., Mt. Sumeru.

The view of the Ōmine Mountain range as the diamond world and the womb store world can already be found in the *Shozan engi* (History of the Mountains), compiled at the end of the Heian period.[10] According to this book, the buddhas of the womb store world are assigned to the various peaks of the Kumano side, while those of the diamond world are assigned to the peaks of the Yoshino side. In those places, images of the Buddha were installed and worshipped. However, from the time of the Middle Ages, this elaborate arrangement was discontinued and, instead, the southern half of the Ōmine Mountain range at the Kumano side was made the womb store world and its northern part at the Yoshino side the diamond world, while a sacred site called the "division between the two peaks" was established as a border between the two. Moreover, the *mineiri* (entering the peak) from the Kumano side was called the womb store world peak (*junbu*, regular peak) and that from the Yoshino side the diamond world peak (*gyakubu*, reverse peak). This gave birth to the idea that a *shugenja* who performed both could realize both worlds together in his body.

Already from about the end of the Heian period, there was a flourishing site for austere practices in the village Zenki, which is located in the central plateau of the Ōmine Mountain range and which maintained the sacred site of Jinzen where the esoteric rituals, i.e., consecration rite and *hashiramoto goma* were performed. In this location, there are several sacred places such as Kontai no Kutsu (cave of the diamond world and the womb store world). Ten no Nijūhasshuku (the twenty-eight solar stages along the zodiac in heaven), Chi no Sanjūroku Kin (thirty-six birds on the earth), Mie no Iwaya (Threefold Cave), and the entire area were apparently believed to have constituted one big cosmos. At the place called Ten no Nijūhasshuku is a chain attached to a steep rock wall, giving the appearance of leading to the heavenly world, while the place called Chi no Sanjūroku Kin is a narrow road along a precipice that gives the appearance of falling down to the bottom of hell. Moreover, the Mie no Iwaya consists of three caves, of which the lower one is considered the Amida world, the middle one the womb store world, and the upper one the diamond world. The Mie no Taki (Threefold Waterfall) is a place for ascetic practices. In this vicinity is the Dainichi-dake, literally, Dainichi peak, where Dainichi Nyorai is worshipped.

In the Ōmine Mountain range we can also find the representations of Mt. Sumeru, which is typical Buddhist cosmology. In the seventeenth century text *Yamabushi benmō*, the concept of Mt. Sumeru was interpreted in terms of the Kusha theory (*Abhidharma-kośa*).[11] In this *Yamabushi benmō*, particular attention was given to the two deities, Bonten and Taishaku, of Mt. Sumeru. It is also believed that the part of Ryōjusen (Vulture Peak) where the Buddha preached flew to Japan and became Mt. Ōmine. Moreover, Mt. Misen in the Ōmine range is said to represent Mt. Sumeru itself. Incidentally, other mountains called Misen or Myōkō, such as Mt. Misen of Itsukushima in Hiroshima Prefecture, and Mt. Myōkō in Nagano Prefecture, all represent Mt. Sumeru. These kinds of mountains are all believed to be golden mountains at the center of the world from which all things were born. Especially on Mt. Misen in the Ōmine Mountain range, Benzaiten is worshipped as the symbolic unity of the golden world and womb store world. The river called Tenkawa, which originates at the summit of Mt. Misen, is said to flow to Yamato, Ise, and Kumano, so the mountain is considered to be a source of water.[12]

ORIGINAL MYTH OF THE COSMOS

The Yamato area's Mt. Katsuragi, known as the place where Shugendō's founder En no Ozunu first performed ascetic practices, is a Shugendō sacred site linked to Mt. Ōmine. Among the tales of origin transmitted by the *shugenja* of Mt. Katsuragi is the *Yamato Katsuragi hōzanki*, ascribed to a monk of Kōfukuji at the beginning of the Kamakura period (early thirteenth century).[13] According to this book, water was the source of heaven and earth. At first, something spiritual resembling a reed sprout appeared and from this a holy spirit (*kami*) was born. This divine spirit had one thousand heads and two thousand hands and feet and was called Jihi Shin Ō (Merciful Divine King). The reed itself was called Ame no Nuboko (jeweled spear), Kongōhōshō (*vajra*-pounder). From the navel of this Jihi Shin Ō a luminous lotus flower emerged. If one looked closely at Jihi Shin Ō, one could see in the middle of the lotus flower the god-man Bonten Ō, a *kami* in human form who radiated light. This Bonten Ō gave birth to eight children, among whom were the sun, the moon, the stars, and also the ancestor of the imperial line. Later the two divinities Izanagi no Mikoto and Izanami no Mikoto used the Ame no Nuboko, a jeweled spear, to bestow supernatural power on the mountains, rivers, trees, and grass, created the country of Japan, and then descended from heaven at the peak of Katsuragi. They set up the jeweled spear in the heart of Yamato and made it the central sacred pillar of this country. This central pillar is also called *vajra*-pounder. This *vajra*-pounder then turned into a *dokko* (a single *vajra*), Kurikara Ryūō (a dragon deity), Fudō Myōō, and Hachidai Ryūō (the eight great dragon diety). Afterward the *vajra* king descended to earth and governed the country.

As we see from the origin myth of Mt. Katsuragi, heaven and earth originated from water, the source of all things, and from a reed (the *vajra*, halberd) sprout Jihi Shin Ō, who seems to indicate a divine earth mother.[14] From the lotus flower in the navel of this Jihi Shin Ō was born Bonten Ō, who governs heaven as a *kami*. The reed gave birth to the land, the streams, mountains, and plants and was erected at the center of Yamato and became the core pillar (*axis mundi*). In turn, all these objects are said to have been transformed into the divinities worshipped by Shugendō, including Fudō Myōō (its main object of worship).

The end of the Muromachi period (early sixteenth century) marked the appearance of Shugendō as an established organization, and also the compilation of books of systematic doctrine. The text *Shugen shūyō hiketsushū*, which even today is a central doctrinal work of Shugendō, has a chapter entitled "The Origin of the World."[15]

According to this account, at the beginning of the world there existed a state of undifferentiated chaos resembling a chicken egg, but it was filled with the sacred letter "a" of Dainichi Nyorai. Soon there separated from this both heaven and earth, and also the cosmic dual forces, *yin* and *yang*; through the union of heaven and earth all things were born, and through the interaction of the cosmic dual forces humans came into being. In this way, these ideas about the origin of the cosmos became the fundamental doctrine of Shugendō and led to a wealth of interpretations during the Edo period.

COSMOLOGY IN THE MYSTICAL PRACTICE OF SHUGENDŌ

The origin of heaven, earth, divinities and the like can also be observed in a later meditation, a rite that envisions the establishment of the ceremonial site for the main deity on the altars. Therefore, I would like to concentrate in this section on altar meditation in the traditional practice of Shugendō.

Figure 42. Kongōhōshō

We first look at the section "Ōmine kai'e mangyō jizaihō," which gives the altar meditation in the work *Ōmine kai'e mangyō jizai shidai*. This work has as its purpose instructions on how one becomes a Buddha. In this section we learn how the ascetics quietly sit down, and see in front of them the earth; in the water at the center of the earth the sacred letter "a" for Mahāvairocana, i.e., Dainichi Nyorai, appears and this becomes Mt. Sumeru. Then, at the summit of Mt. Sumeru a lotus flower blooms, and above it the sacred letter "a" appears, which at full moon turns into a single *vajra*, then a *vajra*-pounder, and finally becomes the main deity itself.[16]

Next we take up altar meditations in the *Shugen saishō e'in sanmayahō rokudan*. In this ritual are worshipped together six different divinities, namely Dainichi Nyorai, Ryūju Bosatsu (Nāgārjuna), Aizen Myōō, Kongō Dōji, Jinshadaishō (dragon deities), and Benzaiten; the altar meditation in this ritual varies slightly for each of the six divinities. However, in almost all cases a common feature is that the sacred letter "a" of Dainichi Nyorai becomes either Mt. Ōmine or Mt. Katsuragi, and on this mountain a palace arises; on a lotus pedestal in the center of the palace appears the sacred letter for every object of worship, each becoming a *vajra*-pounder, and then turning into each of the objects of worship. In this setting, for Dainichi, Ryūju, Aizen, and Kongō Dōji, it is Mt. Ōmine that appears; in both of the rituals for Jinshadaishō and Benzaiten, Mt. Katsuragi appears.[17] But in either case, the same order of appearance is seen in the rituals: the sacred letter of Dainichi, the cosmic mountain, the palace, sacred seeds, *vajra*-pounder, and divinities.

Thus, in the altar meditation found within Shugendō's representative practices, in every case the seeds of Dainichi within the midst of chaos become the very foundation, and then the cosmic mountain appears in the water. On this mountain, a palace is formed and the lotus flower in it becomes the object of worship. We can perceive here in essence a drama resembling the motif of the tradition about the origin of the cosmos in the *Yamato katsuragi hōzanki*.

The origin of the cosmos in Shugendō is seen not only in altar meditation. Actually, the origin of the cosmos is also acted out in Shugendō's most arcane ritual, the *hashiramoto goma*, pillar erection ritual, whose purpose is to enable the practitioner to become a Buddha in his own body (*sokushin jōbutsu*) (see chapter 4, pp. 94–96).[18]

In this way, the *hashiramoto goma* begins with an undifferentiated state of the cosmos; first heaven and earth are separated, and then in their interaction all things are born. Also, through the interaction of the paternal and maternal elements, the practitioner himself (symbolized by the *hashiramoto*, i.e., small pillar) is born. Moreover, since all things born in this way possess the six elements of Dainichi Nyorai, they all are shown to be the same being, and the practitioner himself born in this way is shown to have the nature of the cosmic pillar (*axis mundi*) placed at the center of heaven and earth, as symbolized by the *hashiramoto* in the water cylinder. This pillar is also considered to be Fudō Myōō, the main object of worship of Shugendō.

SHAMANISTIC ELEMENTS IN SHUGENDŌ COSMOLOGY

In the preceding materials I have treated the cosmology of Shugendō in its tales of origin, doctrine, and rituals. What remains is to take another look at all of this as a whole and to extract the shamanistic elements found therein. First, we have to remember that in Shugendō, which is centered on mountain ascetic practices, mountains are considered to constitute the otherworld, the center of the cosmos. In the mountains, mountain ridges and flower fields, showing the heavenly world, coexist with swamps and valleys, feared as leading to the depths of hell. On the peaks, chains are used to reach the heavenly world. At Nachi of Kumano, the world of heaven was supposed to be above the big waterfall. The caves were thought to be the entrance to the otherworld, and from these, tales about people who went to the otherworld were transmitted. In this way, in Shugendō the otherworld of mountains was a sacred place in which pure land and hell, or heaven and earth, coexist.

According to the doctrine of Shugendō, the cosmos is constituted by the mandala of the diamond world and womb store world, and the mountains themselves are widely recognized as being both worlds. Further, the ascetic who has finished his ascetic practices is said to have become in his own body a microcosm endowed with both worlds. The cosmos, which in the beginning was in a state of chaos like a chicken egg or filled with water, is already at that stage the sacred letter "a" of Dainichi Nyorai. Soon, heaven and earth are separated, a reed sprout comes into being, and this turns into a divinity. This *vajra*-pounder is later seen as the axis (*shin no mihashira*) that links heaven and earth and is at the center of the world, while it is believed that this also became Fudō Myōō, the main object of Shugendō worship.

In the esoteric ritual of "becoming a Buddha in one's own body," namely the *hashiramoto goma*, heaven and earth are born from the water, and from their interaction all things come forth, while from the interaction of paternal and maternal elements the practitioner himself is born. He himself is symbolized by the pillar (the *akafuda, hashiramoto*) in the center of heaven and earth (the two *nyūboku*) and he becomes the *axis mundi.* Altar meditation—in which the seeds on Mt. Sumeru and other cosmic mountains at the center of the cosmos become *dokko* and these turn into the divinities—is also related to the cosmological notion that the *axis mundi* becomes the object of worship. Here, too, when perceived in this way, the object of worship and the practitioner himself become one and the same. In this way, in the cosmology of Shugendō, the cosmos is essentially divided into heaven and earth; mountains are considered to be either the axis that links them together or the womb store and diamond worlds that comprise the whole cosmos, including heaven and earth. Also the object of worship itself is seen as the *axis mundi* or the Buddha that represents the cosmos. In the process of entering the mountains, the ascetic practices of the *shugenja* signify that they come into contact with the cosmos itself, and that they themselves turn into the *axis mundi* or into the world. This is expressed and performed in the *hashiramoto goma* and in the concept of the *dōjō* (training hall). In this cosmology, the object of worship and the practitioners themselves become the axis linking heaven and earth, this world, and the otherworld. The practitioners themselves signify by this that beings from this world can freely go to the otherworld, and that spirits of the otherworld by means of this cosmic axis can visit this world. Precisely because this kind of cosmology lies at the basis of Shugendō, I think that there coexist in Shugendō both the possession type and the ecstasy type of shamanism. The *shugenja,* after becoming identical to the *axis mundi,* can go to the otherworld and can induce spirits of the otherworld to enter this world and to possess mediums.

NOTES

1. Yanagita Kunio, "Fujo kō" (A study of female shamans), in *Teihon Yanagita Kunio shū* (Tokyo: Chikuma Shobō, 1962), 9:221–301.
2. Hori Ichirō, *Nihon no shamanizumu* (Shamanism in Japan) (Tokyo: Kōdansha, 1971).
3. Saigō Nobutsuna, *Kodaijin no yume* (Dreams of ancient people) (Tokyo: Heibonsha, 1972).
4. Miyake Hitoshi, *Shugendō girei no kenkyū* (A study of religious rituals in Shugendō), 2d ed., rev. (Tokyo: Shunjūsha, 1985), 107–30.
5. Sakurai Tokutarō, *Nihon no shamanizumu* (Shamanism in Japan), 2 vols. (Tokyo: Yoshikawa Kōbunkan, 1974–77).
6. See Miyake Hitoshi, "Shugendō to shamanizumu" (Shugendō and shamanism), in *Shugendō to Nihon shūkyō* (Tokyo: Shunjūsha, 1996), 21–42.
7. W. B. Kristensen, *The Meaning of Religion*, trans. J. B. Carman (The Hague: Martinus Nijhoff, 1971), 27–28.
8. Nikō Ryōei, "Kumano Nachi no shinkō" (The belief in Nachi Kumano), in *Kinki reizan to Shugendō,* ed. Gorai Shigeru, Sangaku Shūkyōshi Kenkyū Sōsho 11 (Tokyo: Meicho Shuppan, 1978), 247–77.
9. Now Kumano Hongū is located on the hillside, but until 1896 it was enshrined on an island in the Kumano River.
10. *Shozan engi,* in *Jisha engi,* ed. Sakurai Tokutarō, Hagiwara Tatsuo, and Miyata Noboru, Nihon Shisō Taikei 20 (Tokyo: Iwanami Shoten, 1975), 90–102.

11. *Yamabushi benmō* 1 (Oka Kichibe).

12. Gakuhō, *Buchū hiden*, in *Shugendō shōso*, ed. Nakano Tatsue, Nihon Daizōkyō 46 (Tokyo: Ryūbunkan, 1916–19), 1:568.

13. For the Shugendō of Kōfukuji, see Royall Tyler, "Kōfuku-ji and Shugendō," *Japanese Journal of Religious Studies* 16, 2–3 (June–September 1989): 143–80.

14. According to the legends of *Ōmine engi*, Jihi Shin Ō (or Jihi Daiken Ō) has an important role, but the tradition of Mt. Katsuragi emphasizes a divine earth mother.

15. *Shugen shūyō hiketsushū*, in *Shugendō shōso* 2:382.

16. *Ōmine kai'e mangyō jizaihō*, in *Shugendō shōso* 1:94.

17. *Shugen saishō e'in sanmayahō rokudan*, in *Shugendō shōso* 1:50.

18. Miyake Hitoshi, *Shugendō shisō no kenkyū* (Tokyo: Shunjūsha, 1985), 217–35.

Prohibition of Women at Mt. Sanjō in the Ōmine Mountains

A contemporary controversy surrounding Mt. Sanjō in the Ōmine Mountain area, which has drawn much attention from many people, including both ascetic monks and the local population in Yoshino and Dorogawa, is its territorial "off limits" for women. Mt. Sanjō still maintains its prohibition of women, in spite of the fact that some related areas and rituals formerly closed to women have been opened—for example, an esoteric ceremony of consecration (*Jinzen kanjō*) by Shōgoin at Zenki (Ōmine) has been opened to females; and women have been allowed to participate in the mountain pilgrimage of southern Ōmine (*minami-okugake*) conducted by Kinbusen Shugen Honshū at Yoshino. This exclusively male character, however, is precisely why Mt. Sanjō attracts such devoted male trainees.

Of course, there have been demonstrations protesting the prohibition of women, and also movements organized to eliminate this ban,[1] and there have been some women who sought to climb all the way to the top of the mountain. However, notwithstanding these objections, this ironclad prohibition has stood intact.

This chapter has two main purposes: first, to trace the various movements challenging the prohibition of women; and second, to investigate the principle or cosmology underlying the persistent adherence to the prohibition of women despite these movements.

THE HISTORY BEHIND FEMALE PROHIBITION

It is recorded in *Yi Chu liu tie*, edited 945–954 A.D. by Yi Chu in the Latter Chou Dynasty, that Mt. Kinbu in Yamato Province was a sacred mountain prohibiting women, as described in the following account:

There exists Kinbu 500 *ri* south of Japan's Capitol Castle; Bodhisattva Kongō Zaō atop the mountain; pines, cypresses, famed flowers, and poetic plants in the midst of its sacred place; several hundred shrines and temples, small and large; those monks with reputed discipline enter therein; no woman has access to ascend this region; and men afire with the yearning to ascend, having abandoned carnal lust and diet, hurry where their hearts yearn to go.[2]

This kind of esoteric tradition had been recognized in Japan as early as the Heian period. To be sure, many sacred mountains such as Mt. Hiei and Mt. Kōya—not to mention Ōmine, Haguro, Hikosan, Hakusan, Tateyama, and Fuji, all of which are well-known as sacred mountains for ascetic life—had forbidden women from entering and trespassing. At the foot of these mountains, places of worship for women were built in ancient times, with names such as Fushiogami (literally, "kneeling down and worshipping"), and Boshidō (mother-child temple), where a pioneering ascetic monk and his mother are said to have parted from each other. Furthermore, it is not unusual to find on the mountainside sites called Miko-ishi and Uba-ishi (both meaning, literally, "a shamaness who goes beyond the prohibition line, turned into a stone"), and deeper into the mountain, Ashizuri (literally, "stamping the feet in disappointment").

The prohibition against women entering these mountains has been maintained from the medieval era through the modern era. Although in modern times some mountain temples such as Nyonin Koya (Murō Temple) and Nyonin Sanjō (Senkō Temple) opened their doors to women, and pilgrimages to these temples and shrines by the general public have come to be prosperous ventures, they did not amount to a significant number. However, on March 27, 1872 (Meiji 5), the Meiji Government ordered the lifting of such prohibition in Cabinet Act 98, which ordered that:

Heretofore, there were places under the jurisdiction of shrines and temples that have barred women from entering such regions; henceforth, mountaineering pilgrimage, thus far forbidden, will be open to women.[3]

In addition, on April 25 of the same year, the government permitted monks to eat meat and be married, and also to let their hair grow long, and wear secular clothing except when they were performing priestly duties.[4]

Unable to overlook these political orders, Yoshino mountaineering ascetics tried to open Sanjōzaō Temple for female worshippers; however, this attempt was met with outrage and revolt from the Dorogawa side. The village council also decided to protest against permitting this opening. In those days there was already strong resistance against free female access to Mt. Sanjō. Later, on February 2, 1878, the government officially clarified that the act issued April 1872 had no bearing on the religious codes of different sects. As a result, some ascetic monks reaffirmed female prohibition as legitimate because the government had extended the above explanation to mean that such a prohibition could be determined by their own religious codes.

Thus, this prohibition has been maintained practically as law. In respect to Mt. Sanjō, the Yoshino side set its outmost territorial limit at a divergent point on Ōtaki Road running 500 meters to the left of Kinbu Shrine, the Dorogawa side at the temple Hahakodō, and the Kashiwagi side at Amida Forest.

Nonetheless, some women have attempted to ascend Mt. Sanjō. For example, Toyo, a daughter of a chief Shintō priest at Katsuragi Shrine (Mt. Katsuragi), tried to climb the forbidden route along with two monks in 1902 (Meiji 35). Also, at least two women ascended to the summit during the opening of the mountain in 1929 (Shōwa 4). Other than these instances, there seem to have been a few cases in which women ascended Mt. Sanjō from the Kashiwagi direction, during seasons when the mountain was closed. However, we could not find any scheme or serious attempt designed to violate the ban on women from either the Dorogawa or the Yoshino region.

The Ōmine Mountains were designated as Yoshino-Kumano National Park on October 8, 1932 (Shōwa 7). Supported by the fact that eleven other national parks designated at the same time had no internal area forbidding female entrance, the claim was made that male-exclusive areas should be opened to women. The argument was that the tradition banning women ran contrary to the purpose for which these parks were designated, namely the provision of opportunities for the general public to see the grandeur of nature and places for vacation, health care, and leisure. In addition, the local people of Yoshino and Dorogawa began to anticipate an increase in the number of tourists by opening Mt. Sanjō to women. Of course, mountaineering pilgrims such as members of the fraternity called Sanjō-kō firmly resisted this liberal voice, due to their position that the female prohibition had persisted to the present from the days of En no Gyōja (legendary founder of Shugendō, ca. 699), and also that it would not be feasible to have women around during ascetic austerities; quite a few local people also gave their support to this resistance.

In the midst of the conflict between the "pro" and "con" sides on the issue of prohibition of women, the *Osaka Asahi Newspaper* on February 25, 1936 (Shōwa 11), printed an article claiming that Dorogawa had decided in a meeting to lift the ban on Mt. Sanjō and would open the mountain for women in May. Thus, a local movement in Dorogawa supporting the opening of Mt. Sanjō for women had surfaced.

Aghast at this new development, the religious fraternity held a meeting on the 27th of the same month and reaffirmed their absolute position against lifting the ban, and on the following day its representatives submitted a petition to the Nara Prefectural Government, requesting that the upper region bounded by Dorotsuji of Mt. Sanjō be preserved exclusively for men. Along the same lines, Shōgoin and the fraternity called Heian Rengōkai, on March 6 and 7, respectively, submitted similar petitions to the prefectural government for the maintenance of the local tradition at Ōmine. Moreover, there was a joint staff meeting at Yoshino for representatives from Yoshino and Dorogawa, the five temples that alternately managed Ōminesan Temple atop Mt. Sanjō (Gōjiin),[5] and the religious fraternity; they resolved to continue to exclude women from Ōmine. Representatives of this conference appealed to the governor and obtained an official approval stating that authorities would declare the premises of the main building of Ōminesan as a forbidden area for women. Thus, prohibition of women at Mt. Sanjō and its vicinity came to be officially guaranteed. It is true, however, that from time to time some women ascended mountains other than Mt. Sanjō at Ōmine, due to the fact that the Ōmine Mountains were designated a national park. For example, female students from Osaka climbed Misen in 1938 (Shōwa 13), and Okumura Tsurumatsu took several students from Sakurai Girls' School along and climbed Mt. Inamura in 1940 (Shōwa 15).[6]

In the post-World War II period, once more women made attempts to remove the prohibition of females at Mt. Sanjō; perhaps this was prompted by the postwar constitution, which promised equal opportunities for men and women. First, there was an incident in which Matsuyama Keikichi, chairman of the Kinki Alpine Society, tried to ascend from Kashiwagi with fifteen Japanese women, an American female staff member from a U.S. Army base, and her Japanese translator, claiming that they received permission from the Occupation forces. At this point, the district chairman and all the others from Dorogawa rushed to the scene and, after great difficulty, were successful in dissuading them from their ascent. In order to prevent similar incidents thereafter, the people associated with Ōminesan Temple made a great effort and succeeded in obtaining a notice from Lieutenant Colonel S. Henderson in the Temples and Shrines Section, the Nara Prefecture Military Administrative Department, that stated it would respect the privileges and traditions of Japanese religions and officially recognize the prohibition of women that had persisted for over 1,300 years; this notice was then posted at several places on the outer boundaries of the proscribed area.[7]

Nonetheless, despite the above notice, a female ascetic, claiming to have received a divine message from En no Gyōja to overthrow the tradition of female prohibition at Ōmine, attempted a mountaineering pilgrimage (or worship) in July 1947. This attempt was halted prematurely, when she felt the presence of a bright light at an entrance for the mountaineering pilgrimage and received a divine message to halt the ascent. Moreover, a woman who owned the Jirochō Sushi Shop in Tobita, Osaka, tried to climb and complete a pilgrimage but was stopped in September 1948; Yamamoto Satoshi of the Society for Mountaineering and Skiing Promotion from Tokyo, along with two other women, made a similar attempt, only to be stopped at Dorogawa.

In the postwar period the number of female followers rapidly increased for both the Ōmine deity and Hachidai Ryūō (the eight great dragon deity) enshrined within the precincts of Ryūsen Temple in Dorogawa. As a response to the expectations of these women, Ryūsen Temple lifted its prohibition of women in its precincts on the occasion celebrating the completion of its main building, on July 10, 1960. In addition, in 1964 it set aside a place for women to undergo ascetic training in a waterfall, called Ryūō no Taki. Ryūsen Temple also began to manage Dainichi Temple at the summit of Mt. Inamura (known as Nyonin Ōmine because many female ascetics worshipped there); the temple gave ascetics who completed their training there certificates called Inamuragatake Nyonin Shugyō Dōjō (literally, "training at the female temple on Mt. Inamura"), intending to keep them placated. Also, in 1957 Yamaguchi Shinchoku from Dorogawa established a basic training hall for ascetic discipline called Shugen Setsuritsu Konpon Dōjō at Janokura of Mt. Nanao and attracted female followers who could not enter Mt. Sanjō. Furthermore, the headquarters for Kinbusen Shugenhonshū in Yoshino enshrined Nōten Daijin in Ryūō Temple within its precincts and thereby commanded a large female following. Thus, in recent years, several ascetic locations have been established for female ascetics, although male ascetics also undergo austerities in the same locale.[8]

Incidentally, since 1965, there have been waves of depopulation in Dorogawa, where people have relied on forestry and mountaineering visitors to make a living. Consequently, it was no longer possible to manage the labor force in forestry without women. The local people who were inclined to protect the ban on women could no longer belittle women, who as part of the work force entered the forbidden region. This dilemma led to serious discussion about narrowing the boundaries of the areas off-limits to women; representatives from the Gōjiin of Ōminesan Temple (both the local and the district representatives for the followers), and representatives from the religious fraternity Yakkukō[9] participated in these talks. The result was that the Dorogawa side decided to move their entrance to Shojō Bridge and the Yoshino party redefined their entrance at Gobangaseki; the former facilitated access by establishing an entrance gate at Shojō Bridge; the latter erected a new entrance gate at Gobangaseki.

Figure 43. Exclusion of women from Ryūsenji

Figure 44. Gate announcing the exclusion of women at Dorogawa

RATIONALE FOR ARGUMENTS ABOUT PROHIBITION OF WOMEN

As we analyze the grounds of arguments for, as well as against, prohibition of women, we can notice in the argument against prohibition both an ideology of equality between men and women and also the motivation to ensure local profits. From the former perspective, exclusion of women from a national park—which all citizens should be able to fully experience—is evidence of inequality for women; and because there is no distinction between the two sexes in religion, and female ascetics are considered suitable for missionary activities and for receiving inspiration in the ascetic tradition, it is inconsistent to restrict women from Mt. Sanjō (a mecca of the ascetic tradition). Also, the local people of Mt. Sanjō—especially those in Dorogawa, who due to the forest industry and recent depopulation must depend upon tourism for their living—argue that they must attract female tourists by opening the area, and thereby resolve this difficult situation. According to them, by opening the area leading to Kashiwagi and other locales on the other side of the mountain, they will be able to attract a maximum number of female tourists.

Even though some are motivated by the challenge of climbing itself and others have been guided by divine inspiration, like one female ascetic from Mt. Ishizuchi, many of them advocate the idea of equality for both sexes. Local proponents of prohibition of women call such attempts "publicity stunts," because most of them are escorted by men and accompanied by media reporters. It is understandable that mountain aficionados just raise their eyebrows at the whole process.

Furthermore, the people related to Ōminesan Temple, or affiliated with the Shugen sect, and mountaineering pilgrims stand together for the continuation of the prohibition of women. Their argument for its maintenance may be summarized in the following manner.

Just as women at nunneries and women's temples lead ascetic lives by excluding men, we do the same by excluding women.[10] Mt. Sanjō is a region for men to live ascetic lives devoid of carnal desire, and we consider such ascetic exercises as the foundation of religious life. Moreover, the custom of the prohibition of women at Mt. Sanjō has persisted for 1,300 years, ever since En no Gyōja rejected even his own mother. Therefore, it is an obligation for those who follow the same path to preserve this ancient heritage.

In addition, some advocates claim that it will be impossible to live an ascetic life once the area is opened, since it will lead to the construction of leisure facilities. They argue that if it is necessary to provide a place for female ascetics, Mt. Inamura may be designated as a site for the exclusive use of women.

We can imagine local antagonists against female access expressing their resistance in the following manner. Ever since our ancestors were commanded by En no Gyōja to protect this area for ascetic austerities, we have protected it for more than 1,300 years and supported the religious fraternity members among the mountaineering pilgrims. Religious fraternities (*kō*) reciprocated our support by economically supporting the lives of local people. Therefore, it is proper for us to acknowledge their endeavors by seeing to it that men will be able to continue this training without any limitations. Insofar as our ancestors were against the inclusion of women, we must take the same position. Moreover, even if female tourists to our area may increase due to the liberalization of access by women, Mt. Sanjō and the villages below will gradually decline when the mountaineering ascetics and pilgrims, with whom we have kept in close touch, refuse to come. For these reasons, we must maintain the prohibition of women.

The rationale for their resistance to the liberalization of female access apparently stems from the age-old custom of prohibiting women, maintained since the time of En no Gyōja, and also from their resolute faith that ascetics would never be able to undergo true ascetic training unless they adhered to the same tradition. In times past this was reaffirmed by youths in their coming of age ceremony (*seijin shiki*), and by all religious fraternity members.

Where, then, can we look for the cosmological basis for this faith? In the following pages we will look for it in the worldview of beliefs in relation to the ascetic tradition at Ōmine.

RATIONALE FOR BELIEFS ABOUT PROHIBITION OF WOMEN

As recorded in *Yi Chu liu tie*, the Ōmine Mountains have been considered a sacred domain exclusively for men since the Heian period. The local legend that accounts for the origin of this form of exclusion is traced to an event in which En no Gyōja parted from his mother in order to engage in ascetic practices deep within Ōmine. However, according to the oral tradition about Ōmine, as it appears in *Shozan engi* (History of the Mountains), edited early in the Kamakura period, En no Gyōja's mother had lived on Mt. Hōtō in a stone house that looked like a *goko* (a *vajra*-pounder with five points on each end), located a day's walk from Jinzen in Ōmine. En no Gyōja had come here from Jinzen three times every day and humbly worshipped his mother near the prayer altar. Furthermore, En no Gyōja is said to have invited Hokuto-taishi, the third highest hermit of Great T'ang, and to have held a memorial service known as *sentō tōba kuyō* for his mother at Mt. Dainichi. Mt. Dainichi is a mountain immediately to the south of Jinzen, where presently initiates undergo ascetic practice by climbing up a chain; Mt. Hōtō is the name given to its summit.

Although En no Gyōja was exiled to Izu because of the slander of Hitokotonushi no Mikoto, he was later pardoned and returned to Jinzen. He then commanded Zenki (literally, "anterior demon") and Goki (literally, "posterior demon") to thereafter protect those ascetic practitioners who enter Ōmine; then he shaved his beard and, putting his mother in a Buddhist alms bowl, went with her to T'ang (China).[11] This concludes the legend of En no Gyōja, well-known since the medieval era. Furthermore, it is believed that descendants of Zenki have dwelt in Shimokitayama-mura-zenki and have guarded Jinzen, Mt. Shaka, and Zenki Uragyōba, while the descendants of Goki have dwelt in Dorogawa and have guarded Mt. Sanjō and Ozasa. Also, the place where En no Gyōja buried the beard he shaved off has been known down to the present as Higezuka (literally, "beard mound"). According to the legend, En no Gyōja's mother dwelt within the Ōmine Mountains and was paid visits by En no Gyōja day and night, and finally accompanied him to T'ang.

Since the late medieval era, various stories have been told and retold about how En no Gyōja entered the mountains after parting from his mother at the temple called Hahakodō in Dorogawa; or his mother, en route to visit him, advanced to Fushiogami beyond Zaō Temple in Anzen and on to Nakakoba, well beyond the "off-limits" for women, only to find herself unable to go farther; she then stamped her feet in frustration. Another version well-known since ancient times relates that the police captured the mother and kept her in the hamlet in order to lure him there, because he could not be caught during his ascetic practices. The legend claims that his ardent concern for his mother and the strong emotional bond between them are based on the fact that his mother, Shiratōme, divorced Daikaku, her husband, who had been married into her family from Izumo, after giving birth to En no Gyōja, and that she had lived alone with En no Gyōja thereafter. In this way, new episodes, one after another, have been added to the legend.[12]

According to the legend, then, what characterizes En no Gyōja's so-called "mother at the mountain" and "mother in the village," and how can we understand the relationship between the two mother figures? In order to simplify my argument, I shall jump to a conclusion. I would like to interpret the former as a goddess of the mountain, and the latter as an ordinary, profane mother. As a matter of fact, a local identification of a mountain deity with a goddess exists in the Ōmine area, as is widely known. The local mountaineers believe that, due to their unbroken tradition of services to the enshrined goddess and her invisible protection, they are able to conduct their daily activities in a trouble-free manner. Moreover, just as a mountain goddess had disguised herself as a mountain witch and reared the legendary Kintarō, the mountain goddess at Ōmine is endowed with a maternal instinct to nurture the mountain people steadfastly and affectionately.[13] It is believed, however, that if a mountaineer's wife becomes jealous of the mountain goddess and grows arrogant, the husband loses divine protection.

In this connection, another tale, handed down in the region along Totsu River at the foot of Ōmine, is helpful. One day a woman, who had been watching her mountaineering husband go into the mountains every day after shaving his beard, grew suspicious and followed him into the mountains, where she found a beautiful woman accompanying the husband working nearby. When the outraged wife screamed, the woman disappeared, and as a result, the husband fell and was severely injured. This injury is blamed on the wife for disturbing the goddess's guardianship of the husband. It is further believed that the souls of mountaineers who have offered their services to the goddess will be protected by the deity after their death.[14]

GODDESS OF THE MOUNTAIN VERSUS PROFANE MOTHER OF THE VILLAGE

The ascetic life we have been studying, generally, is said to have originated from mountaineers' religious beliefs. If this is so, the aforementioned story of En no Gyōja—who went from Jinzen to Mt. Hōtō to worship his mother, and then after shaving off his beard traveled to T'ang with her in a Buddhist alms bowl—can be viewed as related to belief in the goddess of the mountain. In other words, the significance of the story is that he served the goddess of the mountain as if he were her actual child, and left for the otherworld with the goddess riding in a Buddhist alms bowl (known as a vessel for spirits). In order to serve the goddess as her own child, and thereby to obtain her blessing, moreover, he needed to cut all ties with his profane mother. My conclusion is that this preexisting rationale actually gave birth to the previously mentioned episode of the separation of child from mother.

This kind of interpretation is helpful in understanding the various occasions when people enter Ōmine. First, let us look at a type of mountaineering rite known as *seijin shiki* widely practiced in the Kinki District. It is widely acknowledged that *seijin shiki* performed at a sacred mountain is a ritual essential for becoming an adult man. It is basically designed to sever a youth from his mother and isolate him in the mountains, in order to restore him to life once more upon his completion of training, all under the patronage of the goddess. The ritual ends in his being redeemed as an adult by the founder of his community or its subgroup. The ceremonial phases of this *seijin shiki*, which follow this general rationale, are formulated faithfully according to the *seijin shiki* practiced at sacred mountains elsewhere: having left women behind, the youth enters Ōmine, offers his penitence upon completing the pilgrimage (*dhūta*) practices, leaves Ōmine after experiencing the "departure from the womb" and the austerity of abandoning his body at Byōdō Rock, and finally encounters the esoteric statue of En no Gyōja (the patriarch of asceticism) at Ōminesan Temple. Then, descending from the mountain, he becomes a man by visiting a "foreign woman" (a prostitute) after a banquet at the foot of the mountain. Another feature of the *seijin shiki* is that the youth engages in Okugake (walking through Yoshino to Kumano) and *Jinzen kanjō* (the consecration rite at Jinzen) and climbs the metal chain to the summit of Mt. Hōkan and there undergoes austerities that enable him to meet the goddess. This scenario, too, is patterned after the mountaineers' belief that the separation from a worldly mother and the encounter with the sacred goddess of the mountain endows a man with her protection.

The same pattern holds for ascetics who have entered Ōmine many times. The ascetics, by avoiding worldly women and undergoing austerities in the Ōmine Mountains with the purpose of escaping profane dust and entering the otherworld, attain the spiritual state of feeling as if they were enfolded by the mother goddess in the depths of the mountains; and, eventually they achieve an ineffable mystical experience.

I tend to think that the solemn enshrinement of Shōten, a sculpture in the form of a man and woman embracing each other—in places comparable to the otherworld such as Ozasa and Jinzen in the Ōmine Mountains, and the local worship of these Shōten figures as the secret Buddha in ascetic temples such as Yoshino Sakura Motobō—indicate that such beliefs about the mother goddess had long existed among *yamabushi* (mountain ascetics) at Ōmine. According to Jungian interpretation, this whole pattern of ascetic life may be seen as psychic development in which an ascetic deepens his human nature through these experiences within the mountains, as he encounters his own anima (a feminine figure idealized unconsciously) seated deep in his unconsciousness and thereby obtains the ultimate power for living daily life. Whatever the case, an ascetic is required to shun profane women at least once in his life in order to attain such a spiritual plateau. Can we not see that the ascetics who have entered Ōmine many times will insist on the prohibition of women there; and, should Ōmine be opened to women, these ascetics will vow never to enter there because of these beliefs so dear to their hearts?

The reader may wonder why to this point I have developed the argument in this fashion, and will perhaps judge this chapter to be excessively male-oriented. Therefore, in the remainder of this chapter I would like to shift attention to village women who are left behind at the foot of the Ōmine Mountains. It is widely known that women who live at the foot of a sacred mountain are afraid of entering therein and faithfully abide by the custom of female exclusion. Specifically, they are afraid of being impregnated by evil spirits that may enter their bodies, and of anomalies caused by their curses. It is often asserted that women who have come under the extraordinary and mysterious influence of the mountain develop quite unstable psychological and physical conditions.[15]

Due to this combination of belief and fear, ordinary women worshipped the goddess of the mountain at a shrine known as Fushiogami, at the foot of the mountain. However, holy women, and also women considered to be both holy and profane (such as nuns, shamanesses, and mothers of famous ascetics) have climbed halfway up the mountain. Nevertheless, according to folk belief, if they had tried to trespass beyond the "off limits," they would have come under extraordinary and mysterious influences and would have been transformed into stones. In sharp contrast, the mountain goddess is deified at the peak of the mountain.

Ascetics who had separated themselves from profane women, either at the foot of the mountain or at the mountainside, and entered Ōmine encountered the goddess of the mountain in caverns near or at the summit and tried to absorb her power. *Misoka yamabushi* in particular, who entered Ōmine in autumn and underwent austerities in caverns, and returned on April 8, were revered as the most effective masters of spiritual force in the medieval era, the time when the Ōmine ascetic tradition reached its zenith. April 8 is widely believed to be the day when the mountain deity descends to the village (as a deity of the paddy field) to protect agricultural activities. Therefore, we can conjecture that the ascetics who descended from Ōmine to the village on April 8 were welcomed by the village folk as deities endowed with the fertile power of the mountain deity. And we can assume that the gate-opening ceremony at Ōminesan Temple and also the Mt. Shaka Festival, both of which are celebrated on April 8, are rooted in the ancient practice of welcoming mountain ascetics as mountain deities.

The mountain ascetics who had acquired the power of the mountain deity and descended to the village were greeted by village women outside the entrance to the forbidden area (at places such as Boshidō); these women sought to receive the men's fertile power through intercourse with them. The legend in which a daughter of a wealthy villager gives birth to a

Figure 45. Boshidō with pillar announcing the exclusion of women

child as the result of intercourse with a mountain god is common and widely disseminated; one example is the mythology of Mt. Miwa.[16] For these women, it was perhaps more favorable for them to come into contact with the mountain ascetics, who had acquired fertile power in austerities—and to gain the divine power of fertility through them—than to trespass into the forbidden area and risk the curses from evil spirits and malevolent spirits in their own bodies. Such were the women who became "one-night wives" for the mountain ascetics on their descent. Even today, amulets for conception and safe childbirth are sold at the temple Hahakodō in Dorogawa.

There is also a belief that those who lie in the road and have these mountain ascetics step over them will be blessed with good health. Seen in this light, the brothel in Dorogawa may be a vestige of the ancient belief system among shamanesses and other women who had served the mountain ascetics and tried to acquire their fertile power.

This concludes our analysis of the prohibition of women at Mt. Ōmine, in the light of the Ōmine ascetic belief system drawn collectively from the legend of En no Gyōja, as well as other legends related to mountain asceticism, and also the rituals of the village women. On the whole this tradition can be considered a mutual pact between *yamabushi* and the village women, and also as a custom emerging from the agricultural society based on the rice fields and crops providing their livelihood. Because occupational circumstances and society at large are changing drastically, of course, we may not envision that this configuration of beliefs and customs will continue just as it is. Nevertheless, we can surmise that at the core of the prohibition of women, strictly observed at Japanese sacred mountains such as Ōmine, were concealed the beliefs we have discussed.

NOTES

1. For a book written from this standpoint, see Kizu Yuzuru, *Nyonin kinsei* (Prohibition of females) (Osaka: Kaihō Shuppansha, 1993).
2. Yi Chu, *Yi Chu liu tie* (Kyoto: Hōyū Shoten, 19797), 21:459.
3. Date Terumi, *Nihon shūkyō seidoshiryō ruijūkō* (Historical materials of Japanese religious institutions) (Tokyo: Gannandō, 1931), 620.
4. Ibid., 621.
5. Yoshino side: Tōnanin, Kizōin, Sakuramotobō and Chikurinin; Dorogawa side: Ryūsenji.
6. Itō Sanae, "Ōminesan no nyonin kinsei" (Prohibition of females at Mt. Ōmine) (master's thesis, Keio University, 1988), 28–40.
7. Zenitani Osamu, "Ōminesan no nyonin kaikin mondai tsuiokuki" (Reminiscences of the opening of Mt. Ōmine for females), *Jinben* 724 (1970): 37–44.
8. Miyake Hitoshi, "Shugendō ni okeru seitō to itan" (Orthodoxy and heresy in Shugendō), in *Nihon shūkyō no seitō to itan*, ed. Sakurai Tokutarō (Tokyo: Kōbundō, 1988), 100–6.
9. Yakkukō are the eight old fraternities that are proud of a tradition dating back to the Edo period in Osaka and Sakai: i.e., Osaka—Iwa, Sangō, Kōmyō, and Kyōbashi; Sakai—Torige, Izutsu, Ryōgō, and Goryō.

10. This is also a historical fact: see Ushiyama Yoshiyuki, "Nyonin kinsei sairon" (Reconsidering exclusion of women), *Sangaku shugen* 17 (1996):1–11.

11. *Shozan engi*, in *Jisha engi*, ed. Sakurai Tokutarō, Hagiwara Tatsuo, and Miyata Noboru, Nihon Shisō Taikei 20 (Tokyo: Iwanami Shoten, 1975), 113–14.

12. *En no gyōja honki*, in *Shugendō shōso*, ed. Nakano Tatsue, Nihon Daizōkyō (Tokyo: Ryūbunkan, 1916–19), 3:246.

13. This tradition is dependent on the belief in mother-son deities in Japanese folk religion. See Ishida Eiichirō, "Mother and Son Deities," *History of Religions* 4.1 (1964):30–52.

14. Kinkiminzoku Gakkaihen, *Yamato no minzoku* (Folklore of the Yamato area) (Nara: Yamato Taimuzusha, 1959), 141.

15. Chiba Tokuji, *Nyōbō to yama no kami* (Wife and mountain goddess) (Osaka: Sakaiya Tosho, 1983).

16. According to the mythology of Mt. Miwa, the ancestor of the Miwa clan was the child of a village woman and the deity of Miwa.

Part Two: Folk Religion

Toward a Structural Analysis of Japanese Folk Religion

FOLK RELIGION IN THE CONTEXT OF THE RELIGIONS OF JAPAN

For most Japanese people, religious life involves more than what goes on in Shinto, Buddhism, Christianity, or other religious organizations. In real life, the religious practices the Japanese have developed and maintained in response to daily needs—practices generally called "folk religion"—occupy them even more than the institutional religions.[1]

Folk religion (*minzoku shūkyō*) is essentially indigenous primitive religion onto which elements from Shinto, Buddhism, Taoism, *yin-yang* dualism, Confucianism, and other religions have been grafted. It differs from Shinto, especially Shrine Shinto, in that it has no classic texts like the *Kojiki* or *Nihon shoki* (also known as *Nihongi*) and lacks the hierarchical structure of an organization like the Jinja Honchō (Association of Shinto Shrines). Overlapping at many points with folk Shinto, it is a multilayered phenomenon. Folk religion, unlike the institutional religions, has neither doctrines nor organization; it neither seeks to win converts nor to propagate a faith. It is, rather, something transmitted as a matter of custom among people bound together by community or kinship ties. With its festivals, cycle of annual observances, rites of passage, ceremonies of exorcism and the like, folk religion puts the greatest emphasis not on ideas but on rituals. Among its rituals, particularly numerous are those that serve the aim of securing tangible benefits, such as fertility, growth, prosperity, protection from danger, and healing from disease—immediate, concrete benefits in this world. Perhaps because of rituals like these, Japanese folk beliefs and practices have a distinctly magico-religious character.[2]

What folk religion involves may be presented more concretely. The ordinary Japanese offers worship at the family Shinto and Buddhist altars, before the *kami* of the kinship group (*dōzoku*), and before the stone pillar erected in honor of the *kami* who stands guard at the entrance to the village and drives away misfortune. To each a prayer is offered for protection

161

in daily life. At stated times the ordinary person participates in services for the ancestors, in ceremonies to obtain a good harvest, and in other rituals that occur yearly. At special times he or she takes part in various rites of passage connected with birth, coming of age, marriage, and death. To allay anxieties about the future, a person may request the services of diviners and in time of illness ask for ritual prayers and charms that will drive out bad fortune and attract good. All this belongs to folk religion.

It is true, of course, that weddings and festivals are usually Shinto affairs and that funerals and other mortuary rites are usually Buddhist. In these and other ways the organized religions participate in the customs and usages of folk religion. More to the point, it is within the frame of reference provided by folk religion that the organized religions have made their way into Japanese society. Only as they accommodated themselves to folk religion and its implicit norms did the institutional religions find acceptance and begin to exercise influence on people in daily life. Any attempt to understand the role of Shinto, Buddhism, and other religions in the lives of Japanese people must come to terms with folk religion.

In a historical perspective, folk religion has been the source of many new religious movements in Japan. Not only the various Sect Shinto groups but most of the so-called new religions sprang from the soil of folk religion. Besides providing a base in which the other religions of Japan could take root, folk religion also has a close connection with the Japanese national character and ethos. In view of these considerations it will be evident that no student of the religions of Japan can afford to neglect Japanese folk religion.

JAPANESE FOLK RELIGION AND RITUAL

The most important aspect of folk religion is ritual, and in this chapter, my purpose is to introduce my methodology for the study of Japanese folk religion with reference to the annual observances and rites of passage in rural Japan.[3] My main interest is to make clear the religious worldview that has sustained Japanese folk religion over the centuries, through the interpretation of its religious rituals. Toward this end, I use the following procedures:

1. To construct a model of the structure of Japanese folk religion based both on other academic theories and on the personal understanding of researchers, who have developed an empathy with folk religion through participation. This model will provide the direction of the study.
2. To observe and arrange as data the rites of Japanese folk religion according to this model.

3. To examine the material by comparison and analogy, and to discover the principles that are common to these materials.

4. To interpret the meaning of these principles through the contributions of the study of folk religion and personal empathetic understanding of these rituals.

This treatment is concerned primarily with the first part of these procedures, i.e., construction of a model of Japanese folk religion.

My definition of religious *ritual* is as follows. It is a series of religious actions performed according to a system that is regulated by the sacred. It is also a symbol system that has an irrational character based on religious experience. It is a social custom fixed by a definite religious worldview and it sustains the integrity of the individual and the society. As one may notice, I emphasize the following two aspects of religious ritual in this definition:

a. The religious ritual is a system of actions that is regulated by the sacred.

b. It is also a symbol system that symbolizes a definite religious worldview.

Therefore, I intend to construct a model that will be useful for the elucidation of the religious worldview sustaining the ritual of Japanese folk religion. In this chapter, I take up annual observances and rites of passage in rural Japan that are among the primary rituals of Japanese folk religion.

Annual observances and rites of passage comprise the *whole ritual system*, which includes many individual rituals. For example, annual observances as a whole include New Year, the Turn of the Seasons, the Doll Festival, Equinox (spring and autumn), the Flower Festival, Boys' Day, the Rice-planting Festival, the Drumming Out of Noxious Insects, the Festival of the Water Deity, the Star Festival, the Festival of the Dead, Moon Viewing, the Rice-transplanting Festival, the Harvest Festival, Grand Purification, etc. Rites of passage as a whole include birth, the Festival for Three, Five, and Seven Years of Age, puberty rites, marriage, "years of peril" or "unlucky years," mortuary rites, etc. These individual rituals are *unit rituals* that are the parts of the whole ritual system and have an organic connection with it. First I will explain my method for the study of these unit rituals.[4]

The Method of Structural Analysis of Ritual

Each *religious action* composing the religious ritual is a symbol system that consists of an actor, i.e., a human being (priest, ascetic, diviner, etc.)

and/or a group (a family, village, etc.); an object, i.e., the object of worship and/or the actor himself (in the case of ascetic training); the situation (time, space, and facilities), and the orientation of the actor.

I designate as a *ritual element* a series of religious actions that are included in a definite situation and that are a constituent element of the whole ritual. An individual ritual (unit-ritual) is a combination of a series of these ritual elements in accordance with a system.

Religious ritual is not only a system of actions but also a complex symbol system that symbolizes a *religious worldview* and is related to other symbol systems. Therefore the above constituent elements of religious action (actor, object, situation, and orientation) have a meaning. These meanings are derived from the worldview. As a matter of fact, the ritual element that is the system of these symbolic actions is itself a symbol system. Furthermore, the religious ritual, which is a combination of a series of ritual elements as a symbol system, forms a symbol system as a whole that overarches the ritual elements.

A *symbol* is something that expresses a hidden meaning. Therefore the religious ritual, which consists of a series of ritual elements as a symbol *system*, forms a system of meaning. To put it more specifically, a ritual element forms a system of meaning that consists of the separate meanings of its constituent religious actions. Moreover, the meaning or significance of the ritual as a whole consists of the meanings of these ritual elements.

As the totality of the individual meanings of the ritual elements and the ritual as a whole is called a system, all of the individual aspects of a system have to be guided by something like a theme. I designate as *motif* the theme that guides the system of meaning. The separate meanings of all the religious actions that constitute the ritual elements are organized by the motif, which determines the meaning system of the ritual elements. Then, the motif of the meanings of the ritual as a whole determines the specific meaning of each of the ritual elements. I designate this mode of meaning determined through relationship to motif as *mechanism.*

The motif of religious ritual is created as the most suitable theme for symbolizing the religious worldview of the ritual, connecting the life experience of the practitioner and the function of the ritual. But the practitioners and/or participants are not necessarily aware of this motif and its worldview. These features are extracted from the above structural analysis by the researcher. The model is diagrammed in figure 46.

I have explained the structural model of the religious ritual, starting from the individual meanings of each religious action within the ritual, and leading to the worldview that sustains the ritual. Next, in order to make clearer my structural model of the religious ritual, I will explain it in

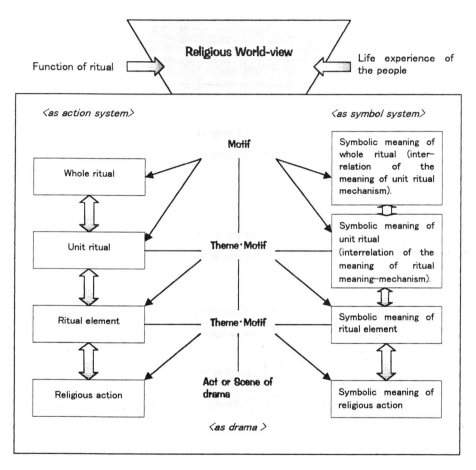

Figure 46. Structural paradigm of ritual in Japanese folk religion

reverse order, i.e., from the religious worldview to each religious action in the ritual. In a word, I think the religious ritual forms a *drama* that is guided by the motif. To phrase it more concretely, the religious ritual is a symbol system that frames the drama. The parts of this drama are determined by the motif. It is something like a theme that is suitable to the functions of the ritual and has an intense connection with the life experience of the people.

As I have explained above, within a given religious worldview, the system of symbolic action within the situation of concrete action in the ritual constitutes the ritual elements of the symbol system of the ritual as a whole. The ritual is framed by the interrelated connection of these ritual elements, guided by the motif. I designate this dynamic construction a mechanism. Therefore each ritual element frames a *system* of meaning that is determined by the motif of the ritual system. This system of meaning (the meaning of the ritual element) is similar to the act or scene of a play that forms a drama. And the subject, object, situation, and orientation of each of the ritual actions that constitute the ritual element are symbols or symbolic actions that symbolize the meaning system of the respective ritual elements. Thus the meaning of the ritual element is like the meaning of the act or scene in relation to the drama as a whole (i.e., the whole ritual).

Next, I take up concrete examples from annual observances and rites of passage. First I will examine the Festival of the Dead (Bon) as an example of an annual observance.[5] The Festival of the Dead is premised on the dualistic worldview that presupposes the existence both of people of this world and of ancestral spirits of another world who take care of them. It is also premised on the worldview recognizing that communication between the living and the spirits of the dead occurs in this world at specific times. The people who observe the Bon festival have a great desire to meet their dead relatives in this world. In their everyday life, they know of people who have gone far away but come back again to their native place to visit their relatives. The Bon festival incorporates in its ritual structure this dualistic worldview, the great desire of the people to see their dead relatives in this world, and their experience of meeting again with friends. Accordingly we can see in this festival a process that involves inviting the ancestral spirits from the otherworld, meeting again with the dead relatives, and entertaining them. In other words, we can discover the motif of "meeting again" in the Bon festival.

The drama of the Bon festival, which is guided by the motif of "meeting again," is celebrated from the first of the seventh month to the fifteenth of the seventh month according to the lunisolar calendar (summer season). The contents of this festival are as follows: At first, people

Figure 47. The altar for the dead at the Bon festival

purify the graves (first day of the seventh month) and their houses (seventh day) where the primary ceremonies are practiced. I classify these situations of purification as the first ritual element (a constituent element of the ritual). Also they erect a special altar for ancestral spirits (*bondana*) inside the house and clean the road from the grave to the house. July 13 (August 13 in some areas in modern Japan) is the day when the ancestor spirits come. Before this time, people hang a paper lantern from the eaves of the house and make horse and cattle effigies out of eggplant and cucumber, which symbolize the means of travel for the ancestor spirits. The spirits of the ancestors come back from the mountains and/or graves to their beloved homes by means of these animals. These situations express an invitation (the second ritual element). Then they enter the special altar. At this time, the hungry ghosts that disturb the people gather. People give them coarse food and exorcize them with special folk dances. (This scene of exorcism is the third ritual element.) Buddhist priests also read sutras in order to appease these hungry ghosts. The ancestral spirits that enter the altar receive a religious service from their descendants and communicate with them (this scene of communication is the fourth ritual element). On July 15 people lead the ancestral spirits to their graves, and then they carry offerings to a stream and set them adrift on the current (this scene of returning is the fifth ritual element).

Thus we can see that the Bon festival has five ritual elements: purification, invitation, exorcism, communication, and returning. These ritual elements are closely interconnected, centering around the ritual element of "communication," which has an intense relationship with the motif of "meeting again." I call this the mechanism of the Bon festival.

The male puberty rite is premised on the religious worldview that holds that boys can obtain new power as adults by enduring a series of trials in the world of ancestral spirits.[6] Its *purpose* is to get the boys away from the protection of their mothers and to make them members of the local community. This worldview and the purpose of the puberty rite produce a *motif* of symbolic death and rebirth. At the same time, we can see its ritual elements, such as separation of boys (initiates), trial, learning, meeting with the ancestral spirits, and rebirth in the puberty rite. Therefore, the puberty rite is a drama that organizes these ritual elements according to the motif of symbolic death and rebirth.

I use the following method in order to concretely analyze the structure of the unit ritual. First, we must observe and record every religious action (especially the actor, object, situation, and orientation) one by one. Second, these symbolic meanings that constitute the ritual action, and the meaning of the action as a whole, have to be interpreted on the basis of the practitioner's interpretation, the local tradition, and the meanings of such symbols and symbolic actions in similar rituals. Third, we compare these individual meanings of ritual action. Then by comparing various ritual actions, we establish groups of similar ritual actions. Thus we obtain the ritual elements (constituent elements) of the unit ritual. Fourth, we discover the interrelationships among each ritual element—the mechanism—and the principle of its interrelationship (motif). In this case, at first we must recognize the primary ritual element. By relating it to other ritual elements, we may recognize its motif. Fifth, we infer the religious worldview that is sustaining this motif. Namely, within the ritual drama that is determined by the motif, we must grasp the expression of the interrelationship among the universe, the object of worship, and human beings. In these procedures we must refer to the symbol, the structure of the ritual, and the worldview of similar rituals that have been studied before.

The Method for Clarifying the Religious Worldview

We have seen that the annual observances and rites of passage that include many unit rituals (for example, the Festival of the Dead, puberty rites, etc.) constitute a whole ritual system. Next it is important to explain my method for analyzing the whole ritual system of annual observances and rites of passage and their worldview. Then I will compare their structure and worldview in order to discover the principles of Japanese folk religion.[7]

As I have explained, each of the unit rituals (New Year, puberty rite, etc.) that are included in the whole ritual system (i.e., annual observances and rites of passage) forms a drama directed by its motifs. The whole ritual system is made up of the unit rituals, in turn forming a larger drama. This drama of the whole ritual system vividly relates the religious worldview and its relationship with human life as a whole. For example, annual observances act out the meaning of the rhythm of one year to the people, by relating it to the worldview. Rites of passage act out human life, by connecting it with the religious worldview. Each unit ritual in the annual events forms an act of the drama that vividly portrays aspects of the seasons. Each unit ritual in the rites of passage forms an act of the larger drama that expresses the important stages of human life including birth, puberty, and death.

A concrete explanation may be helpful. In figure 48, I locate the principal annual observances of rural Japan in a circle that is divided into twelve parts. These twelve parts correspond to the twelve months. Annual observances can be interpreted according to this table. First we can divide the annual observances (unit rituals) into three major categories, i.e., rituals of ancestor worship, agricultural rituals, and rituals of exorcism and purification. Rituals of ancestor worship are practiced at the New Year (originally they were practiced at the Little New Year on January 15) and at Bon. In these rituals, after the rites of exorcism and purification, the people invite their ancestral spirits to their homes, communicate with them, give them offerings, and then send them back.

Typical agricultural rituals are the Spring Festival (April) and the Autumn Festival (October). Besides these two festivals, the rural people have a series of rituals following the growth of rice plants. For example, there is the Little New Year with its divinatory elements and anticipation of blessings to come, the Flower Festival (*hanami*) with its symbolic welcoming of the deity of the rice fields, the Rice-planting (*tanemaki*) Festival, and the Rice-transplanting (*taue*) and Reaping (*kariage*) Festivals. This series of rituals includes prayers to the deity of the rice field for a good harvest. This deity comes down from the mountain to the rice field on April 8, guards agricultural life, and then goes back to the mountain after receiving the celebration of the Reaping and Harvest Festivals.

As for rituals of exorcism and purification, there are the Turn of the Seasons, Doll Festival, Boys' Day, Festival of the Water Deity, Grand Purification, Star Festival, Drumming out of Noxious Insects, and the Festival of the Wind Deity. These rituals of exorcism and purification may be classified under three headings: (1) purification as a preparation for ancestor festivals; this is mainly practiced in June and December (Festival of the Water Deity, Grand Purification, and Star Festival); (2) exorcism of bad spirits and/or deities; this includes the Drumming out of Noxious Insects, and the Festival of the Wind Deity; (3) seasonal festivals such as the Doll Festival and Boys' Day. (But the Doll Festival and Boys' Day have some connection with agriculture;[8] therefore, the rituals of exorcism and purification may be included in the rituals of ancestor worship and agricultural rituals.)

In this light, we can divide the complex annual observances into two categories, i.e., rituals of ancestor worship, and agricultural rituals. As we have seen above, New Year (January) and the Bon festival (July) are typical rituals of ancestor worship. Similarly the Spring (April) and Autumn (October) Festivals are typical rituals for agricultural fertility. Therefore I divide the circle in figure 48 on the horizontal axis (i.e., the line from January to July that symbolizes the time of ancestor worship) and on the vertical axis (the line from April to October that symbolizes the time of agricultural rituals). It is clear that the rituals of ancestor worship converge on the horizontal axis of December and January (Festival of Water

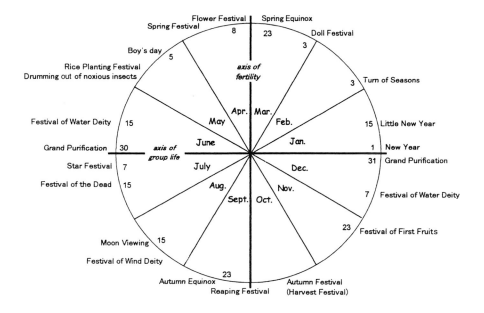

Figure 48. The structure of annual events—macrocosmos

Deity, Grand Purification and New Year) and June and July (also Festival of the Water Deity, Grand Purification and Bon). The agricultural rituals converge on the vertical axis (i.e., March, April, and September, October, December). Needless to say, the rituals of ancestor worship have a function of integration for the kinship group and village society, while the purpose of the agricultural ritual is to insure the abundance of agricultural products. As is well known, these two aspects are the most important dimensions in the life of rural Japan. Therefore I would like to designate the horizontal axis as the *axis of group life* and the vertical axis as the *axis of fertility*. I will use this model with its two primary axes to analyze annual observances in rural Japan.

Rites of passage are rituals that are practiced at critical times of human life, such as birth, puberty, marriage, unlucky years, and death. Every individual overcomes these critical stages under the care of the deities and with the cooperation of relatives and/or neighbors. Then they go on to a new stage of life. Moreover, if a dead person is given a funeral ceremony, the prescribed memorial services for the deceased (on the seventh day, forty-ninth day, one hundredth day and on the memorial days at the first, third, seventh, and thirteenth years after death), and the final memorial service (i.e., completion of the memorial rites at thirty-three or forty-nine years after death), then that person becomes an ancestral deity. All of the deceased go to the land of the dead, but it is believed that sometimes the spirit of an ancestor will enter a newborn baby. This process of rites of passage may be illustrated in a circle as shown in figure 49. Using this circle, we can explain the structure of the rites of passage as a whole and its religious worldview.

The series of rituals of birth is concerned with the merging of souls and the baby. The soul that merges with a body is called a living soul. Human beings grow up under the care of the ancestor spirits and the local shrines. There are special prayers at three, five, and seven years old. When children enter into adulthood, puberty rites are celebrated for them. The general belief is that only married men and women with an heir will have the privilege of being worshipped after death, and thus become ancestral deities. They must pass safely through the unlucky year of peril (age 42 for men, age 33 for women) by special services to the deities. Their years of celebration (i.e., sixty-first, seventieth, etc.) are celebrated by their relatives. These years of celebration may be understood as a precelebration of death.

Death means separation of the living soul from the dead body. The separated soul is called a spirit of the dead. The funeral ceremony is practiced to insure this separation. These processes are shown in the upper

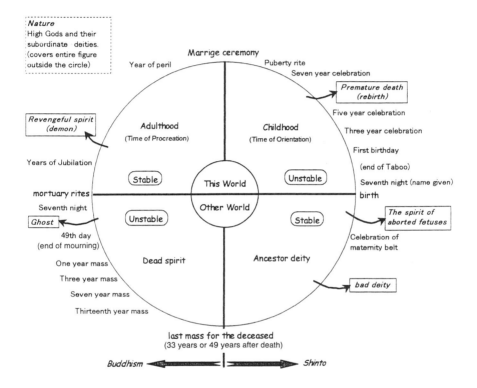

Figure 49. The structure of rites of passage—microcosmos. The left side of the figure has an intense connection with Buddhism and the right side has an intense connection with Shinto.

part of the circle. Figure 49 shows the symmetrical relation between the rites associated with birth and those associated with death. These comprise the celebration of the maternity belt, usually around the fifth month of pregnancy, years of celebration, first bath and last bath, the new name for the baby and the dead, the end of taboo, and the end of mourning. The dead spirits that are given the prescribed memorial services grow up and are purified gradually by means of these ceremonies. This process corresponds to the puberty rites and/or the marriage ceremony. Then, in some cases, this ancestor spirit becomes the soul of a newborn baby, and a new cycle of life begins. This growing process of the spirits of the dead and the ancestor deities is seen in the bottom half of the circle.

Therefore, the upper half of the circle shows this world and the bottom half shows the otherworld. The everyday life of people is under the protection of the dead spirits and the ancestral deities (i.e., bottom half of the circle). Conversely, the condition of the dead spirits and of the ancestral deity depends on their conduct in this world, the circumstances of their death, and the memorial services held by their own descendants. Above all, the devout practice of these memorial services is most influential for their destiny. In this fashion, the upper half of the circle (the beings of this world) and the bottom half of the circle (the beings of the otherworld) are intimately connected with each other.

Moreover this development of the soul is regulated by the high gods, their subordinate deities, demons, and others, which guide the movement of *nature*. The square that encloses the circle shows this area of nature. The high gods have the character of nature gods, such as the sun, moon, and thunder, and have a rather universal character. They have a strong benevolent power and bring their worshipper good fortune.

However, if people do not worship them, they bring misfortune upon humans. The spirits of aborted fetuses, the spirits of premature death, the spirits of accidental death (revengeful spirits, demons), the spirits of the dead who have no descendants (ghosts), and the deities that are neglected (malevolent) deities—all these enter the pantheon of the high gods and also bring misfortune. If people worship these spirits and/or deities courteously, however, they will be guardian spirits and/or deities. This ambivalence between forces of potential benevolence and potential danger (or malevolence) is one of the central features of Japanese folk religion.

It is believed that misfortunes depend on both conflict within the circumference of the circle (the conflict between living persons or conflict between living and dead spirits), as well as the conflict between beings within the circumference of the circle and beings outside of it (i.e., high gods and/or subordinate deities and/or devils and/or ghosts and/or malevolent deities). In such cases, rites of affliction are performed, as seen in the following methods. First the practitioners such as *shugenja* (mountain ascetics) determine by divination the cause of misfortune and the means of treatment. After that, they identify themselves with their respective guardian deity (a high god and/or its subordinate deities). Then, according to the results of divination, they practice the most suitable means for the kind of affliction (such as worship, exorcism, or punishment of the deities.)[9]

To this point I have interpreted the structure of annual observances that are practiced in conformity with the rhythm of the seasons, and the structure of rites of passage that have a close connection with the cycle of life. Next I will compare these structures and worldviews. In this case, the cosmological worldview that can be seen in the ancient civilizations of the near East, medieval Europe, and Asia (especially China and India) will be suggestive for us.[10] This cosmological worldview is based on the idea that the shape and/or destiny of human beings follows the structure of the macrocosm such as the movement of heavenly bodies. We can see this worldview eminently in astrology and in the theory of the divine right of kings. The Tantric worldview, whose influence was pervasive in Japanese religious thought, is based on this cosmological worldview. It is well known that in the Tantric worldview, human beings are believed to have the same character (i.e., Buddha nature) as the Mahāvairocana Buddha that symbolizes the macrocosm.

We may see the same cosmological worldview in the structure of annual observances and rites of passage. In this case the annual observances are in consonance with the rhythm of the macrocosm (i.e., external nature as seen in the transition of seasons). The rites of passage signify the development of human life (internal nature or microcosm) that corresponds to the macrocosm. As I have shown above, in the cosmological worldview, the macrocosm (external nature) corresponds to the microcosm (inner nature of humans). Therefore annual observances (macrocosm) might correspond to the rites of passage (microcosm).

Now let us compare the circles of annual observances and rites of passage according to the above proposition. In this view, first of all, the vertical axis of fertility in the circle of annual observances (spring and autumn festivals) corresponds to the axis of maturity for the rites of passage (marriage and last memorial service). We can interpret the rites of birth and death as the rites of restoring the equilibrium of the group since they treat the loss or gain of a member. Then we can interpret the horizontal axis of annual observances as the axis of intensification of the group integrity, since it treats the communion of the group under the protection of the ancestors. These two axes then correspond to each other, since they both treat the problem of group integrity.[11]

I have compared only the annual observances and the rites of passage by utilizing these two axes. We must examine more closely every unit ritual. But at any rate, the basic two axes (horizontal and vertical) of both circles correspond closely to each other. I think this correspondence shows that the life of a human being as a microcosm is a correlate to the movement of nature as a macrocosm (i.e., the law of the cosmos).

From the above considerations, we can conclude that the annual observances and the rites of passage in rural Japan are based upon the cosmological worldview that perceives the life of human beings as a microcosm in terms of the rhythms of nature as a movement of the macrocosm.

Many of the folk practices described here are found only in ancient and traditional Japan and are no longer observed at present. However, even today, Japanese people faithfully practice many such rituals as New Year, the Bon festival, birth ceremonies, marriage ceremonies, and funeral ceremonies. They feel insecure without these rituals. I think this may indicate that the Japanese people as a microcosm identify themselves with the movement of the macrocosm by practicing these rituals and that they thereby confirm the substantiality of their lives.[12] These beliefs and practices are clear evidence of folk religion as a way of life.

NOTES

1. According to a survey by the Tōkeisūri Kenkyūsho (The Institute of Statistical Mathematics), the people who believe in a specific religion, such as Shinto, Buddhism, or Christianity add up to 31% of the total population. But the people who periodically attend the observances of the respective religions amount to only 36% of the 31% of believers. However, 34% answered that people should follow some custom, even if in their opinion it was mistaken. These answers show how many Japanese people attach importance to custom. The preceding answers are based on data from 3,033 people who were chosen from the survey record of 1968, with random sampling of all strata. Tōkeisūri Kenkyūsho Kokuminseichōsa Iinkai, *Daini Nihonjin no kokuminsei* (Second national character of the Japanese) (Tokyo: Shiseidō, 1969), 357, 361.
2. Miyake Hitoshi, *Nihon no minzoku shūkyō* (Folk religions in Japan) (Tokyo: Kōdansha, 1994), 15–39.
3. Hori Ichirō, *Folk Religion in Japan: Continuity and Change*, ed. and trans. Joseph M. Kitagawa and Alan Miller (Chicago: University of Chicago Press, 1968); Miyake Hitoshi, *Shūkyō minzokugaku* (A study of folk religion) (Tokyo: Tōkyō Daigaku Shuppankai, 1989).
4. For the structural analysis of ritual, see Victor Turner, *The Forest of Symbols* (Ithaca, NY: Cornell University Press, 1967); also Miyake, *Shūkyō minzokugaku*, 150–56.
5. Yanagita Kunio, *About our Ancestors*, trans. Fanny Hagin Mayer and Ishiwara Yasuyo (Tokyo: Society for the Promotion of Science, 1970).
6. Arnold van Gennep, *The Rites of Passage*, trans. Monika B. Vizedom and Gabrielle L. Caffee (Chicago: University of Chicago Press, 1961); originally published as *Les rites de passage* (1909).

7. Bernard Bernier, *Breaking the Cosmic Circle: Religion in a Japanese Village*, Cornell East Asian Papers (Ithaca, NY: Cornell China-Japan Programs, 1975).
8. The Doll Festival is associated with purification for the rice planting, and Boys' Day is related to the exorcism for rice transplanting.
9. See chapter 5 for a more complete treatment of exorcism.
10. Robert Heine-Geldern, *Conceptions of State and Kingship in Southeast Asia*, Data Paper, no. 18, (Cornell University Southeast Asia Program) (Ithaca, NY: Cornell University Press, 1956).
11. Eliot D. Chapple and Carleton S. Coon, *Principles of Anthropology* (New York: Holt, 1942), 484–528.
12. Erik H. Erikson, *Identity and the Life Cycle* (New York: International Universities Press, 1959).

The Idea of Nature in Japanese
Folk Religion

FOLK RELIGION AND NATURE

The core of Japanese folk religion consists of ceremonies such as the ordinary annual observances and rites of passage, and also salvation rites; of narratives from myths, legends, and ancient tales; and of iconographic objects including places of worship, sacred figures and paintings, and ritual paraphernalia. Much of this body of practice was developed by people engaged in the primary industries directly linked with nature, such as agriculture, hunting, fishing, and forestry. Accordingly, these notions and practices are closely related to nature. But while they have been passed from one generation to the next, the need for dissemination to outside parties never arose. Consequently, there is no systematic body of doctrine, ritual, or religious organization; rather it is researchers who have attempted to decipher a cosmology among the rituals, narratives, and images.[1]

As indicated by currently used terms such as "natural science" and "natural environment," nature refers generally to objects and phenomena that have originated and developed in a spontaneous fashion, in opposition to culture, the product of human agency. In this sense objects may be labeled "natural objects" and phenomena "natural phenomena." This usage traces its origin in Japanese to the late 1890s, when the word *shizen* came to be used as a translation of the English "nature." Of course "nature" in English refers not only to natural objects and phenomena, but also to their underlying essences or principles that impart meaning to their existence and govern their formation and development.[2] In this manner the meaning of "nature" in European languages includes natural objects and phenomena, plus their essential qualities and principles.

But the word *shizen*, used to translate "nature," also has the connotation of "naturally occurring" (*onozukara*), deriving from "the original form of all things" as the meaning of the old Chinese *zi-ran*.[3] This Japanese term *onozukara* indicates a self-reliant state and may be likened to that of

178

heaven and earth, in which one's actions are not dependent upon an external power but proceed from within.[4] As a further outgrowth, there developed a concept idealizing the act of living in voluntary accordance with the ultimate rhythms of the universe, or the universe's unifying power; this concept came to be regarded as the Japanese moral ideal.[5] This view may also be found in the ideas of Nishida Kitarō, who regarded the activities of the universe and those of the individual as one and the same, and thus saw virtue in living in accordance with the unifying force of the universe.[6]

The preceding discussion has indicated some of the characteristics of Japanese folk religion and introduced the term *shizen* as a translation of the English "nature," its meaning as generally used today, as well as its older meaning of *onozukara* (naturally occurring, or "just as it is"). From this basis, the present chapter will attempt some detailed observations of the understanding of nature and its relation to humans as seen in Japanese folk religion, especially in premodern times. For this purpose it will help to examine Japanese concepts of nature in closer detail.[7] (Because it is not easy to distinguish sharply beliefs and practices found only in previous times, and those which continue in modified form today, we will use the present tense in much of the following description.)

First, the heavenly bodies, inert substances, plants, and animals can all be seen as included among the phenomena referred to as nature (*shizen*). In its broad sense, humans are also seen as existing within this realm. As the present chapter proposes to examine nature in its relation to humans, a more detailed consideration should be given here of things within this realm having some kind of connection with people.

Heavenly bodies consist of the sun, the moon, and the stars; inert substances include air, rocks, soil, water, and fire.[8] Plants and animals are organic compounds. Plants include seed plants such as trees and grasses; fungi such as ferns, mosses, and mushrooms; seaweeds like kelp and other algae; and bacteria. Animals include birds, beasts, insects, and fish, with humans also belonging to this category. The above items divide broadly into the heavenly realm comprised of the sun, moon, and stars, which are all inorganic objects, and the earthly realm, made of soil, rocks, and water, and which consist of mountains, rivers, seas, lakes, fields, and villages in which plants grow and animals live. Between the two realms there is air. For these reasons, perhaps, the English "nature" was initially translated as *tenchi* (literally, "heaven and earth").[9]

It goes without saying that all earthly things, particularly plants and animals, depend on such natural phenomena as climatic patterns determined by the movement of the sun, moon, and stars, on weather conditions such as wind and rainfall, on the flow of rivers, and on the ebb and flow of the tide. These are all recognized as part of the spontaneous activity of nature. Moreover, even accidental phenomena such as natural disasters that occasionally effect great changes on floral and faunal life are seen as spontaneous events. Further, among these natural elements the ones seen as enveloping man and directly affecting human livelihood are referred to as the natural environment.

Although subsumed under nature, a human's mind and body also exist apart from nature and are thought of as an "internal nature," against which the natural objects and phenomena mentioned above are considered the "external nature." As the embodiment of this internal nature, humans come in contact with external nature and their livelihood is affected by its spontaneous actions. The product of this relationship between external and internal nature is called culture. A variety of things may be recognized within culture, including a religious outlook that sees the sacred element in nature, the arts and letters that discover beauty, the scientific outlook that uncovers natural law, and technology that utilizes and processes natural elements. The part of the natural environment that has been transformed through these activities into a state suitable for human livelihood is referred to as the cultural environment.

Robert Redfield has argued that humans live by positioning themselves among all things in existence, both natural and supernatural, and he refers to this outlook on humanity's place within the cosmos as the worldview. Citing "god," "nature," and "man" as constituent elements of the worldview, he proposed three basic types of worldview according to which of these elements hold eminence. The first is the god-centered worldview in which God is held to create both man and nature and to entrust man with control over nature, as seen in Judaism, Christianity, and Islam. The second is the human-centered worldview of modern rationalism, which originated with the humanistic discoveries of the Renaissance, in which people control nature (although their weaknesses make God necessary). The third is the nature-centered worldview, widely seen in Japanese and other Asian folk religions, in which both humans and gods are positioned within the spontaneous activity of nature.[10] The general view of nature held by Japanese folk religion can be regarded as an example of the third type of worldview, which gives precedence to nature.

NATURE AND THE SACRED

Among the natural objects that surround people in their daily lives, those shaped unnaturally or seen as mysterious in some other way are revered as having extraordinary power. The practice of venerating natural objects as sacred is generally referred to as nature worship.[11] In Japanese folk religion in particular, *kami* (deities) are thought to lead an essentially covert existence, residing in natural objects such as trees, rocks, plants, or animals, manifesting themselves as natural phenomena such as wind or thunder, or possessing humans and making oracles. Such natural objects or human beings are worshipped as *kami*. It is also not uncommon for items such as water, fire, or plants, which are thought to possess sacred power, to be used in rituals or to be regarded as "fetishes." Among such various natural objects and phenomena related to them, the major items regarded in Japanese folk religion as especially sacred will be introduced in this section.[12]

First, the sun in heaven is seen as the *kami* protecting the people's livelihood as a whole, and the practice of worshipping the rising sun, of waiting to venerate the sunrise (*hi machi*), is observed. In earlier times, when rainy weather persisted, entreaties were made for the sun's appearance, and solar eclipses were feared. The *kami* Amaterasu, a deification of the sun, is regarded as the ancestral deity of the imperial line. The moon is seen as reigning over night, and its waxing and waning are regarded with mystery. The moon is venerated through the practice of *tsuki machi* (waiting for the moon), and lunar eclipses are feared. The lunar *kami* is said to be Amaterasu's brother Tsukiyomi. Among the stars, Polaris and the constellation Ursa Major are deified and worshipped as the Bodhisattva Myōken and his subordinates. Also, the five planets of Jupiter, Mars, Saturn, Venus, and Mercury are seen as controlling a person's luck, while falling stars and comets are said to indicate bad fortune. Of natural phenomena related to the heavens, those seen as sacred in nature include thunder, tornadoes, typhoons, floods, rainbows, strange images or shadows seen at the peak of mountains, and mirages encountered at the seashore. Also, the heavens in their entirety are seen as deified and referred to as Tenpushin (literally, "heaven father deity").

By contrast, earth is personified as female and called Chiboshin ("earth mother deity"). Among the elements composing the earth (soil, sand, stone, rock, and minerals) and its waters (rivers, waterfalls, marshes, ponds, lakes, and seas), and among the plants that grow on the earth's surface, those which are unusual and impart thereby a feeling of awe are considered sacred. Once the bulk of the Japanese populace came to reside on flatlands and practice rice agriculture, locations different in topography, such as mountains, forests, seas, beaches, and capes were regarded as sacred places.

Of the inorganic substances related to the earth, those often considered sacred are stone and water. In addition to serving as the objects of worship in small shrines, stones are widely thought to have spirits residing within them as shown by such examples as the small round stones, *ubuishi*, that may impart the soul to the newborn baby, or stones often placed by the pillow of the deceased at his wake (*makura ishi*). In addition, boulders having unusual shapes, rock outcroppings, and caves are considered sacred, and Buddha images may be carved in relief on such sacralized rock outcroppings and caves. Naturally occurring smooth pebbles are often venerated as objects of worship, and minerals such as gold or mercury, or meteorites, may be considered sacred. On occasions such as rites to pacify local spirits, held prior to construction, sand is used to sanctify the ground. As an agent having purifying powers, water is used in ablution rituals performed for purification. Rivers, springs, marshes, ponds, waterfalls, and seas are also regarded as places where water deities or dragon spirits dwell. Waterfalls located at precipices or caves in particular are often used as places for practicing religious austerities. Also, fire is used in votive lamps, and for welcoming the spirits of ancestors. At the end of the New Year's celebration, a festival is held in which a large bonfire called *tondo* is burned.

Among plants, sacred objects are especially plentiful among trees and grasses. First, the five crop plants of rice, wheat, barley, millet, foxtail millet, and legumes are deified as harboring the grain spirit. Straw is used for making religious paraphernalia and is used along with bean husks for making the *tondo* bonfires. In addition, a Chinese bellflower, Japanese bush clover, *Patrinia scabiosaefolia*, a lily, *Dianthus superbus*, and other flowers are commonly used in the Bon festival to help induce the visit of the ancestral spirits. Sacred trees include Japanese star anise used for Bon and other Buddhist offerings, and *sakaki* (*Cleyera ochnacea*) used in Shinto offerings. Also, members of such species as Japanese cedar, pine, Japanese cypress, camphor, zelkova, camellia, wild orange, cherry, plum, bamboo, and others, are frequently regarded as sacred. Individual trees regarded as sacred are long-lived specimens having unusual shapes or cavities at their bases, or large trees with smaller trees growing out of the main branch, scars left by lightning strikes in their upper branches; many of these trees have a *shimenawa* (straw rope used to mark off sacred precincts) hung around the trunk. Further, the fruits of the peach, pomegranate, plum, and other trees are regarded as sacred. Among plants other than these, a fern and an edible seaweed are used on festive (*hare*) occasions. Bacteria are feared as *mono* (demons) that cause disease.

Mountains, forests, seas, capes, beaches, islands, shoals, and so forth are places where soil, sand, rocks, water, and trees come together to provide beautiful scenery, different from that of the village where daily life is conducted. Among mountains there are two types: those with a beautiful green cover of trees, which are called *kannabi*, and those strewn with rocks.

Figure 50. Sacred stone where Kongō Zaō Gongen appeared (on Mt. Sanjō)

The former are smaller hills in the vicinity of the village, having shrines at the base. The latter are high and steep mountains, such as volcanoes, often regarded as places for austerities practiced by members of Shugendō. Further, on many high mountains, shrines are built on the plateaus at the top, or on the slopes. In village shrines, however, the area behind the sanctuary is given over to forest and made a sacred precinct. The pools, falls, and shallows of rivers that draw water from the mountains are also regarded as sacred sites. By the sea, beaches with white sand and lush pines, and also capes and offshore islands are regarded as sacred.

Among animals, bird species considered to be sacred include the domestic chicken, crow, crane, dove, pheasant, swan, and hawk. The crow in particular is seen as the messenger of the sun in ancient times, as Sakugami (agricultural deity), and as a portent of death. The dove is regarded as the messenger of the deity Hachiman. Among animals, sacralized species include the snake, turtle, frog, monkey, deer, wild boar, fox, bear, wolf, ox, and horse. Of these the snake in particular is revered as a manifestation of water *kami* or mountain *kami*, and beliefs in dragons that developed from this are widely known. The deer and wild boar, and the *shishi* (a fictionalized lion), which is an abstraction of the latter, are also seen as manifestations of the mountain *kami*. The frog is associated with the moon and said to be a messenger of water *kami* and earth *kami*. The turtle and crane together are animals celebrating long life. The ox and horse are sacred because they are indispensable to agriculture. The horse in particular is seen as the mount of the *kami*, thus engendering the religious practice of consigning requests meant for the *kami* to tablets bearing the image of a horse (*ema*). Incidentally, these animals are also regarded as messengers of *kami* venerated at various shrines: the snake of the Miwa Shrine, the monkey of Hie Shrine, the fox of the Inari cult, and the wolf of Mitsumine Shrine.

Sacralized insects include spiders, red dragonflies, and silkworms. When thus sanctified, spiders are regarded as omens of good or ill fortune, red dragonflies as messengers from the otherworld, and silkworms are revered as the *kami* Oshirasama. Among fish, those that approach the shore seasonally like bonito and herring, and those that journey from river to sea and back again like salmon and trout, are regarded as sacred. Catfish, which are thought to portend earthquakes, and eels, which are always served in late summer, and carp and red snapper, which are used in celebrations, are also considered sacred fish. Upon examining the above-named sanctified animals, it will be noted that turtles, snakes, and frogs, whose habitats cross the borders between the three locations of mountain, sea (including rivers and ponds), and village, and categorically anomalous animals, like scaleless species of fish (catfish, eel) or thread-producing insects (spider, silkworm), are regarded as sacred.

ONOZUKARA (NATURALLY OCCURRING, OR "JUST AS IT IS")

The natural objects and phenomena introduced individually in the preceding section bear close mutual relationships with each other, relationships that moreover are determined in spontaneous fashion. But among these there are not a few that receive no particular notice from the Japanese people. Accordingly, in this section, the mode by which sacred objects and phenomena stand in spontaneous mutual relation to each other will be examined with respect to the two aspects of time and space.

First, with regard to spatial relations, heaven and earth are seen to stand in vertical opposition. In other words, the sun, moon, and stars are in the heavens above, while the earth (made of soil, rock, and water) is below. In addition, the spaces between heaven and earth and that of the world below can also be specified. The animals and humans on the surface of the earth live amidst the light of the sun, the changes of the moon, the movements of the stars, and the wind and the rain. Incidentally, the sun is linked with the crow, and the moon with the hare and the frog, and many of the constellations bear the names of animals. When these various heavenly phenomena are moving in regular fashion, creatures on the surface world lead normal lives. Accordingly, solar and lunar eclipses, comets, and falling stars are taken as portents of warfare and political upheavals, or of typhoons, torrential rains, floods, earthquakes, and other phenomena that bring great damage to the earth's plant and animal life. Animals like catfish and mice, the first to apprehend these calamities, are considered sacred entities. Also, the subterranean sphere in which corpses are buried, and which absorbs the rotten remains of plants and animals, is thought to be the realm of the afterlife.

Looking next at the horizontal dimension, and taking the village where paddy agriculture is practiced as the central area, a tripartite spatial division can be seen to include the mountains, which are the headwaters of rivers, and the sea to which rivers passing through the village flow. The mountains are places of livelihood for hunters and woodcutters, as is the sea for fishermen and sailors. Among the *matagi* (men who live by hunting) in Shiiba Village, Miyazaki Prefecture, the following story is related. The male mountain *kami* once took the form of a pheasant and went to the sea, where he became intimate with Otohime, daughter of the head of the sea *kami* Ryūō who dwells in the mythical palace Ryūgū beneath the sea. When Otohime, with child, went to the mountains to visit her consort and suddenly felt the onset of birth, she was aided by a passing hunter called Nishiyama. Upon later becoming the female mountain *kami*, she granted this hunter Nishiyama the right to take prey from the mountains. It is also generally held that when hunters enter the mountains to hunt, if they make an offering of an ocean fish called *okoze* (a stingfish) to the mountain *kami*, they will be granted animals. In this fashion, mountains and sea are seen as linked. Also, among fishermen who rely on species like herring and bonito, which approach the shore, these fish are revered as visitors from the otherworld beyond the sea, and sharks and other fish (which chase them closer to shore) are sacralized.

To farmers of the village, the mountains and sea are seen as the otherworld to which the spirits of the dead proceed. In particular, souls that have gone to the mountains are believed to become mountain *kami* after the thirty-third anniversary of their death. These kami descend to the village in early spring, watch over the agricultural activities of their descendants, and return to the mountains in autumn. Decorations and offerings left over from New Year and Bon are thrown into the rivers and the sea, as are other significant objects: straw or wooden toy boats (*shōryōbune*) carrying souls unable to attain salvation, surrogate images made to carry off pollution, and harmful insects that attack the rice crop. At the same time, the banks of rivers, together with the seaside, are regarded as sacred spots where souls come from the otherworld of the mountains or sea and enter newborn infants.

This cycle, from village to mountain or sea, and then back again, may be observed in Japanese folk religion in various other contexts as well. In the *ondamatsuri* of Mt. Hiko in Kyushu, mountain ascetics (*yamabushi*) who have descended from the mountains along the rivers to the sea, scoop up tidewater and return to the mountains, and make offerings to the *kami* of seed rice that was purified with this water, which they then bestow upon the villages. At Mt. Ishizuchi in Shikoku, after seawater is poured into a pond at the top of a mountain, water from the pond is then taken back and poured into the fields to entreat rainfall. At Yahanmēutaki (a sacred place), a mountain cave in Nakagusuku Village in Okinawa, childless couples carry home a small stone taken from within the cave, and when a child is born they take a stone from the shore that they then deposit back in the cave. And as just seen, at the Bon festival, offerings made to spirits welcomed from the mountains, along with boats bearing souls unable to attain salvation, are set adrift down river. Malicious *kami* (*yakujin*) and pollution are also washed away. Seen in this way, it may be supposed that the souls unable to attain salvation, polluted spirits, and malicious *kami* thus washed downstream were believed to climb up from the horizontal realm to heaven, having been purified by the sea, and after being reborn descend again from the mountains back to the village. Incidentally, the custom of releasing fingerlings of salmon in mountain streams, in expectation that they will mature in the sea and return upriver to spawn, may also be seen as based on a belief in the spontaneous vitality of this cycle between mountain and sea, with the river as medium.

Time is basically divided according to the movements of the sun and the moon, the activities of animals, and so forth. Even today, almanacs listing these events are in use. According to these almanacs, the day divides into daytime, based on the movement of the sun and spanning the sunrise and sunset, and into nighttime when the moon and the stars shine, with daytime being the workaday realm of pursuing one's daily living, and night being a sacred time. The change from night to morning, and the twilight of evening, are regarded as temporal boundaries. Moreover, all of these times are associated with various plants and animals, such as daytime with sunflower, nighttime with primrose, fox, and badger, morning with morning glory and domestic fowl, and evening with moonflower and crow. The week is also divided into days bearing names based on the sun and moon, and the planets, Mars, Mercury, Jupiter, Venus, and Saturn.

Calendars may be solar, based on movement of the sun, or they may be based on the moon like the traditional lunar calendar (*taiinreki*); the latter was in use in Japan until 1872, and the waxing and waning of the moon have thus provided markers for daily life. For example, the native word *tsuitachi*, designating the first day of any month, means the appearance of the moon (*tsukidachi*). The seventh day, called *jōgen* (literally "upper half-moon"), the fifteenth day *mangetsu* ("full moon"), and the twenty-third day *kagen* ("lower half-moon") are all designated as festival days, and the thirtieth day *tsugomori* (deriving from *tsukikomori*, meaning the moon's hiding away) marks the beginning of a period of abstinence. In this manner the conduct of daily life is derived from the waxing and waning of the moon. In addition, as indicated by the fifteenth of January being celebrated as Koshōgatsu (literally "Little New Year"), and the fifteenth of July being the Bon festival, the full moon on the fifteenth day is taken as the beginning of the lunar cycle and of the year. In the case of the solar calendar, the apparent annual path of the sun can be divided into an ecliptic having twenty-four equal parts. Such a division yields the twenty-four intervals called *sekki*. The *sekki* have individual names: *shōkan* (literally, "lesser cold," beginning in early January), *daikan* ("great cold," late January to February), *risshun* (first day of spring, early February), *haru no higan* (vernal equinox), *rikka* (first day of summer, early May), *geshi* (summer solstice), *risshū* (first day of autumn, early August), *aki no higan* (autumnal equinox), *rittō* (first day of winter, early November), *tōji* (winter solstice), and so forth. As is well known, the summer solstice (around June 21) is the day with the longest period of sunlight, the winter solstice (around December 22) is the shortest, and during the vernal and autumnal equinoxes daytime and nighttime have the same duration.

The four seasons of spring, summer, fall, and winter, based on changes in natural phenomena, form the most familiar annual division for the Japanese. The birds and flowers of each season are common motifs in poetry, especially haiku. The spring cherry blossoms, the green pines and cedars of summer, the autumn colors, the early blooming plum of winter, the spring nightingale, the morning glories and goldfish of summer, autumn's red dragonflies, the winter swans, all of these are woven into poetry as signs of the coming of the seasons. In addition, the change of the seasons is sensed in various natural phenomena, such as the recognition of spring given by the melting of snow and the opening of buds, of summer in the shape of clouds or the sight of fireflies, of autumn in the cries of insects and the coming of typhoons, of winter in the first snowfall and the flocking of migratory birds. A dual division of the year is also sometimes undertaken by distinguishing the spring and summer seasons of economic production from the dormant spell of autumn and winter, or by separating the year into spring as the time when mountain *kami* and animals end their hibernation and descend into the village, and autumn as the time of their return.

In Japanese folk religion it has been held from ancient times that the spatial divisions of the natural realm and the mutual relations between them, and the movement of time based on the solar and lunar standards as described above, are all naturally occurring phenomena of heaven and earth far beyond the limits of man's own doing, and that it is good to live in accordance with these phenomena.

INTERNALIZED NATURE

As seen in the previous section, humans live in conformity with the naturally occurring temporal and spatial aspects of the external natural realm. From this has arisen the concept of an "internal nature" (*uchinaru shizen*) in opposition to the realm outside.[13] This contrast between an external nature and an internal nature corresponds to the contrast between extrinsic and intrinsic nature, and between macrocosm and microcosm, as well as between external and internal. Incidentally, in Japanese the word for "cosmos" (*uchū*) is formed by two characters indicating "space" and "time."

In India, during the Vedic age (ca. 1000 B.C.), the natural and human realms were viewed according to the same law. In other words it was held that when nature conforms to cosmic principles, order and balance are maintained, but when cosmic principles are transgressed, disorder erupts. For humans, cosmic principles are truth and justice; transgressions of these amount to falsehood and iniquity. Cosmic principles are also the rules governing ceremonies, and when rites are conducted at the designated times and places according to these predetermined rules, they conform to the cosmic principles and are deemed effective. A view of nature can thus be discerned in which the gods are the observers and protectors of cosmic principles.[14] In the Chinese view of nature, even while taking the proper state of the external realm (composed of heaven and the physical world) to be one and the same as that of the interior realm (of human inner experience and of the self), it is the latter, or namely the true form of the spirit (one's innate nature) that is fundamental.[15] Drawing upon these two examples, the following discussion will attempt some observations on the contrast between external nature and internal nature, and on the elements constituting them, as seen in Japanese folk religion.

With regard first to the constituent elements, the internalized nature of humans and the external nature (comprising all things) have in common the existence of a soul or spirit (*seirei*) as the basis of life. Of course there are different varieties of spirit: in the case of humans this is *reikon* (differentiated as *seirei* for the living and *shirei* for the deceased), whereas for natural objects it is *seirei*, and for deified beings it is *shinrei*, but fundamentally these are all the same. Also, the belief in spirit *ki* (or *ch'i* in Chinese) as the foundation of all life has been incorporated into Japanese folk religion. It is derived from the concept found in Chinese divination of a Great Ultimate as the foundation of all things. In other words, as seen in the way Japanese speak of a state of good health as being in good or vigorous spirit (*genki*), and of a weakened state as a decline in spirit (*kiyowa ni naru*), a loss of spirit (*ki o ushinau*), or a diseased spirit (*byōki*, used generally for illness), they locate the wellspring of life in spirit (*ki*). At the same time, in indicating the condition of external nature, as shown by the term for "climate" (*kikō*), itself a product of "weather" (*tenki*) and "atmosphere" (*kūki*), the same expression, "spirit," is used. Similar assumptions of unity are apparent in the concept that humans and all things in creation partake of the two principles of *yin* and *yang*, and in the notion that all things are made of the five forces (*gogyō*) (wood, fire, earth, metal, water). This is also seen in esoteric Buddhism, which in Japan goes back to the priest Kūkai (774–835), in the concept that all things beginning with the Buddha and bodhisattvas are created by the six elements (*rokudai*) (earth, water, fire, wind, space, and consciousness) and possess the three secrets (*sanmitsu*) (the suprarational activities of body, speech, and mind). A similar assumption is seen again in the Tendai *hongaku* doctrine, which formed the nucleus of the Buddhism of the Kamakura period (1185–1333), in its notion that starting with man, all things possess Buddha nature and are capable of attaining buddhahood. These beliefs have had great influence on folk religion and Shinto in Japan.[16]

In folk religion the contrast between external and internal nature can be discerned in the beliefs of farmers that liken human death and rebirth to the waxing and waning of the moon, the growth of plants on the earth, and conception and childbirth for women. As stated previously, at first the moon appears on the first day of each month, and from the upper half-moon stage on the seventh day it grows rounder daily until it becomes a full moon on the fifteenth. From then it begins to wane, becoming the lower half-moon of the twenty-third, then disappearing on the thirtieth. In this manner it repeats a cycle of emergence, maturity, decline, and disappearance. Japanese pictorial interpretations of the face of the moon show a hare pounding steamed glutinous rice into a rice cake. This image may be regarded as the hare, representing a female *kami*, producing or spawning the glutinous rice cake (*mochi*), which is the refined form of the rice spirit.

Until 1872, agricultural practice in Japan followed the traditional lunar calendar. The name given the apotheosis of the moon, Amaterasu's brother Tsukiyomi, means "read the moon" (*tsuki o yomu*); in other words, the name refers to divination of the weather or the auspiciousness of a given day from the phase of the moon, from the clouds that cover it, and so forth. In addition, the *Kojiki* (compiled 712 A.D.) relates that agriculture began when Tsukiyomi killed an earthly deity, Ukemochi, and the five grains that sprang from various parts of the latter's corpse were cultivated. From its association with the low and high tides, the moon is thought to exercise control over tides and currents and over water itself and is thus associated with rain and lightning, snakes, and so on.[17] The label of *samidare* applied to the early summer monsoon rain, vital to paddy agriculture, is an expression made by combining the name for the fifth month of the lunar calendar (*satsuki*) with the term for "making rain" (*midare*). Also, from the six cycles of lunar waxing and waning that mark the time from planting of the rice paddies until their harvest, the year was divided by the lunar calendar into two parts: the six months from the fourth through the ninth when rice is cultivated under the protection of the *kami* of the rice fields, and the slack period starting when the *kami*, having ended their watch, depart in the tenth month named *kannazuki* (literally, "month of no *kami*"), and continuing to the third month.

Agriculture is the task of tilling mother earth with a hoe, planting a seed therein, and making it sprout with the water brought by the moon and the light of the sun, thus raising the plant to bear fruit. This enterprise may be likened to the conception of a child and its development in the maternal womb, followed by birth and the child's maturation. Specifically, the wetting of the hoe with water, prior to turning the soil, is sometimes said to represent the male organ with seminal fluid, and rainwater, too, is likened to this fluid.[18] Also, in addition to games and music traditionally played in the rice fields as a prelude to celebrating a bountiful harvest, pantomimes imitating intercourse, conception, and childbirth are performed in combination with ritualized imitations of sowing, transplanting, and harvest. Perhaps because of these beliefs, the primary agents in ancient agriculture were women.

A woman's conception, followed by the swelling of the womb with the development of the fetus, then childbirth, are linked with the waxing and waning of the moon, with birth coming after ten lunar cycles. It is the swelling of its belly that also links the frog with the moon. The moon and the female principle are regarded as *yin*, in opposition to the sun and male principle, which are *yang*. In addition, the menstrual cycle is called a "monthly passing" (*gekkei*) or "monthly course" (*gessui*, from "moon" plus "water"). This identification is based on the same idea as that which views the water brought by the moon as indispensable to agriculture. Partly because of this, on the twenty-third of the month, when the waning moon reaches its half-moon phase, married women belonging to a voluntary association called the "twenty-third evening fraternity" (*nijū sanya-kō*) gathered at a meeting place, where they hung a scroll with the image of the *kami* Tsukiyomi and awaited the rising of the moon while praying for conception.

The view of death and rebirth as a naturally occurring phenomenon, thus seen symbolically in the moon, in vegetation, and in women, is reflected in understandings of life and death found in folk religion. As noted in the previous section, in earlier times human remains were interred in the soil, either directly after death, or as the bones that were washed and interred after the corpse was allowed to decay upon exposure to the elements. Later, when cremation came to be practiced, the remains were gathered as ashes from the pyre and then interred. At this juncture the umbilical cord of the deceased (saved from the time of birth) may also be placed in the coffin. As mentioned previously, the earth in which such burial is made is likened to the maternal womb. This being the case, burial may be regarded as the act of returning the deceased once again to the womb for rebirth. The account of grains sprouting from the body of the *kami*

Ukemochi in the *Kojiki* was previously cited. Bleached bones are called *shari* (in the strict sense, a reference to the bones of the Buddha or a bodhisattva, but loosely applied to all cleansed human bones); rice is called *ginshari* (*gin* meaning "silver"). Further, at the final lifting of mourning observed on the thirty-third anniversary of death, a living tree with foliage called *uretsuki tōba* is erected, and when this takes root it is believed that the deceased is transformed into a *kami*. It is thus held that humans embody as part of their essential nature, in the same manner as rice and other plants, and in accordance with the naturally occurring movement of nature, the repetition of death and rebirth. Of course, for humans it is in general as a Buddha or *kami* that rebirth is seen to take place. For example, at Shimokasaka in Oku County, Okayama Prefecture, Buddhist nuns (*bikuni*) propagating the Kumano faith used illustrated texts to preach that the soul of a deceased man, conceived as a spirit when his wife passes the night with him at his wake, is reborn on the third anniversary of his death, and becomes a fully developed Buddha on the thirty-third anniversary.[19] The ritualized motif of fictive death and rebirth is also visible in the puberty rite, which symbolically kills the child who is then reborn as an adult. Further, the earth that envelops withered plants and the corpses of humans and beasts also nurtures the buds of new plant life and the eggs of animals. For this reason, the earth is taken as the locus of death and rebirth of all things. From this it is believed that, in the same manner as the moon and plant life, humans bear within them the proper form of nature's spontaneity, or natural occurrences, regaining life after death and returning from the dead.

DESTRUCTION OF THE NATURAL ENVIRONMENT

Recall now the three basic types of worldview cited at the beginning of this work. It is universally recognized that recent centuries have witnessed humanity's technological domination of nature, based on a human-centered worldview and supported theoretically by the perspective of Cartesian dualism. Secularization increased in the twentieth century, giving birth to the theological perspective that God is dead. At the same time, technological advances have brought about the destruction of the natural environment on a worldwide scale, and conceptual and practical countermeasures are now being called for. As one such response, an environmental ethic is being proposed that respects the rights of nature to free it from human domination.[20] The aim of this chapter, however, is to seek a worldview through comparison with the three basic types cited earlier that will serve as corrective to the human-centered perspective that has led to the death of God and the destruction of the natural environment. Two conceivable means to such an end are, first, to return to the god-centered worldview as found in Christianity and other religions, and seek in it a new path, and, second, to search in the worldview centered on the spontaneity of nature, as seen in Asian folk religions, for a way in which humans and nature can coexist.

Examples of the first means include the environmental theism that claims all living things within the Kingdom of God to be equal, or the attempt to discover within the Bible a God who places humans within nature, or in other words, a God from the perspective of self-denial.[21] But I prefer to take the second position given above, i.e., seeking a path for coexistence of humans and nature in terms of nature-centered modes of existence of people and gods, as found in the worldview of Japanese folk religion.

In this worldview, both humans and gods are positioned within the spontaneity or natural occurrences of nature. Of course, in this case it is the spontaneous activity of nature itself that tends to be seen as deified. Early examples of this are the Mahāvairocana Buddha (Dainichi Nyorai) of Tantric Buddhism and Amaterasu (a manifestation of Mahāvairocana Buddha as the deified sun)—in other words, *suijaku*, manifestation of Buddhist deities in Japan. Later, the moon and stars of the heavens and all natural phenomena such as wind and rain came to be seen as manifestations of nature's spontaneity, with the changes of the moon being an especially important indicator of such. In accordance with the moon's rhythms the majority of farmers applied themselves to growing rice in the paddies from the fourth through the ninth lunar months, and resting from the tenth through the third month of the following year. During this slack period in the autumn a festival was celebrated, in which the new grain was shared with the *kami*; in the winter festival the soul force of the deity was infused in the body, and in the spring festival, the soul force was expressed.[22] The *kami* were also seen to be present in the village to watch over its agriculture from the fourth through the ninth months and to rest in the mountains from the tenth month to the third month of the following spring. The Shinto priests and mountain ascetics, who secluded themselves in the mountains during this period for religious training, were regarded as embodying the power of the *kami*, and the animals that hibernate at this time were revered as messengers of the *kami*.

Later on, the New Year's celebration and the Bon festival took on importance as days for ancestral worship. New Year's Day was observed as the time when children were given presents of money (*toshidama*, a New Year's gift that symbolizes new souls) and were counted as one year older, and the Bon festival was celebrated as the occasion for memorial services for the dead, in which a Buddhist priest took part. In conjunction with these, the spring festival was observed in the fourth month, and the autumn festival in the tenth. The former prayed for a bountiful crop by welcoming the *kami* from the mountains; in the latter, the *kami* were sent back, after being thanked for an abundant harvest with offerings of new grain. In this way the New Year, Bon, and the spring and autumn festivals came to be the most important events of the year. Year after year, by practicing agriculture in the midst of natural occurrences, farmers worked to enjoy the benefits of nature by performing various rituals, especially this sequence of four rites.

For humans, life in the fullest sense is obtained at birth, following conception and development in the maternal womb, when a soul enters the body, having been washed downstream from the mountains (a part of the otherworld), or alternatively, having drifted ashore from beyond the sea. Then, under the blessing of nature and the care given by the family, the child undergoes the puberty rite, marries, produces children of his or her own, and finally dies. This process is likened to the germination and growth of crops, or to the various trees during the four seasons in the manner of the small child being a plum, a youth a cherry, someone in the prime of life a pine or cedar, a middle-aged person being the colors of autumn, and an aged individual like a tree that has shed its leaves. After death, by receiving memorial offerings and rites from one's descendants at Bon and the New Year, which purify the soul, one's spirit grows gradually more and more refined and finally goes to the mountains, and after celebration of the thirty-third anniversary of death and the final lifting of mourning, becomes a *kami*. From that time the spirit is believed to descend from the mountains in spring to watch over the agricultural activities of descendants, and to return to the mountain after seeing the crop come to harvest in autumn, as described above.

The annual festivals that proceed according to this rhythm of nature are the law of the macrocosm. In opposition to this, the microcosm formed by the life of an individual can be referred to as internal nature. Incidentally, the course of a human life as this internal nature, and the cycle of annual observances demonstrating the spontaneity of the macrocosm, are linked in a coordinated fashion: birth aligning with the New Year in which a new soul is received and matures, marriage with the spring festival that is celebrated in anticipation of a bountiful harvest, death with the Bon festival in which the ancestral spirits are welcomed, and the end of mourning and transformation into a *kami* with the tenth month's harvest festival. This relationship is thought to indicate that the human life as microcosm is played out in accordance with the spontaneous movement of external nature that forms the macrocosm, and moreover, that it thus constitutes an internalization of nature.[23] For the Japanese, to live out one's life un- eventfully in this manner, in accordance with the natural law that is dei- fied as the Tōgyoshin (the overarching divinity of natural occurrences), and later to be worshipped as *kami* by one's descendants, has been consid- ered to be the best fortune possible.

But there are not a few who fail to follow this proper path. These are the unborn fetuses that were deliberately aborted by their parents, the children who die because of the neglect of their parents or others around them, those who die harboring resentment over human entanglements, strife, or warfare and become vengeful ghosts, those whose souls go unmemorialized by their descendants, and those who, as unworshipped *kami*, fall from grace and turn into demons. These beings, unable to be- come ancestral *kami* like persons who end life satisfactorily and are me- morialized by their descendants, come under the influence of *shizenshin* (a deification of nature), and together with that *kami* (who vents rage at the human destruction of the natural environment), they wreak revenge on those who reduced them to their current state. Disease, loss of work, natural calamities, and so forth, are explained as harm brought about by the souls of aborted fetuses or small children in league with *shizenshin*, and caused by vengeful ghosts, or as pranks played by specters and other demons.

Among these it is the curse of vengeful ghosts in particular that takes the form of nature's fury as earthquakes, blasts of lightning, typhoons, and so forth. In order to appease these it is necessary to propitiate the vengeful ghosts as venerated spirits, and seek their protection. The ven- eration of Sugawara no Michizane (845–903, who challenged the power- ful Fujiwara family and was sent into exile where he died in disgrace) at Tenman Shrine, and of Taira no Masakado (?–940, who led the first major rebellion of the warrior class against the central government, and was killed) at Kanda Myōjin are representative examples. In order to avoid interference from unborn fetuses and the souls of young children, pin- wheels and the like are offered at places where they are thought to be present, as though these spirits were still alive, and through the offering of votive tablets (*ema*) for school entrance and marriage, an attempt is made to satisfy their unfulfilled longings.[24] Also, by making offerings to ghosts and venerating demons, an attempt is made to placate their dis- content.

However, when the normal human desire to become a *kami* through the cycle of birth, marriage, death, and mourning is distorted in the extreme, through the selfishness of a particular individual or enterprise, into a pursuit of lavish tastes or excessive profits, and destruction occurs in the surrounding natural environment that supports the naturally occurring activities of heaven, earth, plant and animal life, then the *kami* of nature bring natural calamity upon people. It will be recognized that in fact among the causes of calamities in nature, man-made disasters due to the destruction of the environment through the arrogance of people and industry are many. In these cases—much like the physical embodiments of the notion of people who have died harboring resentment, and who become vengeful ghosts, cooperating with *shizenshin* (and particular natural *kami*) to wreak natural disaster—the families and friends of those who have died because of pollution, brought by the pursuit of profit and self-interest of industry, conduct the struggle against such pollution and for the preservation of nature, holding aloft photographs of their lost loved ones or flags inscribed with words proclaiming their grievance. Although the protectors themselves may not realize it, their stance is surely grounded in the view of nature held by folk religion.[25]

As stated in this chapter, in the view of nature held by Japanese folk religion, the original law of natural occurrence or spontaneity is regarded as divine, and accordingly, living in harmony with that spontaneity is taken as the ideal. In addition, in recognition of the sacred soul or spirit, or Buddha nature seen to exist in all things, the concept of revering all things is maintained. But from recent times, people who have used nature for their own benefit have dominated it in high-handed fashion, losing this understanding of nature seen in folk religion. In order to put a halt to this destruction of the natural environment now proceeding on a global scale, in conjunction with the various protest movements that arise in each situation, more than anything else it is necessary for humans to live in accordance with the spontaneity of nature, having internalized nature by returning to the bright and pure spirit, or spirituality, or Buddha nature, that is shared by all things in the universe.

NOTES

1. See Miyake Hitoshi, *Nihon no minzoku shūkyō* (Japanese folk religions) (Tokyo: Kōdansha, 1994).
2. Yanabu Akira, *Honyaku no shisō: shizen to neichyā* (The idea of translation: nature and *shizen*) (Tokyo: Heibonsha, 1977), 32–50.
3. On the meaning of the Chinese word *zi-ran*, see Ikeda Tomohisa, "Chūgoku tetsugaku ni okeru shizen" (The idea of nature in Chinese philosophy), in *Shizen*, manuscripts prepared for the Fourth Public Symposium of the Philosophy Division, Science Council of Japan, 1994; Hachiya Kunio, "Shizenkan" (The idea of nature), in *Chūgoku no shii* (Chinese thinking) (Kyoto: Kyoto Hōzōkan, 1985), 32–46.

4. Sagara Tōru, "Hajime ni" (Introduction), in *Kōza Nihon shisō* (Lectures on Japanese thought), ed. Sagara Tōru et al. (Tokyo: Tōkyō Daigaku Shuppankai, 1983), 1:iv.

5. See Sagara Tōru, "Shizen to iu kotoba o meguru kangaekata ni tsuite—shizen keijijōgaku to rinri" (About the way of thinking on the word nature—metaphysics of nature and ethics), in *Shizen—rinrigakuteki kōsatsu* (Nature—ethical considerations), ed. Kaneko Takezō (Tokyo: Ibunsha, 1979), 252–53. Takeuchi Seiichi, "Nihonteki onozukara ni tsuite" (About the idea of naturally occurring in the Japanese thought), in *Shizen*, Fourth Public Symposium of the Philosophy Division, Science Council of Japan.

6. Nishida Kitarō, *Zen no kenkyū* (A study of Zen) (Tokyo: Iwanami Shoten, 1950), 221–33; Sagara Tōru, "Shizen to iu kotoba," 250–51. This view, as expressed by Takeuchi Seiichi at the symposium mentioned in note 3, is believed to originate in the Tendai doctrine of original enlightenment or immanent buddhahood (Tendai *hongakuron*).

7. See Nakano Hajime, "Shizen tetsugaku no jidaiteki shiten" (Current thought of natural philosophy), in *Shizen to kosumosu* (Nature and cosmos), ed. Ōmori Shōzō et al., Shin Iwanami Kōza Tetsugaku 5 (Tokyo: Iwanami Shoten, 1985), 241–68. A recently published volume of essays in English emphasizing the variety of "Japanese images of nature" is Pamela J. Asquith and Arne Kalland, eds., *Japanese Images of Nature: Cultural Perspectives* (Richmond, Surrey: Curzon Press, 1997).

8. Although the sun, moon, and stars are composed of inorganic matter in the same manner as rocks, soil, etc., I would like to make a conceptual distinction between the two classes of items.

9. The English term "nature" was first translated as *tenchi* (meaning "heaven-earth"), *banbutsu* ("all things"), *zōka* ("creation"), or *shinra banshō* ("all things in nature"); see Yanabu, *Honyaku no shisō*, 32–50. In Chinese philosophy, there was an attempt to analyze the concept of "nature" by replacing the English term with such Chinese words as *t'ien* ("heaven") *sho* ("character"), *ch'i* ("spirit"), *tzu-jan* ("spontaneity") and *tao* ("way"). See Uchiyama Toshihiko, *Chūgoku kodai shisōshi ni okeru shizen ninshiki* (The understanding of nature in ancient Chinese thought) (Tokyo: Sōbunsha, 1987).

10. Robert Redfield, "Primitive World View and Civilization," in *The Primitive World and Its Transformations* (Ithaca, NY: Cornell University Press, 1953).

11. Harada Toshiaki, *Kodai Nihon no shinkō to shakai* (Belief and society in ancient Japan) (Tokyo: Shōkō Shoin, 1948), 53–68.

12. Among various works treating natural objects regarded as sacred and interpreting the basis of their sacred nature are Mircea Eliade, *Patterns in Comparative Religions* (New York: Sheed and Ward, 1958). Treatment of sacred natural objects in Japanese folk religions include Saitō Shōji, *Nihonteki shizenkan no kenkyū* (Study on the idea of nature in Japan) (Tokyo: Yasaka Shobō, 1978), 2:103–270.

13. Minamoto Ryoen, "Nihonjin no shizenkan" (The idea of nature among the Japanese), in *Shizen to kosumosu*, 352.

14. Hattori Masaaki, "Indo no shizenkan" (The idea of nature in India), in *Shizen to kosumosu*, 299. See also Hattori Masaaki, "Kodai Indo no shizenkan" (The idea of nature in ancient India), in *Shizen*, Fourth Public Symposium of the Philosophy Division, Science Council of Japan.

15. Fukunaga Mitsuji, "Chūgoku no shizenkan" (The idea of nature in China), in *Shizen to kosumosu*, 345.

16. Tamura Yoshirō, "Nihon shisōshi ni okeru hongaku shisō" (The idea of innate enlightenment in the history of Japanese thought), in *Kōza Nihon shisō* 1:123–42. Hagiyama Jinryo, "Nihonteki shizenkan no ichi yōso to shite no sōmoku jōbutsu shisō" (The enlightenment of grass and trees as one aspect of the Japanese view of nature), *Shūkyō kenkyū* 299 (1994):315–16.

17. Mircea Eliade, *Patterns in Comparative Religion*, trans. Rosemary Sheed (New York: Sheed and Ward, 1958), 154–87.

18. Ibid., 332–34.

19. Miyake Hitoshi, "Tsuizen kuyō no etoki—Tōzanha Shugen no chiiki teichaku" (The explanation by a picture of a memorial service for the dead—local indigenization of Tōzanha Shugen), *Keiō Gijuku Daigaku Daigakuin Shakaigaku Kenkyūka kiyō* 36 (1997):65–68.

20. Roderick F. Nash, *The Rights of Nature: A History of Environmental Ethics* (Madison: University of Wisconsin Press, 1989).

21. Arai Sasagu, "Seisho no shizenkan ni yosete" (On the idea of nature in the Bible), the Public Symposium of the Comparative Religion Division, "Environment and Religion," Science Council of Japan, 1994.

22. See Origuchi Shinobu, *Nenjūgyōji* (The yearly round of observances), *Origuchi Shinobu zenshū*, vol. 15 (The complete works of Origuchi Shinobu) (Tokyo: Chūō Kōronsha, 1976).

23. The endeavor to position human life as a microcosm within the movements of the macrocosm may also be discerned in the art of fortune telling, which reads an individual's fate by the person's placement within the constellations of the heavens.

24. Helen Hardacre, *Marketing the Menacing Fetus in Japan* (Berkeley: University of California Press, 1997).

25. See Miyake Hitoshi, "Nihon no minzoku shin'i—onjō to jōnen to" (Japanese folk mind—or beneficence, favor, and sentiment), in *Nihon shūkyō no kōzō* (The structure of Japanese religion) (Tokyo: Keiō Tsūshin, 1974).

Japanese Religion and Worldly Benefits

The term "worldly benefits" (*genze riyaku*) is an awkward one, often used with pejorative connotations.[1] Religious leaders frequently brand the "suspect" healing activities that are practiced by faith healers or others as being conducted for "worldly benefit," and claim that their own religious activities are of a more sophisticated or advanced nature. In such cases the term "worldly benefits" is understood as synonymous with pseudoreligious or religious-like activity that cannot be encouraged as authentic.

Among intellectuals or people in general, however, practices for "worldly benefits" refer to the prayers and invocations offered by those involved in the whole gamut of Japanese religion, be it Shinto, Buddhist, the new religions, or folk religion. In this case "worldly benefits" refer to the direct benefits people seek to obtain for their daily lives through religious means, that of relief from disease; safe birth and the raising of children; a stable supply of the necessities of food, clothing, and shelter; prosperity and commercial success; secure production; maintenance of good human relationships, and so forth.

However, there is hardly any religion in Japan that is not involved in activities directly connected to those aspects of daily life such as healing disease and assuring safe delivery of children, prosperity, or other daily needs.[2] This fact indicates that the various problems and meanings indicated by the term *genze riyaku* may hold the key to understanding Japanese religion.

What is the role of *genze riyaku*, or "worldly benefits"? What place does it hold in religion, and in the daily life of human beings? What kinds or types of *genze riyaku* are there, and how do Japanese religions respond to the peoples' demand for these "worldly benefits"? What kind of religious worldview supports the belief in *genze riyaku*? Those are the questions that will be examined in this chapter.

UNDERSTANDING *GENZE RIYAKU*

Genze riyaku originally was a Buddhist term referring to "the blessings *obtained in this present world* from the bodhisattvas or buddhas by believing in the scriptures and chanting or keeping them, and by chanting formulae (*shingon*, Skt. *dhāraṇī*) or the names of the buddhas."[3] Terms such as *genyaku* (present benefits) and *genzeyaku* (benefits in the present world) were also used in the same way, as terms in contrast to the seeking of benefits for the next life after death.[4] Thus the original meaning of the term was for useful benefits and blessings within this world rather than in the next. Concretely speaking, it referred to obtaining worldly requests for healing, lengthening of one's life span, accumulation of wealth, and so forth through religious means. Tamamuro's comment that "*genze riyaku* religions are those which grant one's wishes for long life, protection from misfortune, and prosperity"[5] and Takagi's definition of *genze riyaku* (referring to the new religions) as "an opportunity to break out of an impasse situation in one's life"[6] are uses of the term based on this understanding of *genze riyaku*.

This obtaining of benefits, both in this world and the next, is based on the Buddhist idea of *riyaku*, which refers to "obtaining good fortune and blessings (*kōfuku, onkei*) from following the teachings of the Buddha."[7] As mentioned above, those benefits include both those that are obtained in the present world, as well as those obtained in the next life. However, this idea is based on the theological (or "Buddhological") premise that there is another life, or world, beyond this present one. The term originally arose to contrast the benefits obtained in this present world rather than in the next.

From the perspective of religious studies, however, the concept of "benefits in the next life" is of value because it provides security and stability to people in this present life and world through a specific faith in those future benefits. In this sense even those "future" benefits are actually astute ways for dealing with life in the present world and are thus another type of "worldly benefits" obtained by religious means, though admittedly indirect and latent. "Worldly benefits," on the other hand, are directly and obviously connected with the problems and requirements of daily life. I would therefore define *genze riyaku* for the purposes of this study as "the obtaining of benefits by human beings with regard to problems faced in daily life through an association with a supernatural reality."

I have attempted to place *genze riyaku* within the framework of religious faith in obtaining worldly benefits. In other words, the idea of *riyaku* refers to the activity of obtaining benefits by human beings through religious faith or belief for one's daily life, whether direct and obvious or indirect and latent. The former type constitutes "worldly benefits," and the latter type includes benefits in a later life.[8]

THE ROLE OF *GENZE RIYAKU*

The view of religion as something that is beneficial to the daily lives of human beings is the same as that proposed by the theory of religious functionalism.[9] This view attempts to define the role of religion in terms of its contribution to, or function within, the daily life of human beings. Thus, I will attempt to define the role of what is generally called "worldly benefits" within the framework of the theories of religious functionalism.

Religion, in the theories of religious functionalism represented by Paul Tillich, is defined as that which has to do with the relationship between human beings and "ultimate reality."[10] The function of religion in human life is to provide salvation or relief from ultimate frustrations, and to provide meaning that serves as the ultimate support for human life.[11] It goes without saying that the content of the ultimate—ultimate frustrations or ultimate support—is a matter for the person who is a believer in that religion.

Let us analyze this view to see how it fits with the question of "worldly benefits." It is an obvious fact that the primary objective facing human beings is the maintenance of their lives, and that their daily lives are their immediate and predominant occupation. The daily life of a human being is directly concerned with individual preservation centered around various concerns for health, growth, and nourishment: the economic concerns that accompany production and commerce, and that include consumption of food, clothing, and shelter; the social life with regard to the family and local society; political problems that include the advancement of the individual; and the spiritual aspects of life centered around religion that endow life with meaning and depth.[12]

In living such a daily life with those various concerns, one has the expectation that things will go smoothly, and one attempts to proceed in certain directions. However, there are times when things go wrong and one is faced with difficult situations. At these times one seeks ways to remedy the situation. This may involve visiting a medical doctor or seeking counseling. However, sometimes these methods do not produce adequate results. When people are forced into such situations, on what should they rely?

The kind of religion outlined above comes to the fore in these situations. Religion is generally thought to apply to the spiritual life of human beings. However, this is not the only area of human life for which religious activity is relevant. Religion is also related to health, growth, production, commerce, the basic necessities of food, clothing, and shelter, human relations, politics, and so forth. Religion provides guidance for human activity in all these areas, and provides a way to deal with situations where one has reached an impasse—through providing a relationship with "ultimate reality"—a symbol of the supernatural.

If we understand *genze riyaku* in terms of obtaining benefits from "ultimate reality" within this world, then in the broad sense of the word it signifies the overcoming of disappointments and frustrations that arise when one's aspirations in all of the aforementioned areas of human life fail to progress smoothly. In the way Takagi uses the term, as "an opportunity to break out of a deadlocked situation in one's life," *genze riyaku* refers to deliverance/salvation from ultimate frustration/defeat in areas other than the spiritual life, i.e., health, growth, commerce, obtaining the daily necessities of food, clothing, and shelter, human relationships, politics, and so forth. This would be the narrow sense of the word. I understand the term *genze riyaku* more generally as the attitude that seeks assistance from supernatural powers in all areas of life other than the spiritual, including the solution to a seeming impasse in one's life.

What role do these kinds of "worldly benefits" play in religion? Let us first examine the role of "worldly benefits" in an individual's belief system. Kishimoto Hideo divides the belief system of an individual into three categories of attitudes: petition (*seigantai*), aspiration (*kikyūtai*), and enlightenment (*taijūtai*). "Petition" refers to the use of religious means to resolve immediate problems in daily life such as sickness, misfortunes, and so forth. "Aspiration" refers to the search to solve religious problems through religious means. The final aspect of "enlightenment" is to be engrossed in seeking the highest religious values. It is clear that as one's belief becomes deeper and more profound, one's attitude also advances from that of making petitions, to aspiration, to enlightenment.[13]

Robert Bellah, on the basis of Talcott Parsons' action theory, suggests that religious action consists of four kinds: ethics, worship, religious therapy, and faith.[14] Those four kinds of action are sustained by or based on the concept of a righteous god for ethics, a loving god for worship, ancestor veneration or the Tao for religious therapy, and natural law for faith. It could be said that the categories of worship and religious therapy in this analysis are similar to Kishimoto's concept of "aspiration." And it is an ancestral, "loving" god, or a concept such as the Tao, that provides the basis for such religious attitudes. In such a case, aspiration is related to worship, and the overcoming of frustrations is related to religious therapy.

Bellah adds that religious therapy includes diagnosis (divination), the therapeutic process, salvation, and theories on the origin of these evils and the ways to overcome them.[15]

TYPES OF WORLDLY BENEFITS

So far I have considered some theoretical approaches to the problem. Next let us examine the types of worldly benefits offered by various religions.[16] First let us take a look at Shinto, the ancient religion of the Japanese people. Hiraoka Yoshifumi's standard reference work on Shinto rituals records a total of fifty-five ritual types for various rituals and festivals.[17] One can surmise on the basis of those rituals how Shinto attempted to respond to the appeal for worldly benefits by the common people. These rituals can be characterized as: rites of passage (including birth and death)—11; general Shinto rites—7; removing misfortune—6; the festival of the *kō* (religious fraternity)—5; building, construction, and agriculture—4 each; natural phenomena—3; consumption, bridge ceremonies, ceremonies of the household *kami*, ceremonies of the occupational *kami*—2 each; opening ceremony, safe journey, occupational safety—1 each. If one considers that most of the Shinto observances are concerned with agricultural rituals, one can safely conclude that the major Shinto ceremonies performed for the sake of worldly benefits are those of rites of passage, agricultural rites, ceremonies for avoiding misfortune, *kō* ceremonies, prayers for occupational safety, and so forth. It is also well known that in Shinto there is a fear of the spirits of those who died an accidental or violent death or of the *kami* of pestilence (*ekijin*), and that Shinto provides ceremonies for exorcising or pacifying those spirits. Of course such purification (*harai*) is a central part of all of the aforementioned ceremonies.[18]

Worldly benefits are also widely accepted in Buddhism. Sutras such as the *Kannon* chapter of the *Lotus Sutra, Yakushi ruriko nyorai hongan kudokukyō, Kanjōkyō,* and *Konkōmyō saichōōkyō* teach that worldly benefits can be obtained through Buddhist practices such as chanting the sutras or the names of the buddhas and bodhisattvas. Even in the Pure Land tradition, which is generally thought of as a faith centered on the next world, texts such as Hōnen's *Senchaku hongan nenbutsu shū* and Shinran's *Jōdo wasan* (Hymns on the Pure Land) contain teachings on worldly benefits. The "hymns on worldly benefits" in the *Jōdo wasan*, for example, speak of the merits (*kudoku*) that can be accrued through the practice of *nenbutsu*, such as avoiding misfortune, long life, and the extinguishing of seven kinds of difficulties.[19]

Worldly benefits are an especially important part of esoteric Buddhism, which places a high premium on prayer and incantations. It is well known that prayers and incantations (*kajikitō*) were performed frequently during the zenith of esoteric Buddhism, from the Heian period through the Middle Ages, in response to peoples' anticipation of worldly benefits. The content of worldly benefits in this case can be inferred from the records of the various kinds of esoteric Buddhist rituals. A look at the purposes for the ceremonies given in one of these records, the *Shoson yōsho* (Essential Summary of All Deities) shows 30 for avoiding misfortune, 28 for granting wishes, 17 for safe birth and growth of children, 9 for extinguishing sins, 7 each for help against curses and natural calamities ("acts of God"), and 3 each for protection from bad dreams and help for attaining enlightenment. If one disregards the general category of "granting wishes," then the great majority of those ceremonies concern the two categories of "avoiding misfortune" and "safe birth and growth."[20]

According to Kūkai's *Misuhō sōjō* there are two types of esoteric ceremonies, the *senryakushu* and the *himitsushū*. The *senryakushu* refers to the use of elementary passages from sutras, which is compared to the diagnostic role of explaining the cause of disease or the nature of certain medicine. The *himitsushū*, in contrast, refers to the use of *dhāraṇī* or spells, to heal disease directly, as in the direct application of medicine in accordance with the cause of the disease. In other words, the esoteric ceremonies are effective only when diagnosis and treatment are applied together.[21]

A religious tradition that actively responded to the people's requests for worldly benefits from the Heian up to the modern period, and which can be seen as a popularization of esoteric Buddhism, is Shugendō. The types of worldly benefits offered by Shugendō can be seen in the *Shugen jinpi gyōhō fujushū* (Collection of Secret Shugen Spells and Ceremonies), a collection of secret practice papers (*kirigami*) carried around and passed down by *shugenja*, the practitioners of Shugendō. These include 105 for health and safe birth and growth, 88 concerning production and consumption, 71 concerning human relationships, and 58 concerning the spiritual life. If these are categorized into the two areas of the attainment of one's wishes and deliverance from frustrations, there are 138 for attainment of one's wishes, and 185 for deliverance from frustrations. One can see that for Shugendō, the most common requests concerned health and safe birth and growth, and from the content of the ceremonies one can see that this usually took the form of deliverance from calamities caused by evil influences, rather than the form of obtaining one's wishes.[22] For Shugendō, the causes of those calamities were attributed to the interference or curse of evil *kami* (*jashin*) or evil spirits (*jarei*). Therefore in order to remove the source of the possible misfortune or put an end to the anger of the evil *kami* or spirit, the nature of the curse must first be identified through divination, and then proper prayers intoned in accordance with the nature of the curse.[23]

In the modern period much of the demand by the common people for worldly benefits has been met by the so-called "new religions." A sampling of 308 converts to Tenrikyō, one of the religions founded toward the end of the Edo period (nineteenth century), shows that their motivation for joining Tenrikyō was as follows: disease—273 (eye disease—51, general sickness—48, stomach disease—26, birth-related—20, chest disease—14, psychological disorder—11, injuries—9, neuralgia—8, women's complaints—6, 5 each for cholera, tumors, lumbago, and cripples, and 60 for other diseases). There were 31 cases where the motivation came from circumstances other than diseases (attracted to the teachings—9, misfortune in the home—6, attracted by the virtuous example of a Tenrikyō believer or teacher—4, 3 each through the experience of a possession or the death of one's parents, prayer for rain—2, and 4 others).[24] A quick glance will show that disease is the most common motivating factor. This is due to the fact that Tenrikyō is engaged in active proselytization with the offer of physical healing as its main worldly benefit.

The same tendency can be seen in other post-World War II new religions. A random sampling of 100 professions of faith in Risshō Kōsei Kai between 1952 and 1953, for example, gives as reasons: illness—68, bad personal conduct—16, problems in the home—6, misfortune—6, unemployment—2, and 1 each for loneliness and "no special reason."[25]

In contrast, many of the new religions teach that the cause for misfortune or frustrations in life is the lack of ancestor veneration. Or the explanation given to their followers as instructions from the object of worship is that they "lack humility," "are too selfish," or "lack feelings of gratitude." In the first case divination, e.g., on the basis of one's surname, is performed, and in the latter case often some form of personal counseling or advice is given. In the case of personal counseling, problems are usually resolved by changing one's own attitude, a kind of "logic of substitution" (*surikae no ronri*) rather than by getting rid of some sort of evil curse. Many followers of the new religions resolve the impasses and frustrations in their lives not only by this "logic of substitution" but also through attaining a new sense of values and an incentive to renew their lives.[26]

WORLDLY BENEFITS AND THE RELIGION OF THE JAPANESE PEOPLE

We have taken a quick look at some of the types of worldly benefits offered by various religions such as Shinto, Buddhism, Shugendō, and the "new religions," and the ways they respond to the demand for such worldly benefits. As I suggested before, the Japanese have absorbed those various religions as appropriate and in accordance with their daily, personal needs. No contradiction is felt. It is considered a matter of course by most Japanese concerning religious activity that one visits a shrine on New Year's Day, goes to a Buddhist temple for equinoxes to visit the family grave, attends church on Christmas Day, and participates in a group pilgrimage sponsored by a new religion. There is the religion of the common people, and within this structure aspects of various religions have been absorbed.[27] Let us then take a look at the sorts of religious activity through which the common people attempt to fulfil their hope for their own worldly benefits by referring once again to the structure and categories proposed by Bellah.

First, let us examine the attempt to find direction to resolve problems in one's daily life through a supernatural power. The most general and common example of this type is the prayers to the supernatural Shinto and Buddhist deities (*shinbutsu*) for the smooth working out of one's daily existence. This would include *hatsumōde*, the first visit to a shrine of the New Year, or the daily morning and/or evening prayers in front of the family *kamidana* or Buddhist altar (*butsudan*). It is also common in Japan that certain deities are sought out and petitioned for certain purposes, such as a water deity for safe childbirth or Akiba to prevent fire, or Tenmangū for passing the entrance examinations for school, or Inari for success in business. To present these prayers one must purify oneself, solicit the deities with the presentation of offerings, pray for the smooth progress of one's daily life, and then send off the deities. Most shrines also sell charms (*fuda*) for prosperity in business or safety in the home. Prayer for smooth progress in one's life is offered at certain occasions and annual observances throughout the year. Festivals at field planting time or other celebratory occasions are good examples. Rites of passage, such as *shichi go san* (celebration for the seventh, fifth, and third years of a child), initiation, unlucky years (*yakudoshi*), and so forth are times when one prays for safe and smooth progress in one's daily life.

It goes without saying that anxiety for the future remains no matter how hard one may pray. It is at this point that divination plays a role. People seek guidance for their lives. This would include *omikuji* (a kind of written oracle), divination by physiognomy, palmistry, fortune-telling, analysis of one's surname, astrological divination, and recently even computer-assisted divination. Lucky and unlucky days, the geomancy of a house (*kasō*), divination of compatibility before marriage, and so forth are all ways of dealing with anxiety concerning the future. Such divination and fortune-telling assumes that there are set laws governing the universe, that human beings are subject to those laws, and that by knowing these laws one can predict one's future or fate.

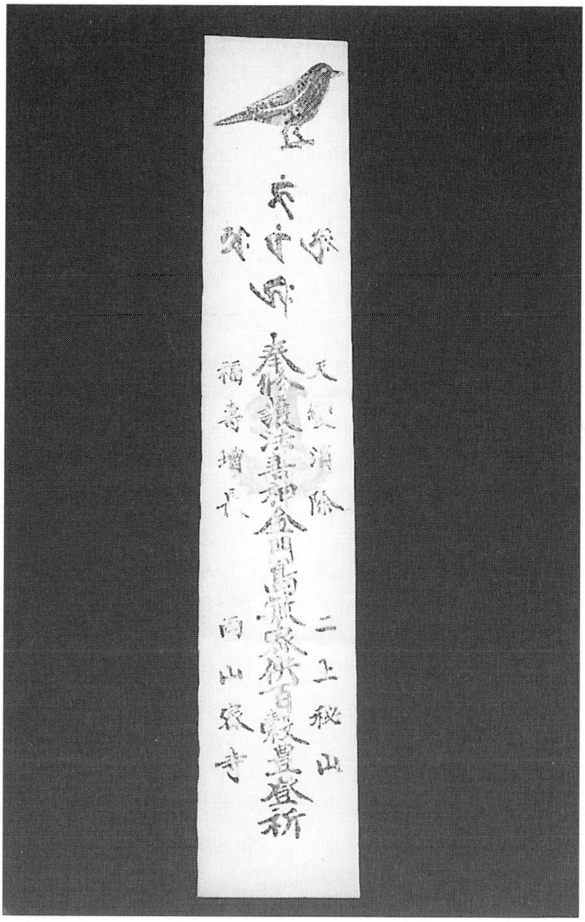

Figure 51. *Fuda* for a good harvest

Another type of divination is to invite spirits to possess someone and communicate through messages given at that time. The oracles given by shamanesses (*miko*) or roadside faith healers (*ogamiya*) are of this type. There are also special forms of divination that are called *yorigitō*. In these rituals, practitioners (mostly *shugenja*) use a medium as a means for possession by the deity, and then request an answer about the cause of the misfortune.

Then what method of supernatural salvation can handle the ultimate frustrations of everyday life that cannot be resolved by secular means? The most familiar method for the average person is to say a prayer at a shrine and/or a temple; in this case the appropriate place is determined by the person's personal preference. But if the person feels some anxiety, he or she will ask a priest to perform a special ritual. Let us take as an example the *goma* ritual of an esoteric Buddhist temple. The *goma* ritual is the practice of lighting a fire at a sacred fire altar prepared in front of the object of worship. This ritual is performed in four stages: *katendan* (ritual for Agni, the deity of fire), *yōshukudan* (ritual for star deities), *honzondan* (ritual for the main object of worship), and *setendan* (ritual for *deva*, or guardian deities).

The significance of these rituals is, first, that the practitioner invokes Agni (the messenger of heaven) and then asks the star deity of a client the cause of the person's misfortune. Following these rituals the practitioner invokes the main deity, and using its supernatural power, burns up the misfortune, and finally asks the *deva* to protect his client. So we can see in this ritual the elements of religious therapy: i.e., diagnosis, and the therapeutic prescription, as well as salvation and the theories about the origin of such evils and the ways to overcome them—as Bellah has phrased it.

It is a common experience that when the progress of everyday life comes to an impasse, a person wonders why he or she has come to such a situation. But often the person cannot find a good reason. At last he or she goes to a diviner, shamaness, or a practitioner of magical cures for a resolution of the problem. When a consultation is requested, these practitioners explain the supernatural cause of the misfortune, the method of resolution, and also the proper time and place for the appropriate ritual. Sometimes they threaten their client by explaining that the cause of misfortune is spirit possession or a curse, and indicate that the client must rely on their rite of exorcism.

For this reason rites of healing and "salvation" sometimes take the form of exorcism. The practitioner first, in his mind, becomes one with a higher deity such as Fudō Myōō; then he instructs the malevolent force or spirit of possession, and if necessary subdues it or drives it out. In this ritual the practitioner hits, cuts, beats, and burns the symbol of the devil

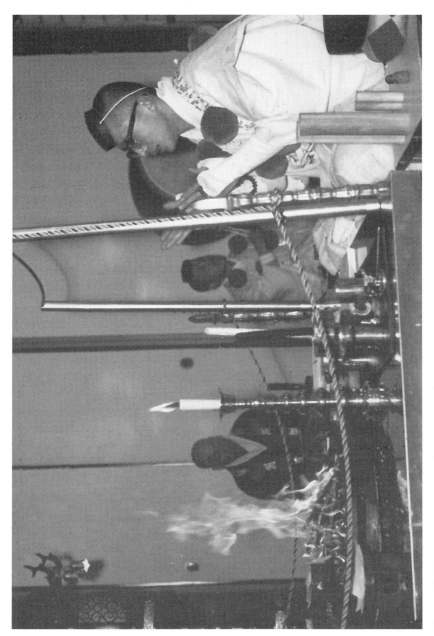

Figure 52. *Shugenja* performing the *goma* ritual

or possessing spirit and expels it from the client. Sometimes he uses amulets or magical means to prevent such sickness or misfortune from occurring.[28] Religious consultation is a fascinating spiritual technique that has been used by the Japanese people from ancient times. Formerly clients consulted priests and shamans about the cause of their troubles, and the supernatural means of resolving them.

In more recent times, new religions such as Risshō Kōsei Kai have adopted the technique of *hōza* (discussion circles), formed by a teacher of a new religion and his or her believers. In this technique, believers suffering from a personal problem (*nayami*) or misfortune confess their troubles to the circle members. Then the teacher explains that this misfortune is not simply an unfortunate situation, but actually the instruction of the deity that can lead a person in the right direction. Through this explanation the individual does not feel the suffering so much but recognizes the suggestion of the deity that takes into account the person's own bad deeds. Taking advantage of this opportunity, the person develops a strong belief that, even though misfortune has befallen him or her, the individual would like to live under the protection of a supernatural reality. The truth is that many urban middle-class and lower-class people are attracted to this logic of substitution (which interprets their misfortune as the instruction of the deity).[29]

The Religious Worldview Supporting the Acquisition of Worldly Benefits

What is the religious worldview that supports these religious rituals corresponding to the wishes and demands for worldly benefits? The reason these rituals become feasible is the fact that they make sense of everyday life within the greater framework of the entire cosmos. We can understand from the foregoing description the existence of the belief in supernatural realities, i.e., deities and buddhas, and also the law of the universe, spirits, and evil spirits. (I use these terms without explicit definition, as ruling over and influencing human destiny.)

What kinds of deities are these supernatural beings, and what are their mutual relationships? How do Japanese people accept this worldview? I will try to answer these questions through the methods of folklore, which seek to understand Japanese religion from the standpoint of popular believers and their actual practices rather than from the viewpoint of specific religious sects and their doctrines.

According to the folklore studies pioneered by Yanagita Kunio, everything in the universe has its own spirit, and human beings consist of both soul and body. After death the body rots away, but a person's soul exists forever. The soul continues in this state until the thirty-third memorial service of the person, as a "fresh" or new *hotoke* (Buddha or spirit of the dead) with its own individuality. After the thirty-third year it turns into a purified being and becomes a deity. Actually this is a kind of guardian deity that possesses the character of an ancestral deity. However, in order to become an ancestral deity, the soul of the dead must be worshipped by the deceased's descendants. The souls of the dead that are not able to become ancestors, as well as unworshipped deities and buddhas, turn into evil spirits and demons that bring misfortune.

But even these beings, if worshipped and honored by the people, can become guardian spirits and deities. Moreover, these benevolent supernatural beings—guardian spirits and souls of the dead—never act in an arbitrary fashion. These supernatural beings, humans, animals, and in fact all phenomena in the universe operate according to the rules that govern them.[30]

According to Bellah, Japanese religion has two basic ideas of deity. One is the superordinate being who gives people food, regulations, and love. The ancestor is this type of being, and a human's appropriate action toward this being is to show respect, gratitude, and to make repayment for benevolence.

Another basic idea is the deity who is the foundation of existence and the inner essence of reality. This notion is expressed in such terms as *michi* (or *dō*, way of life), and *busshō* (*buddhatā*, Buddha nature). The religious action appropriate for this deity is to identify oneself with this reality. That is to say, the two kinds of deities of Japanese religion are the superordinate being (which includes ancestral deities) and beings representing the foundation of existence. Accordingly, the religious action appropriate for these different realities are repayment of benevolence to the former, and identification or union with the latter.[31] This is another way of phrasing the religious thought of the Yanagita folklore school, which emphasizes the ancestral deities and angry evil spirits that are regulated by the law of the cosmos.

Takagi summarizes the characteristics of Japanese religion, focusing on the relationship between deities and humans, in four points:

> 1. There is an almost infinite number of deities that generally are called "gods and buddhas" (*shinbutsu*). Also, both the religious environment and the average person's religious actions are based on syncretism.
> 2. The relation between humans and the deities (gods and buddhas) is very ambiguous. Accordingly, gods and buddhas easily enter the human world, and humans are able to become either gods or buddhas.

3. Gods and buddhas bring worldly benefits to the person who is earnest in religious practice. However, if people do not engage in religious practices, gods and buddhas will bring them harm and evil (and if people neglect the gods and buddhas, they are punished by the gods and buddhas).

4. The worldly benefits of gods and buddhas are divided by their function and according to when people want new benefits as a result of the demands of their circumstances (an example is amulets for traffic safety after the introduction of the automobile).

In these four points Takagi points out the diversity and syncretism of the gods and buddhas, their proximity to human beings, and both their benefits that can be gained by worship and also their punishments that are brought on by the deficiency of worship; he also notes their functional character.[32] Even though Takagi's considerations are drawn mainly from materials of the new religions, we can find the same ideas in Yanagita's folklore and in Bellah's work: i.e., the gods and buddhas have a familiar relationship with human beings, bring worldly benefits when they are worshipped, but also cause harm and punishment if they are not worshipped. As we can see in the above description, the spirits, gods, and buddhas that have the character of ancestral spirits or ancestral gods usually protect people who are their descendants. When people need their blessing, if these deities are worshipped at the time of annual festivals and other prescribed times, they make people's lives go smoothly. If we use Takagi's phrase, they give "favor" (*okage*) to the people. It goes without saying that prayer sustains this worldview. But the spirits, gods, and buddhas that are ignored and left unworshipped become envious spirits and evil gods who get angry and bring injury and punishment to people. Almost all suffering, such as illness and accidents, results from the activities of these spiritual forces. Therefore, in order to get rid of such distress, it is necessary to identify the evil spirits and deities that caused the misfortune and then to worship them; or, by using the power of higher deities, to use persuasion or coercion and stop or expel these negative events. All incantation, prayer, and magic depend on this kind of religious worldview.

Incidentally, these spirits, deities, and buddhas all act in accordance with the rules that govern the cosmos. We can recognize such rules in the prescribed procedures of people and their attempts to identify with the supernatural being. In the former case of prescribed procedures, we are dealing with the worldview of divination, and in the latter case of identification with the supernatural being, it is the pattern of shamanistic practice. These methods are used both for the orientation of the people who worry about the future, and as the instruments of diagnosis for incantations and prayers.

The above mentioned worldview of worldly benefits presupposes the existence of the spirit world and the world of the deceased—in other words, an otherworld or future life that is different from the world of everyday life. But the spirits, buddhas, and deities that dwell in the world of the deceased or the future world exist in relationship to the everyday life in the present world. To put it in plain language, these spirits and deities exist to protect the life of this world, to explain everything in this framework, and also to explain the cause of misfortune and impasse. In a word, this religious worldview is centered in this world.

The Japanese people endeavor to live diligently. Fortunately, Japan's natural environment and the people's living conditions are not so severe as to negate their sincere efforts. The Japanese people have been able to eke out an existence through their exertions. Therefore, what makes life worth living is to gain a subsistence, however meager, and to live daily life safely. People consider this a happy life. Of course, they suffer hardship. And they utilize religious means, as mentioned above, in order to ameliorate this suffering. They presuppose the existence of another spiritual world in addition to the present world. But knowledge of an otherworld did not remove their dependence on a worldview centered on this world. Actually, the otherworld exists for the sake of the life of this world. The spirits and deities of the otherworld exist in order to protect the daily life of this world.

In conclusion, I would like to look again at the rituals that correspond to worldly benefit, because these constitute the wisdom of everyday life that emerged from the sincere activities of the Japanese people who prized above all the life of this world. In the background we can find the generous and bright worldview affirming the present world, which does not attempt to escape to the otherworld.

Of course in Japan there is also the worldview that is oriented to the otherworld—such as the pure land and the world of Maitreya—which in fact denies the reality of the worldview oriented to the present world. But we should remember that the worldview of otherworldly orientation only appeared at times when the small measure of happiness for the people was destroyed.

NOTES

1. For other studies on this term see Ikado Fujio, "Genze riyaku—sono ronri to shinri" (Worldly benefits—its logic and psychology), *Nihon bukkyō* 34 (1971):1–23. Fujii Masao, "Genze riyaku" (Worldly benefits), in *Girei no kōzō—Nihonjin no shūkyō* II (Structure of ritual—Japanese religion II), ed. Tamaru Noriyoshi, Muraoka Ku, and Miyata Noboru (Tokyo: Kōsei Shuppansha, 1972), 179–238. For the bibliography on *genze riyaku*, see Fujii Masao, Tamamuro Fumio, Miyake Hitoshi, Miyata Noboru, Kiuchi Gyōei, eds., "Genze riyaku kankei bunken mokuroku" (Catalogue of documents related to "worldly

benefits"), *Nihon bukkyō* 34 (1972):42–47. The first major work on this topic in English is Ian Reader and George J. Tanabe, Jr., *Practically Religious: Worldly Benefits and the Common Religion of Japan* (Honolulu: University of Hawaii Press, 1998).

2. Nihon Bukkyō Kenkyūkai, ed., *Nihon shūkyō no genze riyaku* (Worldly benefits in Japanese religion) (Tokyo: Daizō Shuppansha, 1970).

3. Nakamura Hajime, *Shin bukkyō jiten* (New dictionary of Buddhist terms) (Tokyo: Seishin Shobō, 1962), 150.

4. Mochizuki Shinkō, *Bukkyō daijiten* (Encyclopedia of Buddhism) (Tokyo: Hōzōkan, 1944), 1:973.

5. Tamamuro Taijō, *Sōshiki bukkyō* (Funeral Buddhism) (Tokyo: Daihō Rinkaku, 1963), 38.

6. Takagi Hiroo, *Shinkō shūkyō* (The new religions) (Tokyo: Kōdansha, 1958), 86.

7. Nakamura, *Shin bukkyō jiten*, 537.

8. It goes without saying that not all "indirect" and "latent" benefits are those that one obtains in the next world after death.

9. Yanagawa Keiichi, "Shūkyō shakaigaku ni okeru kinōshugi riron" (Functional theories in the sociology of religion), *Shūkyō kenkyū* 161 (1960):167.

10. Paul Tillich, *Dynamics of Faith* (New York: Harper and Brothers, 1957).

11. This position is taken by many scholars such as Paul Tillich, Talcott Parsons, Robert Bellah, Kishimoto Hideo, and Hori Ichirō.

12. Minami Hiroshi, *Taikei shakai shinrigaku* (The system of social psychology) (Tokyo: Kobunsha, 1957), 589.

13. Kishimoto Hideo, *Shūkyōgaku* (The study of religion) (Tokyo: Taimeidō, 1961), 37–41.

14. Robert N. Bellah, "The Systematic Study of Religion," in *Beyond Belief* (New York: Harper and Row, 1970), 260–72.

15. Ibid., 271.

16. For details see Nihon Bukkyō Kenkyūkai, *Nihon shūkyō*.

17. Hiraoka Yoshifumi, *Zōsaishiki tenpan* (Standard reference of Shinto ritual) (Tokyo: Kyōbunsha, 1938).

18. See Tamamuro Taijō, "Chibyō shūkyō no keifu" (The genealogy of religions of healing), *Nihon rekishi* 186 (1963):2–15.

19. Matsuno Junkō, "Shinshū no genze riyaku" (Worldly benefits in Shinshū), in *Nihon shūkyō*, ed. Nihon Bukkyō Kenkyūkai, 134–35.

20. Jitsuun, *Shoson yōsho*, no. 2484, in *Taishō shinshū daizōkyō*, vol. 9, *Zokushoshubu*, ed. Takakusu Junjirō (Tokyo: Taishō Issaikyō Kankōkai, 1930), 289.

21. See Kūkai's *Shōryōshū*, in *Sangōshiki*, vol. 9, ed. Watanabe Shōkō and Miyasaka Yushō, Nihon Koten Bungaku Taikei 71 (Tokyo: Iwanami Shoten, 1765), 386–87. A similar interpretation can be found in the *Makashikan* (*Mo ho chih kuan*) by the Tendai (T'ien-t'ai) priest Chigi (Chih-i), no. 1911, in *Taishō shinshū daizōkyō*, vol. 46, *Shoshubu*, general editor Takakusu Junjirō (Tokyo: Taishō Issaikyō Kankōkai, 1990), 3:102–9. According to Chih-i, the first step in treating disease is to clarify the causes for the disease. These causes can be any of six types: imbalance of the four elements, improper eating or drinking habits, improper practice of *zazen* meditation, disease caused by demons, disease caused by evil spirits, and disease caused by karma. Six types of prescriptions are available in accordance with the diagnosis of the causes: use of cessation-type meditation (*śamatha*), use of *ki* (vital energy), use of breathing practices, *kesō* (imagination), meditating on the mind, and "techniques (magic)." Thus, the mind is altered and finally one can perfect the stable mind of *śamatha-vipaśyanā*.

22. Miyake Hitoshi, "Shugendō to shomin seikatsu—Shugen jinpi gyōhō fujushū o chūshin to shite" (Shugendō in the life of the common people), in *Sangaku shūkyō to minkan shinkō no kenkyū*, ed. Sakurai Tokutarō, Sangaku Shūkyōshi Kenkyū Sōsho 6 (Tokyo: Meicho Shuppan, 1976), 204–30. See chapter 5 of the present work for a detailed analysis of *kirigami*.

23. Miyake Hitoshi, *Shugendō girei no kenkyū*, 2d ed., rev. (A study of religious rituals in Shugendō) (Tokyo: Shunjūsha, 1985), 664–78.

24. Oguri Junko, *Nihon kindai shakai to Tenrikyō* (Tenrikyō and modern Japanese society) (Tokyo: Hyōronsha, 1969), 51–65.

25. Tsurufuji Ikuta, *Risshō Kōsei Kai no shinkō* (The faith of Risshō Kōsei Kai) (Tokyo: Kuretake Shobō, 1954), 1–9.

26. Takagi Hiroo, *Shinkō shūkyō* (New religions) (Tokyo: Kōdansha, 1958), 158–60.

27. Miyake Hitoshi, "Shūkyō no shakaigaku" (The sociology of religion), in *Nihon shūkyō no kōzō* (The structure of Japanese religion) (Tokyo: Keiō Tsūshin, 1974), 166–69.

28. Miyake, *Shugendō girei no kenkyū*, 443–510. See chapter 5, above, for a more complete treatment of exorcism.

29. Helen Hardacre, "Hoza: Dharma Seat," in *Japanese Buddhism: Its Traditions, New Religions and Interaction with Christianity*, ed. Minoru Kiyota (Los Angeles-Tokyo: Buddhist Books International, 1987).

30. Yanagita Kunio, *About Our Ancestors*, trans. Fanny Hagin Mayer and Ishiwara Yasuyo (Tokyo: Society for Promotion of Science, 1970).

31. Robert N. Bellah, *Tokugawa Religion: The Values of Pre-industrial Japan* (Glencoe, Ill.: Free Press, 1957).

32. Takagi, *Shinkō shūkyō*, 80.

Revitalization of Traditional Religion

New Religions and Traditional Religions

New religions have emerged one after another amid the social upheavals from the late Tokugawa period until the present day.[1] They have attracted wide public attention as well as academic interest because of their unique teachings based on the founders' personal religious experiences, their acceptance among the lower strata of society and their corresponding mass movements, and their strong organizational structures. As is well known, these new religions have gained great influence in the Japanese religious world by offering salvation to people afflicted with the feelings of alienation and deprivation in an industrialized society.

Generally speaking, the salvation offered by new religions takes two different directions. One direction affirms industrialization and teaches salvation in pursuing modern ideas such as humanism, equality, and peace. The other direction stresses negative aspects of industrialization such as alienation, and offers spiritual salvation elsewhere. In the former case the focus of salvation is our human-centered world; by contrast, in the latter case the focus of salvation is a quest in the distant future—including the next life or in the past, and in the natural or supernatural world in space. To put it more concretely, the orientation to the future is discernible in messianism or eschatology, and that to the past in the emphasis of relations to traditional folk belief, Shinto, and Buddhism. The orientation to the supernatural world manifests itself as mysticism and shamanism.

As scholars have often noted, orientations to such ideas as humanism, eschatology, traditionalism, and shamanism are observed in most of the new religions. It is not rare for a new religion to start with a strong orientation to messianism or shamanism that is critical of industrialization. After the new religion's organization expands, however, it will often begin to emphasize humanism and peace along with an acceptance of industrialization.[2]

These new religions can be classified roughly into two groups according to the above-mentioned orientations. Among the religions placing a high value upon modern humanism are large organizations such as Risshō Kōsei Kai, Sōka Gakkai, PL Kyōdan, and Ōmotokyō. Among the religions with an anti-industrialization orientation, Genri Undō (known as the Unification Church of Reverend Moon), Jehovah's Witnesses, and Iesu-no-Hakobune are all strongly tinged with eschatology. Religions emphasizing a close relationship to traditional religions include Kōdō Kyōdan, which is related to the Tendai sect of Buddhism, and Shinnyoen, Gedatsukai, and Agonshū—all of which are related to the Shingon sect of Buddhism. GLA, Shinreikyō, and Mahikari Kyōdan can be cited as religions having a strong tendency to mysticism and shamanism. However, it is no simple task to classify these religions into distinct categories. Eschatology-oriented or tradition-oriented religions have a strong inherent tendency to mysticism.[3]

In the study of these new religions, attention has focused mainly on the large organizations that have expanded in conjunction with the industrialization of Japan. Examples of the study of large-scale new religions are the numerous reports that have been published on (1) Tenrikyō and Konkōkyō, both of which have the longest history among the new religions dating back to the closing years of the Tokugawa period; on (2) Ōmotokyō and Hito no Michi (PL), which gained great influence after World War I; and on (3) Risshō Kōsei Kai and Sōka Gakkai, which have expanded remarkably since World War II. In contrast, study of the new religions oriented toward anti-industrialization, as classified in the present paper, has been somewhat neglected. Only in recent years has attention begun to be paid to the Christianity-based, messianism-oriented new religions such as Genri Undō and Iesu-no-Hakobune, or ones with occult tendencies such as GLA and Mahikari Kyōdan.[4] Tradition-oriented new religions are still almost unstudied, probably because they lack novelty. It is essential also to pay attention to such new religions that are forms of the revitalization of traditional religious teachings.

"Traditional religion" here refers to the religion formed and developed by the Japanese people over a long span of time, and with which the Japanese people feel emotional familiarity. Today what is generally considered traditional Japanese religion is the pattern that was formed between the Muromachi period and the Azuchi-Momoyama period (fifteenth to sixteenth century A.D.) and was supported and maintained mainly in agrarian communities. This religious heritage included three main practices: worship of the guardian deity of the community, ancestor worship, and incantations and prayers. These three activities represent the aspirations of common people for protection, for repose for the souls of the deceased, and for the desire to avoid misfortune. Therefore, Buddhist and Shinto priests often performed rites of exorcism.

What lies at the root of such traditional Japanese religion is belief in *kami* or animism, as has been noted by many scholars. The awe and reverence for the spirits of all natural objects or living beings, and for the souls of dead persons (including ancestors), formed the core of Japanese religious thought. Many people believed that if, after their death, services were carried out in their honor by the priests of their family temples or by their descendants, their souls would be purified, enabling them to become benevolent spirits who could protect their descendants; therefore, they harbored strong desires to become such purified spirits. It was believed that if the dead were not honored properly, they would become malevolent, vengeful spirits (*goryō*), bringing harm and trouble to people. People asked exorcists to identify the causes of such misfortunes and drive the evil forces out. Such belief in guardian spirits and malevolent spirits is the major content of traditional Japanese religion.

After the Meiji Restoration, State Shinto was formed on the basis of the emperor system as represented in the Ise Shrine and the creation of the Yasukuni Shrine.[5] Through school and social education, this ideology became all-pervasive. At the same time, traditional religious practices— such as the worship of tutelary deities, ancestor worship, and supplication rituals seeking this-worldly benefits—were not forgotten.

After the end of the Second World War, however, State Shinto collapsed, and many traditional religious practices lost their place among the people. Amid such circumstances, the tradition-oriented new religious movements continue to actively support traditional religion by teaching their followers to worship at the household shrine or Buddhist altar, visit their family temples, or hold services to appease malevolent spirits who are thought to cause misfortune in the absence of such services. The traditional religious teachings as revitalized in the new religions take somewhat different form. The new religions are reviving the traditional teachings, using logical arguments to convince their followers instead of the past practice of "rote" teaching. It seems that an answer to the query of what traditional Japanese religions will be in the future may be found in the way traditional teachings are being revived in these new religions. In other words, study of tradition-oriented new religions is significant not only because it fills in a neglected gap in the study of new religions, but also because it may hold clues to the reexamination of the course traditional religions in Japan will take in the future.

With this in mind, I conducted a joint research project with H. Byron Earhart and a team of graduate students, taking Gedatsukai as an example of a tradition-oriented new religion. We examined how teachings of traditional Japanese religion were being revitalized in Gedatsukai and also uncovered the matrix for the revitalization, from such diverse viewpoints as history, sociology, and psychology. Partial results of this study were published (in Japanese) in 1983 in a volume of essays entitled *Dentōteki shūkyō no saisei—Gedatsukai no shisō to kodō* (Revitalization of Traditional Religion—Belief and Practice of Gedatsukai).[6] The next section reports on another dimension of the joint study, with special attention to the way traditional religious teachings have been revitalized in Gedatsukai.

OUTLINE OF GEDATSUKAI[7]

Gedatsukai was started in 1929 by Okano Eizō (Seiken) in his native village of Kitamoto City, Saitama Prefecture. Okano (1881–1948), who had established himself as a successful businessman in the marine transportation business, had a mystical experience during a critical illness when he drank hydrangea tea, and this experience led to the founding of Gedatsukai. It is a layman-based, tradition-oriented religion influenced by folk beliefs, Shinto, esoteric Buddhism, and Shugendō. Its pilgrimage center and Sacred Land (Goreichi) are in Kitamoto City, with the administrative main office at Araki-chō, Shinjuku-ku, in Tokyo.

The founder, Okano Eizō, was born the second son of Okano Makitarō and Okano Kise at Kitamotojuku, Nakamaru-mura, Kita-adachi-gun, Saitama Prefecture. The Okano family was a well-respected family that served for generations as the village representative both for the Tenmantenjin Shrine enshrining the tutelary deity of the village, and also for the family's parish temple Tamonji (Shingon sect). After graduation from primary school, Okano was apprenticed to a sake dealer in Tokyo, but in 1895 he returned home and started a weaving machine leasing business. The business failed and he ran away from his village to Korea. After wandering through Korea, he returned home and founded an association of villagers for joint distribution of drapery. For some time the business was successful, but it too failed, forcing him once more to leave Kitamoto. He went to Tokyo, where he led a wandering life. Early in the Taishō period he began working in the office of a marine transport agent, and became the chief clerk of the shop. Later, he left the shop to establish Hokkai Kyōdō Kumiai (Hokkai Shipping Company), his own marine transportation agency, which eventually was successful. In those prosperous days he worked hard for the interests of his native village, donating fertilizer to the farmers living there, and working for the opening of the Kitamoto Station on the Takasaki railway line.

In 1925, after contracting a severe case of pneumonia, he hovered between life and death. Given a drink of hydrangea tea (*amacha*)[8] by his mother, he underwent a mystical experience, and was brought back from the brink of death. He came to possess a mysterious power after the experience, and took up religious activities such as making pilgrimages to shrines and temples, and associating with ascetic devotees. In 1929, at Kitamotojuku inside a small shrine (the present Tenjin Chigi Shrine) in which the deity Ama no Tajikarao no Mikoto[9] was enshrined, he had a revelation. This deity ordered him to found Gedatsukai. In another experience of inspiration he discovered a *Daranikyō* (Skt. *Dhāraṇī sūtra*) inside the Hōkyōintō (pagoda[10]) in the precinct of Tamonji, in Kitamotojuku. Later, in 1930, Gedatsukai was officially founded in Okano's own house at Araki-chō, Shinjuku-ku, Tokyo, which became the headquarters. In those days Okano formulated the doctrine of Gedatsukai by referring to the doctrine of the Moralogy sect.[11] He also took the Buddhist tonsure at Daigo Sanbōin (Shingon sect), and by registering Gedatsukai as a branch organization of Daigo Sanbōin, he obtained legal recognition for Gedatsukai activities. Later, he was influenced by the teachings of a Shinto sect, Amatsukyō.[12]

By 1937 Okano developed the foundation of the organization, establishing the teaching of the Five Principles (*Gohō soku*), fixing the services at the Sacred Land (pilgrimage center), constructing facilities such as the All Souls' Festival Tower, (Yorozu Mitama Matsuri Tō, "tower for the repose of all souls"), and publishing a monthly journal to solidify the belief of his followers. However, because at the time inspiration-based activities were banned, Gedatsukai came to have a mountain ascetic character under the guidance of the legally recognized Buddhist group Daigo Sanbōin. As World War II broke out, the organization was actively engaged in efforts in line with or supporting the national policy, such as the erection of the Dainippon Seishinhi ("great Japan spirit monument," presently the Sun Spirit Monument), pilgrimages to the three sacred sites of Ise Shrine, Kashihara Shrine, and Sennyūji,[13] visits to children of dead soldiers for consolation, and war donations. After the end of the war, Okano worked to help his followers economically; in 1948 he passed away. With the posthumous name of Gedatsu Kongō, his remains were consigned to Gedatsu Kongō Hōtō (treasure tower) in the compound of Sennyūji.

After the death of the founder, Okano Shōhō, a son of the founder's nephew, succeeded him as spiritual leader of the organization. Administratively, it was managed by a group of councilors with Nagata Hideaki as leader. In 1962 Kishida Eizan became the top administrative leader, and under his direction, Gedatsukai refined its doctrine and religious observances and its membership. With the death of the dynamic leader Kishida late in 1981, Gedatsukai was faced with a new situation. After Kishida's death, Gedatsukai's expansion of branches and members has continued, but at a slower pace.

Gedatsukai worships three divinities: Tenjin Chigi Ōmikami (Divine God of Heaven and Earth), which is the deification of the life of the universe; Gochi Nyorai (the *tathāgatas*, the five wisdoms), which represents the working of the Tenjin Chigi Ōmikami; and Gedatsu Kongō (literally the *nirvāṇa vajra* or diamond man liberated from worldly attachment) as the spirit of the late founder Okano Seiken. Tenjin Chigi Ōmikami is enshrined in the Tenjin Chigi Shrine at the Sacred Land, and to its left are the Gorin Hōtō (five-storied pagoda) dedicated to Gedatsu Kongō, and the Gochi Nyoraidō (temple). These three divinities are enshrined also at individual training halls, branch offices, and homes of believers. At the Sacred Land there are also the All Souls' Festival Tower, the Shrine of Goshugo Ōkami in six forms (great god in six forms for protection), and the Roku Jizō (Jizō of the six states of existence). The nucleus of the doctrine is *Misatoshi* (Admonition) written by the founder and published in 1942, which makes up the most important part of the canon of Gedatsukai, *Shinkō* (True Deeds).[14] Also the *Hannya shingyō* is taken as the basic scripture, and it is chanted at the morning and evening services.

Important rituals include (1) the "service of hydrangea tea" (*amacha kuyō*) for the repose of souls of the deceased, including those with and without surviving relatives; (2) "purification" (*hihō* mediation or *okiyome*); and (3) the "meditation of five principles" (*gohō shugyō*[15]). These are called collectively the "three secret rites." Adherents of Gedatsukai perform these rites as occasion requires: for the repose of souls of the dead, for salvation, and for their spiritual development.

Important annual observances in which all adherents of Gedatsukai are expected to participate include the festival commemorating the establishment of the Sun Spirit Monument held on February 11; the pilgrimage to the three sacred sites of Ise Shrine, Kashihara Shrine, and Sennyūji in the period from April 1 to 3; the Spring Grand Festival of May 7 and 8; the Autumn Grand Festival of October 9 and 10; the Gedatsu Kongō Memorial held on November 4, the date of the founder's death; and the Gedatsu Kongō Birth Festival of November 28. All these events are held at the Sacred Land, except for the pilgrimage to the three sacred sites, and the Gedatsu Kongō Anniversary that is held in front of the Gedatsu Kongō Hōtō at Sennyūji.

As of 1995, Gedatsukai is managed by Okano Shōhō as spiritual leader, and the administrative leader Okano Takenori, an adopted child of the founder. Gedatsukai divides Japan into 33 parishes, and has 6 training centers supervised directly by the headquarters, 382 branches, and 8 gathering places. There are 474 ministers and about 225,000 followers according to 1995 statistics.[16] Local branches play a very important role in Gedatsukai activities. At each branch, a thanksgiving service (*kanshasai*) is held once a month, when the three sacred rites are performed, and counseling by the branch leaders is also provided.

In the United States there is a Gedatsukai Church of America. Gedatsukai activities in the U.S. began in an internment camp of Japanese Americans during World War II, led by Ine Kiyota who had been taught by the founder. Later, the Gedatsukai Church of America was officially founded by Kishida Eizan.[17]

TRADITIONALISM

As can be seen from the foregoing outline, Gedatsukai is deeply imbued with traditional religion. Specifically, one should first note that the founder Okano Seiken grew up under the strong influence of traditional religion. He was born as the second son of the Okano family, a respected and well established family which for generations served as the representative of villagers for both the village shrine and temple. His grandfather and also his elder brother made pilgrimages to Ise Shrine. His father was a *sendatsu* (leader) of a *fuji-kō*, a fraternity of the traditional Mt. Fuji worshippers. He himself seems to have had a deep belief in traditional religion, as can be seen in events that took place while he was wandering around Tokyo after the failure of his business. He frequently returned from Tokyo to Kitamotojuku late at night to worship at the village shrine and temple and at his ancestors' graves. Traditional religion must have been a great spiritual support for him in those days of adversity.

During the period between his mystical experience at the time of his serious illness in 1925, and the start of Gedatsukai in 1929, he underwent religious training at various shrines, temples, and in the mountains, and he associated with many ascetic devotees. In other words, he lived a life of spiritual seeking during that period. He carried out religious training in the Tanzawa Mountain area of Kanagawa Prefecture, and the shrines and temples he visited included the Izusan Shrine, Hikawa Shrine at Ōmiya, Tsurugaoka Hachiman Shrine, Toyokawa Inari Shrine, Fushimi Inari Shrine, Benzaiten Shrine at Ueno Shinobazunoike, and Benzaiten Shrine at Shakujii. He associated with traditional religious spiritualists, such as Shimada Kenshō of the Nichiren sect. Therefore, during the almost five-year period between his first mystical experience and the start of Gedatsukai, Okano had many active contacts with traditional religion.

It was inside a small shrine at Kitamotojuku in 1929 where he experienced the divine revelation urging him to found Gedatsukai, and the founding was supported by the discovery of a *Daranikyō* (*Dhāraṇī sūtra*) inside the Hōkyōintō (stone pagoda containing the *Dhāraṇī sūtra*) of Tamonji Temple. For a time Gedatsukai became a subsidiary organization of the Daigo school of the Buddhist Shingon sect, in order to obtain legal recognition. Okano also sought contact with Amatsukyō, which considered itself a traditional Shinto sect. As seen from these examples, even after the foundation of Gedatsukai, Okano maintained relations with various traditional religions.

When the first Grand Festival was conducted at the Sacred Land in May 1931, Okano's followers visited and paid homage at Tenmantenjin Shrine, Tamonji, and the Okano family grave. Okano also urged members to visit shrines of their tutelary deities and their family temples, and to worship at their household Shinto and Buddhist altars. After World War II broke out, in 1940, when Japan celebrated the 2,600th anniversary of the founding of the nation, Okano erected a monument in celebration of that anniversary (the present Sun Spirit Monument). The next year he initiated the pilgrimage to the three sacred sites. After his death, in accordance with his dying wish that his spirit be devoted to the service of the founder of the imperial family and the imperial ancestors, he was enshrined in the Gedatsu Kongō Hōtō in the temple compound of Sennyūji. This shows that Okano's activities during the war period expressed a strong inclination toward traditional religion, including worship of the emperor and State Shinto.

The total configuration of facilities at the Sacred Land, designed by the founder Okano Seiken himself, represents three parts, as shown in figure 53. This configuration also illustrates the elements of traditional religion. The left part (west) is a forest that resembles the grove of a tutelary shrine. On the far left are the facilities dedicated to the major divinities worshipped by Gedatsukai: the Tenjin Chigi Shrine, the Shōtokuhi (monument in honor of the late founder's virtues), the Gorin Hōtō, the All Souls' Festival Tower, the Gochi Nyoraidō, and the Goshugo Ōkami Shrine. Here important rituals of Gedatsukai, such as the spring and autumn grand festivals, are performed. To the right of the tutelary shrine's grove-like forest is a road, and the area between the road and the Takasaki railway line is a field where stands the Gedatsu Kongō Memorial House (in which the founder lived his last years), the Museum of Gedatsu Kongō, and the training facilities. This is the site where believers come to cherish the memory of the founder and learn his teachings and sacred rites. These two areas can be considered the holy realm related directly to Gedatsukai.

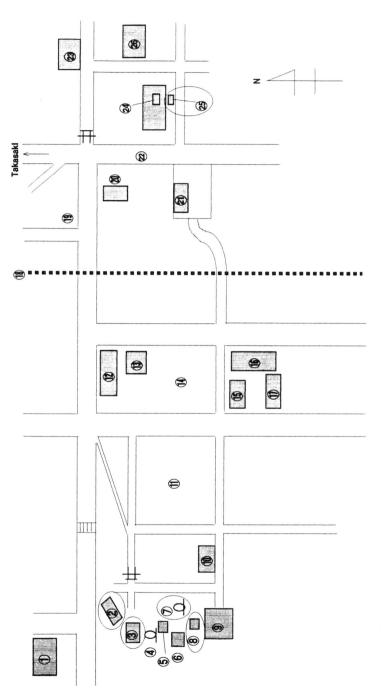

Figure 53. Configuration of facilities at the Sacred Land: 1. Training Center, 2. Goshugo Ōkami (Great Tutelary God) Shrine, 3. Tenjin Chigi Shrine, 4. Shōtokuhi (memorial monument), 5. Gorin Hōtō (pagoda), 6. Jyakkōkutsu (cave), 7. Yorozu Mitama Matsuri Tō (All Souls' Festival Tower), 8. Gochi Nyoraidō (temple), 9. Training Hall, 10. Roku Jizō (Six Jizō), 11. Forest, 12. Gedatsu Kongō Memorial House, 13. Museum of Gedatsu Kongō, 14. Field, 15. Spiritual Training Building, 16. Study Center 1, 17. Study Center 2, 18. Takasaki Railway Line, 19. Town Area, 20. Dainippon Seishinhi (Sun Spirit Monument), 21. Birth House of the Founder, 22. Nakasendō (highway), 23. Tenmantenjin Shrine, 24. Okano Family Grave, 25. Hōkyōintō (stone pagoda containing *Dhāraṇī sūtra*), 26. Main Hall of Tamonji (temple)

In the town area between the Takasaki railway line and the Nakasendō (highway), we find the Sun Spirit Monument and the house where the founder was born. In the wooded area at the right side of the Nakasendō are the Tenmantenjin Shrine enshrining the tutelary god, the family temple Tamonji, and the Okano family grave. Therefore, this area at the right of the Takasaki railway line can be regarded as representing the traditional religion that influenced the founder.

Analysis of the spatial structure of the Sacred Land reveals that various elements of traditional religion are found therein. First, in the forest at the left side that resembles the grove of a tutelary shrine, there are the Shinto elements exemplified by Tenjin Chigi Shrine and the Goshugo Ōkami Shrine, both dedicated to Gedatsukai's own gods, and also the Buddhist elements seen in Gochi Nyoraidō and the Roku Jizō[18] in the Rokudō. As I will show in a following section, Gedatsukai gives its own interpretation to these constructions and divinities, but the scenery is that of traditional religion. On the other side of the Sacred Land, the facilities observed at the right of the Takasaki railway line, such as the Tenmantenjin Shrine, Tamonji, the Okano family grave, the house of the founder's birth (main family or *honke*) and the Sun Spirit Monument, are all related to the elements of traditional religion.

In the spatial landscape, the line from the right (east) to the left (west), i.e., the line starting with and passing through the area containing the tutelary shrine, temple, graveyard, main family house, and the Sun Spirit Monument, and finally reaching the Tenjin Chigi Shrine *via* the training facilities, represents the development in the faith of the founder. The movement from left to right appears to suggest that the present activities of Gedatsukai allow its followers to come into contact with traditional religion through exposure to the teachings of Gedatsukai.

The spring and autumn grand festivals of Gedatsukai held at the Sacred Land resemble the spring and autumn festivals of villages. Several observances give adherents opportunity to confirm the traditional national spirit: the festival commemorating the erection of the Sun Spirit Monument held on the National Founding Day, February 11; the pilgrimage to the three sacred sites of Ise Shrine, Kashihara Shrine, and Sennyūji; and the joint memorial service on behalf of the departed adherents at the Gedatsu Kongō Hōtō on the occasion of the Gedatsu Kongō Anniversary. In addition, quite a few group activities at local branches of Gedatsukai are related to traditional religion, such as the cleaning of tutelary shrines and the visitation at traditional shrines and temples. Furthermore, Gedatsukai urges individual followers to visit tutelary shrines and family temples, and to worship at household Shinto and Buddhist altars. Its doctrine is also colored

Figure 54. Goshugo Ōkami

Figure 55. Tenjin Chigi Shrine

Figure 56. Gochi Nyoraidō

Figure 57. Hōkyōintō

deeply with the hues of traditional religion, teaching the importance of worshipping the tutelary deity and the ancestors, and of repaying the favors provided by the nation, parents, teachers, society, and the universe.

As a matter of fact, our survey, conducted in 1979 by distributing questionnaires to Gedatsukai adherents (5,667 samples out of the total 220,680 adherents), revealed that after they became Gedatsukai members, they participated more positively in traditional religious practices than before. Worship before a household Shinto altar was practiced by 85.97% of the respondents (as against 55.1% before they became Gedatsukai members; hereafter figures in parenthesis represent statistics before they became Gedatsukai members); worship before a household Buddhist altar was performed by 86.8% (66.8%); visitation to the tutelary shrine was undertaken by 88.5% (63.3%); visitation to one's family temple by 74.0% (57.7%); possession of a picture of the imperial family by 24.0% (20.4%); pilgrimage to Ise Shrine by 44.2% (22.8%); and pilgrimage to Yasukuni Shrine by 24.5% (17.6%).[19]

GOING BEYOND TRADITION

As we have seen in the preceding sections, the various influences of traditional religion are quite obvious in the words and deeds of the founder, the spatial structure of the Sacred Land, and in the rituals and the teachings of Gedatsukai. They constitute important elements of Gedatsukai. Closer examination reveals, however, that Gedatsukai does not adopt such traditional religious teachings and practices exactly as they are, but modifies them and throws new light on the old teachings and practices. In other words, Gedatsukai reinterprets traditional religious teachings and practices from a novel viewpoint and resystematizes them when incorporating them into Gedatsukai's own system. The following discussion explores how the founder adopted traditional religion and resystematized its teachings and practices.

It was the mystical experience Okano had when he drank hydrangea tea at the time of his critical illness that led him to begin a new life as a teacher of religion. Okano later said that, while in the coma, he traveled to another world where he met his father and grandfather, and through their guidance he met Shaka Nyorai (Śākyamuni Tathāgata, i.e., the Buddha) who gave him a gold-colored fluid. Upon drinking it, he had a feeling as if everything were squeezed out of his body. In fact, at that time he vomited a great deal as if all the poisonous matter was squeezed out of him, and in that way he recovered from the illness. After that experience, he set out on a life of religious seeking, which may be interpreted as his quest for the confirmation of his mystical experience. He sought contacts with ascetic devotees of traditional religion, and came into close relationship with the Moralogy and Amatsukyō movements. The conclusion he reached after all his religious seeking was, in short, that a person can reach a state of unity with God after the person humbles himself or herself and seeks communion with God.

The chief deities of Gedatsukai are Tenjin Chigi Ōmikami and Gochi Nyorai (who is viewed as representing the actual function of Tenjin Chigi Ōmikami). In Gedatsukai's basic teaching *Shinkō*, Tenjin Chigi Ōmikami is explained as the law governing the whole universe and the cause for the generation and development of everything, both good or bad. This explication of Gochi Nyorai as a working manifestation of Tenjin Chigi Ōmikami suggests that Dainichi Nyorai of esoteric Buddhism is its prototype. However, as described above, Gedatsukai adds a new meaning thereto in order to create its own interpretation. Also, the Goshugo Ōkami in six forms, which are the dependents of the chief deity, represent Gedatsukai's own explanation of deities of traditional religion, such as *tengu*, Inari, and Benzaiten. Another object for worship by Gedatsukai is Gedatsu Kongō, or the spirit of the founder. At the Sacred Land there are the Shōtokuhi and the Gorin Hōtō representing the essence of the founder.

Let us look closely again at the configuration of facilities at the Sacred Land. With the founder's Shōtokuhi and Gorin Hōtō at the center, one sees the Tenjin Chigi Shrine and Goshugo Ōkami Shrine. These Shinto-styled shrines located on one side are related to life. On the other side, one sees the death-related Buddhist constructions of Jyakkōkutsu, Gochi Nyoraidō, All Souls' Festival Tower, and Roku Jizō. This configuration may suggest Gedatsukai's interpretation of the universe with the founder at the center.

A new member of Gedatsukai is first urged to write a letter of apology to the tutelary god in whom he or she has had faith so far, apologizing for the sins committed in the past, and stating his or her desire to withdraw the previous supplicatory prayers that were presented out of selfishness. This apology is directed to the tutelary god, who is believed to pass the message on to all gods. Then, it is believed, all these gods, and eventually the Tenjin Chigi Ōmikami, who is the source of all these gods, accepts the apology and thereafter protects the person. The gods who have come to protect the Gedatsukai adherents after such a procedure are called faith-related guardian gods (*shinkō kankei shugoshin*).

A human consists of flesh and soul, according to Gedatsukai's view. One part of the soul (*kon*) is expounded as the internal representation of the cosmic life. The other part of the soul (*haku*) appears as a human character that is divided into six parts. Before a person practices spiritual exercises, his or her character is composed of the six qualities as described in the left column of table 2. He or she can improve this character so that it includes the qualities shown in the right column by transporting the soul to the Sacred Land by means of the individual's guardian god and letting the soul undergo spiritual exercise under the guidance of Goshugo Ōkami, as indicated in the central column of the table. He or she must do this while observing moral principles in daily life. By improving oneself in this way and by praying to the Tenjin Chigi Ōmikami by means of the faith-related guardian god, Gedatsukai teaches that one is given divine protection for one's life. The tutelary god, who is the nucleus of traditional religion, is given the role of mediator to connect individual human beings to the universal god, Tenjin Chigi Ōmikami. Through the intermediation of the tutelary deity, a person is forgiven sins if he or she repents of them. Through the guidance of the tutelary god, the human soul is led to the Sacred Land where it achieves improvement under the direction of Goshugo Ōkami.[20]

Gedatsukai expounds on the causes of misfortunes and the ways to obviate them as follows. Misfortunes are caused by the spirits to whom the letter has not been submitted apologizing for past sins and declaring withdrawal of selfish supplications, or by the souls of dead persons who have not been memorialized because they lack surviving relatives (*muenrei*). Gedatsukai adherents identify (mainly by the *gohō* meditation) which spirits or souls are bringing misfortunes and why. The *gohō* meditation resembles the traditional prayer of possession *yorigitō* where misfortune was believed to be caused by the sufferer being possessed or cursed by a malevolent spirit. The exorcist then tried to identify the cause of the misfortune and change the location of possession from the sufferer to some other receptor. In the case of *gohō* meditation, the meditator (the Gedatsukai believer) holds a talisman (*reifu*) between both palms and discovers through his or her body's movements the reason for the misfortune caused by the vengeful spirit. The *reifu* is believed to generate a holy power that guides the spirit to the person's body and pacifies it. This *reifu*, on which is written the "seed" of Gochi Nyorai, was discovered by the founder through his mystical experience. At present the *hosshu* (archbishop) of Gedatsukai inscribes the seed of Gochi Nyorai on each *reifu* and presents it to each follower. Here also we see how Gedatsukai has adapted the practice of traditional religion and created its own practice for driving out bad fortune.[21]

When the spirit causing the misfortune is identified in this way, the suffering person tries to propitiate the spirit by submitting a letter of apology

Table 2   Goshugo Ōkami and the Soul

Soul before practice	Goshugo Ōkami	Subordinate	Soul after practice
Arrogance	Amegoshiki Daitenkū Ōkami	Tengu	Nobleness
Misused talent	Amekokuzō Itsuhashira Inari Ōkami	Fox	Wisdom
Vindictiveness	Amegoshiki Benzaiten	Snake	Tolerance
Idleness	Ameōkuninushi Ōkami	Cat	Bring in fortune
Narrow-mindedness	Sansha Ōguchishin Ōkami	Wolf	Honesty
Looseness	Santoku Daimyōjin	Badger	Virtuous talent

Figure 58. *Gohō* meditation

and performing the *amacha kuyō*. This is called *anrei* or spirit propitiation in Gedatsukai. The *amacha kuyō* is derived from the belief that the hydrangea tea rescued the founder from death, and it is believed to have the holy power to purify spirits not yet resting in peace. There are several ways to perform *amacha kuyō*: pouring the tea over a *kuyō fuda* (memorial name tablet); offering the tea to the gods; and spreading the tea over places where malevolent spirits are supposed to be present, such as ancient graveyard sites, battlefields, and shrines. The most general form of *amacha kuyō*, practiced in Gedatsukai adherents' households, is to pour the tea over the *kuyō fuda* of the souls of one's ancestors, and of dead persons who have no surviving relatives but apparently had some relationship with one's ancestors. The hydrangea tea service is performed at local branches, training halls, and the headquarters, as well as at the households of Gedatsukai adherents.

The most impressive *amacha kuyō* is performed at the All Souls' Festival Tower at the Sacred Land on the occasion of the grand festivals held twice a year, in the spring and autumn. This service, attended by a large number of adherents as well as the leaders of Gedatsukai, is designed to appease all the spirits considered to be causing evil (according to the petitions of Gedatsukai adherents across the country). The spring and autumn grand festivals are celebrated mostly in front of the Tenjin Chigi Shrine, and the scene of the festival is reminiscent of the festival of a tutelary deity. However, the climax of the festival is the *amacha kuyō* at the All Souls' Festival Tower. Therefore, the main purpose of the spring and autumn festivals can be understood as driving out bad fortune and bringing in good fortune by what Gedatsukai calls *anrei*.[22]

As described above, Gedatsukai's service for driving out bad fortune and bringing in the good has each adherent utilize his or her own body in the *gohō* meditation in order to identify the spirit causing the misfortune. All members perform their own services to appease the spirit; this is different from similar practices of traditional religion where the service was entrusted to professional persons such as Buddhist monks and mountain ascetics. Gedatsukai uses its own material, *reifu*, or the holy talisman discovered by the founder, making it possible for Gedatsukai adherents to perform the service by themselves. In other words, it can be seen that Gedatsukai has absorbed traditional religious practices and made ingenious adjustments so that they may be incorporated into Gedatsukai's own religious system and applied universally. This way, as Gedatsukai leaders phrase it, each believer may repent of his sins, devote himself to the exercise for self-furtherance, identify the cause of his misfortune through his own body, and drive it out by his own efforts.

MATRIX FOR REVITALIZATION OF TRADITIONAL RELIGIOUS TEACHINGS
IN GEDATSUKAI

In various aspects of Gedatsukai, such as in the words and deeds of the founder and in doctrine and ritual observances, revitalization of traditional religious teachings is evident. What brought this about? It hardly needs mentioning that the model according to which doctrine and ritual observances of a religion are formed consists of the words and deeds of the founder. In the case of Gedatsukai, too, an orientation toward revitalization of traditional religion is evident in the career of the founder, Okano Seiken, as previously described. What factors motivated Okano to act in this way? To answer this question we look once more at Okano's personal history.

In his early life he repeated the cycle of failure, flight, and wandering: apprenticeship in Tokyo in his boyhood, failure in the textile machine business in his home village, and wandering in Korea during his youth; and later failure again in business in his home village and yet again wandering. Through repetition of this cycle, in the mind of Okano a strong feeling arose over his absence from his native province, and at the same time a strong feeling of love for that province. This complex feeling may explain the events that took place while he was wandering in Tokyo; he frequently returned home at night to pay a visit to his family tutelary shrine, family temple, graveyard, and the main family (*honke*). In the depths of despair he alleviated his feeling of loss for his native province by resorting to traditional religion. After his success in business, his contributions to his native province by promoting local industries and setting up the Kitamoto Station of the Takasaki railway line are best understood as coming from his love for his native province. However, at the same time they may be seen as his attempt to conquer the feeling of loss of home by providing material goods for the people of his village.

Following the mystical experience he had while he was seriously ill in 1925, he undertook religious activities and went on pilgrimages to shrines, temples, and holy mountains, seeking contacts with the ascetics of traditional religion, as if he were trying to obtain the evidence to substantiate his mystical experience. He eventually founded Gedatsukai on the basis of the divine revelations he experienced at a small shrine and at a pagoda of his family temple in his home village. That is to say, traditional religion was involved in the very foundation of Gedatsukai. He designated the place where he had the revelations as the Sacred Land (Goreichi), and there grand festivals are performed as the most sacred rites of Gedatsukai. Through these actions Okano conquered in a spiritual way his feeling of loss toward his native province.

While young Okano was living in Korea, he was impressed by the greatness of Japan and became conscious of its national spirit. When Japan was escalating its military involvement in China as a prelude to World War II, Okano must have felt the national crisis. In 1940 he erected a monument in celebration of the founding of the nation, and the next year he started the pilgrimage to the three sacred sites. Further, he actively participated in efforts to support the government in waging the war, such as visiting orphans of dead soldiers to comfort them, and raising donations for the government for military expenditures. When he died, his remains were buried at Sennyūji, in accordance with his dying wish that his spirit would serve Japan for her reconstruction. By such words and deeds Okano indicated his desire to save the Japanese from the crisis resulting from the loss of the native province (Japan). It appears that Okano's feeling of loss for the native province and his strong will to conquer this feeling was a basic element for his propensity to revitalize the practices of traditional religion in Gedatsukai.

Regarding the demography of Gedatsukai adherents, which we documented in the previously discussed survey, there are more female adherents (64.9%) than males (35.1%). The largest age bracket of the adherents is 45–60 years old, with the average age of 50.35. In terms of occupation, housewives and those engaged in agricultural, forestry, fishery, or office work constitute the major groups, and the majority are graduates of junior high school under the new (postwar) educational system, or of higher elementary school under the prewar and wartime educational system. When this data on educational attainment is combined with the data on age referred to above, we can see that the majority of Gedatsukai adherents received elementary school education during the war period. As regards the geographical distribution of adherents, the largest distribution is found in the suburbs of Tokyo and Osaka as well as in rural outlying districts.

Many of them became Gedatsukai believers in their thirties or early forties, through the recommendation of relatives or neighbors, when troubled by illness or mental problems. Gedatsukai has found acceptance in people who moved from rural districts to city areas and experienced the feeling of loss for their native province, or in people who live in a rural area, where traditional religion is still flourishing, and who work in the primary industries. In addition, many of them had a feeling of familiarity with traditional religion through the prewar and wartime school education and life. When such people were plagued by illness or mental worries, they became Gedatsukai believers, seeking explanations for such troubles and also solutions. In this way we can consider that Gedatsukai adherents, like the founder, had the complex feelings of loss of their native province on the one hand and familiarity with traditional religion on the other hand. This is why they were responsive to the revitalized teachings and observance of traditional religion taught by the founder who had overcome those complex feelings.

Traditional religious teachings revitalized in Gedatsukai are not, as has been noted, what they were before. They have been shaped in such a way that they fit into Gedatsukai's own doctrinal and ritual system. Gedatsukai exposes its adherents to traditional religious practices through its own practices, such as the *gohō* meditation and *amacha kuyō*. Through such practices Gedatsukai adherents absorb traditional religion, deepen belief therein, and translate traditional religious practices into their own religious activities. In this mechanism lies the key for the revitalization of traditional religion in Gedatsukai. This is how the theme of Gedatsukai's adaptation of traditional religion and its modification and eventual revitalization is acted out.

As described above, when one becomes a Gedatsukai member, one submits to the Tenjin Chigi Ōmikami through a letter of apology submitted to one's tutelary deity. The god in whom one previously had faith before becoming a Gedatsukai adherent is acknowledged as the faith-related guardian god by Tenjin Chigi Ōmikami. The Gedatsukai adherent has his or her soul transported to Goshugo Ōkami (who is made up of six deities) for spiritual training under the Goshugo Ōkami. This Goshugo Ōkami is Gedatsukai's version of several deities found in traditional religion such as *tengu*, Inari, and Benzaiten. Gedatsukai incorporated these traditional deities, who have a defender-of-religion-like character, into its pantheon. In this way, in the pantheon of Gedatsukai, deities of traditional religion are given their place as ushers needed to guide people to Gedatsukai's chief god, Tenjin Chigi Ōmikami, and also as the direct guardians of individual adherents of Gedatsukai. In other words, one comes into contact with Gedatsukai's original chief god through gods of traditional religion with whom one had familiarity before conversion to Gedatsukai.

Gedatsukai teaches, just as traditional Japanese religions also generally do, that misfortunes are derived from the souls of dead persons having no surviving relatives or not resting in peace. As the method of identifying these souls causing misfortunes, Gedatsukai teaches the *gohō* meditation, and as the method to appease these souls it teaches the *amacha kuyō*. These two rituals, described above and unique to Gedatsukai, were developed by the founder through his mystical experience. Gedatsukai incorporates the thought of traditional religion, which followers accept implicitly, concerning the cause of misfortune and the way to get rid of it.

Figure 59. Sacred pillar of *amacha kuyō*

Such acceptance allows the followers to reaffirm traditional thought through Gedatsukai's unique rituals. The *amacha kuyō* held in front of the All Souls' Festival Tower on the occasion of the spring and autumn grand festivals is regarded as the most important ritual of all. In its practice, we note the philosophy of Gedatsukai that spirits not resting in peace are purified by the power of Tenjin Chigi Ōmikami. The belief and practice of traditional religion concerning the discovery of the cause of misfortune and its removal have found a new application in Gedatsukai through the presence of Gedatsukai's original deity.

In this way, Gedatsukai adherents, who accept unconsciously the concept of traditional religion concerning misfortunes and their removal, discover the causes and attempt to eradicate them by using their own bodies to carry out Gedatsukai's unique rituals, such as the *gohō* meditation and the *amacha kuyō*. Through such rituals they reaffirm the orthodox nature of traditional religion and deepen their faith in Gedatsukai, which in turn sanctions orthodox traditional religion.

In Gedatsukai, traditional religion plays an indispensable role in introducing Gedatsukai's own doctrine and rituals to the adherents. The adherents are guided to the original deity of Gedatsukai (Tenjin Chigi Ōmikami) through their tutelary gods, and conversely, they reaffirm the concepts of traditional religion concerning the causes of misfortunes and the method of their elimination by performing Gedatsukai's original rituals, knowing full well that at the root of such practices lie the workings of Tenjin Chigi Ōmikami. We may conclude that ritual and doctrine of this kind are the very reason why traditional religion has been revitalized in Gedatsukai.

NOTES

1. The new religions of modern Japan appeared during three periods of social upheaval, i.e., the end of the Tokugawa period, (Kurozumikyō, Tenrikyō, Konkōkyō, and Maruyamakyō); during the great panic-depression after the First World War (Ōmotokyō, Reiyūkai); and after the Second World War (Tenshō Kōtai Jingūkyō, PL Kyōdan, etc.). For a general introduction to the new religions in modern Japan, see Murakami Shigeyoshi, *Japanese Religion in the Modern Century*, trans. H. Byron Earhart (Tokyo: University of Tokyo Press, 1980).
2. Miyake Hitoshi, *Minzoku shūkyō e no izanai* (Introduction to folk religion) (Tokyo: Keiō Tsūshin, 1990), 9–14.
3. For a brief outline of these new religions see Inoue Nobutaka, Kōmoto Mitsugu, Tsushima Michihito, Nakamaki Hirochika, and Nishiyama Shigeru, eds., *Shinshūkyō jiten* (Dictionary of new religions) (Tokyo: Kōbundō, 1994).
4. For the trend of new religion studies in Japan, see Inoue Nobutaka et al., *Shinshūkyō kenkyū chōsa handobukku* (Handbook for the study and research of new religions) (Tokyo: Yūzankaku, 1981). For studies and materials on Japanese new religions in Western languages, see H. Byron Earhart, *The New Religions of Japan: A Bibliography of Western-language*

Materials, 2d ed., Michigan Papers in Japanese Studies, no. 9 (Ann Arbor: Center for Japanese Studies, The University of Michigan, 1983).

5. See Daniel C. Holtom, *Modern Japan and Shinto Nationalism: A Study of Present-Day Trends in Japanese Religions*, rev. ed. (Chicago: University of Chicago Press, 1947).

6. H. Byron Earhart and Miyake Hitoshi, eds., *Dentōteki shūkyō no saisei—Gedatsukai no shisō to kōdō* (Revitalization of traditional religion—belief and practice of Gedatsukai) (Tokyo: Meicho Shuppan, 1983). Also H. Byron Earhart, *Gedatsukai and Religion in Contemporary Japan: Returning to the Center* (Bloomington: Indiana University Press, 1989).

7. For the outline of Gedatsukai, see Minoru Kiyota, *Gedatsukai: Its Theory and Practice* (Los Angeles-Tokyo: Buddhist Books International, 1982).

8. A type of tea prepared by roasting the dried leaves of the hydrangea shrub during the *kanbutsu-e* ceremony held in commemoration of the Buddha's birthday. It is the custom to pour *amacha,* in place of the original *kanro,* over an image of the infant Buddha. The Japanese term *amacha* is usually written with the two Sino-Japanese characters *ama* (sweet) and *cha* (tea), in other words, "sweet tea"; in Gedatsukai the second character (*cha,* tea) remains the same, but the first character is the homophone *ama* (heaven), in the sense of "heavenly tea."

9. When Amaterasu Ōmikami (the Sun Goddess) had hidden in the rock cave of heaven, Ama no Tajikarao no Mikoto opened the door and brought her out.

10. Originally the *Hōkyōin Dhāraṇī sūtra* was kept in this pagoda, but later the structure was used as a grave and/or memorial pagoda.

11. The new religion that was founded by Hiroike Chikurō (1866–1933). At first he believed in Tenrikyō, but after he studied ethics, he initiated the Moralogy sect.

12. Amatsukyō was founded by Takeuchi Kiyomaro (1874–1985). He was a *shugenja* of Mt. Kiso Ontake. This sect emphasized the legitimacy of sovereignty of the world by the *tennō* (emperor).

13. Ise is the tutelary shrine of Japan. Kashihara enshrines the Emperor Jinmu who is believed to have founded Japan. Sennyūji is a temple enshrining spirits of the imperial family.

14. *Shinkō* (True deeds) was published in 1942. In this book, Okano interpreted the relationship between the spiritual world and human according to his mystical experience.

15. The practitioner (believer of Gedatsukai) holds the *gohō* talisman that contains the written letter or "seed" of Gochi Nyorai between both palms. Then, under the guidance of the mediator who sits facing the practitioner, the practitioner's hands move. The mediator judges the cause of the practitioner's misfortune by interpreting the direction of this movement and gives advice about the ritual suitable for purification of the evil spirit. See the description of *reifu* later in this chapter.

16. Bunkachō, ed., *Shūkyō nenkan 1996* (1996 Yearbook of religion) (Tokyo: Bunkachō Shūmuka, 1997).

17. For the Gedatsu Church of America, See Ishii Kenji, "Transformation of a Japanese New Religion in American Society: A Case Study of Gedatsu Church of America," in *Japanese Religions in California: A Report on Research Within and Without the Japanese American Community*, ed. Yanagawa Keiichi (Tokyo: Department of Religious Studies, University of Tokyo, 1983), 163–95.

18. The six manifestations of Jizō, each of which is active in one of the six worlds (*rokudō*), in order to lead suffering beings to enlightenment.

19. Earhart and Miyake, *Dentōteki shūkyō no saisei,* 240–63.

20. Kawatō Hitoshi, "Gedatsukai no shūkyōteki uchūkan" (Religious cosmology of Gedatsukai), in ibid., 149–85.

21. Gedatsukai, *Ongohō shugyō no tebiki* (Guidebook for *gohō shugyō*) (Tokyo: Gedatsukai, 1984).

22. Gedatsukai, *Warera ga taisai: taisai sanka no igi to kokoroe* (Our Grand Festival: the significance and understanding of participation in the Grand Festival) (Tokyo: Gedatsukai, 1979).

The Cycle of Death and Rebirth

In Japan the cessation of the heartbeat has always been considered the criterion of death. In recent years, however, there has been a growing body of opinion, especially in the Ministry of Health and Welfare and among doctors concerned with organ transplants, advocating official recognition of brain death.

THE SOURCE OF LIFE

On January 23, 1992, an ad hoc advisory commission set up by the prime minister to consider brain death and organ transplants delivered its recommendations. The commission's report defined life as the state in which the organs of the body maintain organic cohesion and function to sustain mental and physical activity and the body's internal environment, and death as the state in which this cohesion no longer exists. Since it is the brain that sustains this cohesion, the commission concluded, the cessation of brain activity should be recognized as a criterion of death.[1]

This definition of life, however, which considers the brain as having the central role in maintaining the organic cohesion of the organs of the body, runs counter to the view of life found in Japanese folk religion. Since ancient times the Japanese have regarded blood as the source of life and the heart, which circulates blood throughout the body, as the most important organ—a view based on the experience of watching injured people die from loss of blood. This, too, is the reason that women, who shed blood on giving birth and in menstruation, yet do not die, used to be regarded with religious awe.[2]

In addition to blood—a physical substance—life was seen as something conveyed by the spirit that attaches itself to the body upon birth and is sustained through the agency of the spirit of grain inhering in rice, the traditional staple. This is why on occasions calling for especially vigorous spiritual activity—festivals and other sacred events, rice planting, rice harvesting, school sports meets and hikes—people would eat *musubi*, triangular rice balls, or *mochi*, cakes of glutinous rice. The word *musubi*, "joining" or "tying," indicates the activity of spirit power. Yanagita Kunio (1875–1962), the pioneer of Japanese folklore, believed that the triangular shape of *musubi* was intended to represent the shape of the heart.[3] Thus, the Japanese believed that life was established through assimilation of the spirit inhering in rice and through the action of the heart as the source of blood.

BETWEEN LIFE AND DEATH

When one is mortally ill, one is assailed both by fear of the suffering associated with dying and fear of death itself. Many Japanese would prefer euthanasia to either the suffering that attends death or to subsistence in a vegetative state, and quite a few old people make pilgrimages to Buddhist temples dedicated to buddhas or bodhisattvas who are believed to grant the boon of an easy death.[4] People sometimes kill terminally ill family members or severely handicapped children to spare them future suffering. Underlying these phenomena, of course, is the belief that life continues after death, as I shall discuss later.

Fear of death is hard to bear alone. People seek to alleviate that fear by dying at home surrounded by the family members with whom they have shared the joys and sorrows of life. When a man dies before his wife, his death is eased by her promise to follow him and by his children's and grandchildren's pledge to hold the proper Buddhist memorial services in his behalf. Nowadays a growing number of people approach death in hospitals, but even then the doctors often permit them to go home at the end.

Fear accompanies all forms of death: not just death from illness but also suicide, death in battle, and death by execution. When a woman kills a child and then herself, by dying with her child she is trying to overcome the fear of death that grips her even though she has resolved to die. Joint suicide by lovers stems from the same motivation. The kamikaze pilots of World War II hurled themselves to death in two-man planes, so that each pilot met death with a comrade. And war criminals gained peace of mind by dying with fellow prisoners. The suffering of those who died in battle or by execution as war criminals was ameliorated most, though, by the love of other family members, especially their mothers.[5]

There is controversy in Japan over whether people with cancer and other incurable diseases should be notified of their condition. To be sure, it may be advisable to tell people who have carefully thought-out life plans, and who know exactly what they wish to accomplish before death, so that they can live out their remaining days to the fullest extent and bring their lives to a satisfying conclusion. But the practice of notifying patients of cancer is not followed much among the Japanese, most of whom believe in life in the next world and therefore think they should die peacefully, without having to fret over matters having to do with this world.[6] This is also why so many people die without making out wills, even though making wills is urged to prevent family conflict.

HOPE OF THE NEXT WORLD

If one regards death as an absolute severance from life, one must find a way to continue living in order to avoid anxiety over death. This quest has spurred the development of preventive medicine and of new drugs, as well as the present interest in exercise and sports clubs. Certainly modern medicine is dedicated to prolonging life. It is now possible in many cases to sustain life indefinitely through artificial means. Those who advocate organ transplants from brain-dead people are also motivated by the wish to prolong other patients' lives. Turning to religion, we see that the same attitude underlay the Chinese Taoists' quest for eternal youth, which they sought to achieve through taking elixirs and undergoing austerities on sacred mountains.[7] Taoism, spreading from China to Japan, influenced Japanese attitudes.

Nevertheless, physiological life is finite; death is inevitable. The wish for immortality cannot be fulfilled. Once people see death as the negation of life and as unavoidable, they seek to alleviate the distress associated with death by expanding the definition of life. One way to do this is to hope for continued life for oneself or family members, albeit in a different form, by having organs transplanted into other living bodies. The same psychology underlies the veneration of dead family members' bones, teeth, nails, and hair, which change little after death, as if they contained the person's life. There are many customs associated with this belief: burying the ashes remaining after cremation, enshrining a dead person's Adam's apple, worshipping relics of the Buddha, placing teeth in sacred sites, treating dead people's teeth and hair with the same reverence as their ashes, and so on.

The wish for continued life is also seen in folk customs that express the importance attached to the lineage of blood linking one with one's children and grandchildren, and to perpetuation of the family line. Before dying, people entrust the continuation of the family to the remaining family members, who are also expected to fill the dead person's last wishes by devoting themselves to furthering the endeavors and causes dearest to that person's heart. Many people in the arts, for example, die with the wish that their works may enjoy eternal life.

REBIRTH IN THE OTHER WORLD

I have already mentioned the Japanese belief that life begins with a spirit entering a newborn infant's body and ends with the spirit leaving the body to become a spirit of the dead. Just as a child grows along with the growth of the spirit, so in the otherworld, it is believed, the spirit that has received new life there is nurtured through its descendants' prayers and eventually becomes a *kami*, or divine entity.

At the time of death, the family attempts to revive the spirit by calling out the dying person's name, setting a bowl of rice by the deathbed, washing the body, and so on. If these measures do not work, the dead person, having been prepared for the journey to the next world, is placed in a coffin and bid farewell by the family at the *tsuya*, or wake. At the funeral, the spirit of the dead person is transferred to his or her memorial tablet, the person is given a posthumous Buddhist name, and the body is cremated.

This is followed by Buddhist services every seven days until the forty-ninth day. On this day, which marks the end of the mourning period, the ashes are placed in a grave. Further Buddhist services are held on the hundredth day and on the first, third (actually two years after death), seventh, and thirteenth anniversaries. With the thirty-third anniversary and the end of memorial rites, the spirit of the dead person is believed to become an ancestral *kami*. At this time a *sotoba*, or wooden grave marker, is carved from a living tree with branches and leaves attached, and is planted on the grave site. When the tree takes root, the spirit is believed to have completed its metamorphosis into a *kami*.[8]

This series of rites associated with the birth and growth of ancestral spirits corresponds to various rites performed in connection with the growth of the spirit of a living person. The latter include, in the case of a difficult birth, the custom of the father's leading a horse into the mountains to call forth the baby's spirit; the rice offered the *kami* of childbirth upon the baby's birth; the bathing of the newborn infant; the naming of the baby; the celebration on the seventh day of the baby's life; the end of the taboo period; the child's first Girls' Festival (the Doll Festival, March 3) or Boys' Festival (May 5); the child's first birthday; *shichi go san*, when children of seven, five, and three are dressed up and taken to visit Shinto shrines; coming of age ceremonies; and finally the grown child's wedding.

The practice of a woman's spending the night with the body of her dead husband at the time of the *tsuya* is also interpreted as initiating the

Figure 60. Buddhist funeral in a temple

Figure 61. Buddhist service in a home for the anniversary of a spirit of the dead

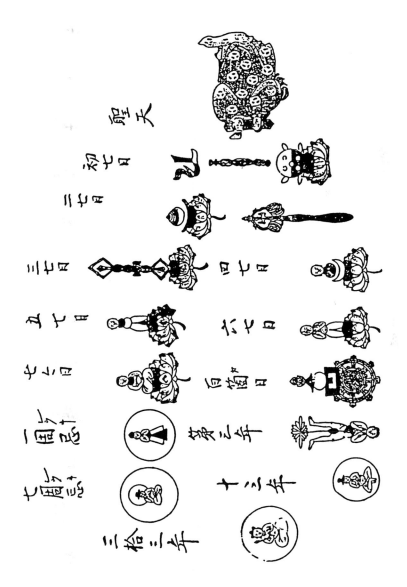

Figure 62. Growth of the soul of a dead person after conception in the womb of Mother Earth

process by which the new spirit of the dead is conceived and grows until it is finally reborn as a *kami*, a process marked by the rites beginning with the seventh day after the funeral and ending with the thirty-third anniversary of death. In other words, it is believed that a dead person's spirit, after leaving this world, receives new life in the otherworld and develops into a *kami*. This belief is based on the idea that the dead are nurtured in the womb of mother earth and finally are reborn.[9] Pursuing this line of thought further, we can see it as a metaphor of the growth of plants: seed potatoes and seed rice, planted in the ground, send forth shoots and finally bear fruit.

THE RETURN TO THIS WORLD

There are many tales of people believed to have died who have revived and described the scene on the banks of the Sanzu no Kawa, the Japanese equivalent of the River Styx, at the entrance to the otherworld. The story is also told of a Buddhist priest who died but returned to life after being ordered by King Enma, lord of the underworld, to tell people of the horrors of hell. We also hear of dead children reborn into other families relating events of the previous life or taking revenge on those who had tormented them in that life. It is said that such a child can be recognized by the fact that the ideographs written on the palms of the hands and the soles of the feet after death are still visible when the child is reborn and that these ideographs can be erased by washing the hands and feet in soil from the child's grave.[10] Moreover, a person is not always reborn as a human being but may return as a horse or a cow. A popular World War II slogan was "Seven lives to repay the country," signifying the pledge to be reborn seven times in order to repay one's debt of gratitude to the homeland.

The custom of burying the body of a dead child in the garden in the hope of the child's rebirth into the same family has been recorded, as has the belief that a baby born immediately after a grandparent's death is that person's reincarnation.[11] Children are often named after grandparents to perpetuate ancestral names.

Taking this line of thought further, the belief that the spirit that enters a newborn baby comes down the river from the mountains in which the ancestral spirits and *kami* dwell or from across the sea leads to the conclusion that ancestral spirits and *kami* are believed to be reborn into this world. At the midsummer Bon festival and at the New Year, ancestral spirits return to this world to visit their descendants' homes, where they are warmly welcomed. The idea of repeated visits to the world of the living is thought to have evolved into the belief that ancestral spirits living in the otherworld, in the mountains or over the sea, attach themselves to new-born babies and thus gain life in this world once again.

To the Japanese, then, life is not just a matter of continued existence in this world; life is thought to continue both in the otherworld and through rebirth in this world.

NOTES

1. As to the standard of brain death, the commission's report adopts the Takeuchi standard that was established by the brain death study group in The Ministry of Public Welfare, 1985. According to this standard, brain death is determined by the following six conditions: (1) deep coma, (2) cessation of spontaneous breathing, (3) fixation of the pupil, (4) loss of brain stem reflection, (5) flat brain wave, and (6) elapse of six hours after passing from condition one to five.

2. Namihira Emiko, *Kegare* (Pollution) (Tokyo: Tōkyōdō Shuppan, 1985), 92–137.

3. Yanagita Kunio, *Shokumotsu to shinzō* (Food and heart) (Tokyo: Sōgensha, 1940); reprinted in *Teihon Yanagita Kunio shū* (Tokyo: Chikuma Shobō, 1969), 14:234–38.

4. Kimura Hiroshi, *Shi-bukkyō to minzoku* (Death-Buddhism and folk customs) (Tokyo: Meicho Shuppan, 1989), 42–94.

5. Morioka Kiyomi, *Kesshi no sedai to isho* (The generation who resigned themselves to certain death in the Second World War and their wills) (Tokyo: Shinchi Shobō, 1991; Tokyo: Yoshikawa Kōbunkan, 1995).

6. Namihira Emiko, *Nōshi, zōki ishoku to gankokuchi* (Brain death, organ transplants, and notification of cancer) (Osaka: Fukutake Shoten, 1988).

7. Murakami Yoshimi, *Chūgoku no sennin: Hōbokushi no shisō* (The hermits of China: thought of Hōbokushi) (Kyoto: Heirakuji Shoten, 1977).

8. Inoguchi Shōji, *Nihon no sōshiki* (Funeral rites in Japan) (Tokyo: Chikuma Shobō, 1977).

9. Miyake Hitoshi, "Tsuizen kuyō no etoki—Tōzanha Shugen no chiiki teichaku" (The explanation by a picture of a memorial service for the dead—local indigenization of Tōzanha Shugen), *Keiō Gijuku Daigakuin Shakaigaku Kenkyūka kiyō* 36 (1997):65–68.

10. Matsutani Miyoko, *Ano yo e itta hanashi, shi no hanashi, umare kawari* (Tales of visiting the otherworld, death, and rebirth), Gendai Minwa Kō 5 (Tokyo: Tatekage Shobō, 1986), 425–39.

11. Yanagita Kunio, *About Our Ancestors*, trans. Fanny Hagin Mayer and Ishiwara Yasuyo (Tokyo: Society for the Promotion of Science, 1970), 170–76.

List of Characters

Agonshū	阿含宗
Aizen Myōō [Rāgarāja]	愛染明王
ajari [ācārya]	阿闍梨
aka	閼伽
Akiba	秋葉
aki no higan	秋の彼岸
aki no mine	秋の峰
amacha	天茶
amacha kuyō	天茶供養
amagoi	雨乞い
Amegoshiki Benzaiten	天五色弁財天
Amegoshiki Daitenkū Ōkami	天五色大天空大神
Amekokuzō Itsuhashira Inari Ōkami	天囹蔵五柱五成大神
Ame no Nuhoko	天の瓊矛
Amenotajikarao no Mikoto	天手力雄命
Ameōkuninushi Ōkami	天大囹主大神
anrei	安霊
Aramatsuri no Miya	荒祭の宮
Ashikaga Takauji	足利尊氏
Ashizuri	足摺
Asuga	阿須賀
ayaigasa	綾藺笠
Azuchi-Momoyama	安土桃山
Baramon Sōjō [Bodhisena]	婆羅門僧正 (菩提僊那)
bettō	別当
bikuni	比丘尼
Bishamonten [Vaiśravaṇa]	毘沙門天
Bitchū	備中
bokusen	卜占

bon	盆
bon dana	盆棚
Bon matsuri	盆祭
bon odori	盆踊り
bonten	梵天
Bonten Ō	梵天王
bosatsu [bodhisattva]	菩薩
bugyō	奉行
buninjō	補任状
bunke	分家
bunshin	分身
bushi	武士
busshō (buddhatā)	佛性
butsu	佛
butsudan	佛壇
butsumetsu	佛滅
byōki	病気
chiboshin	地母神
Chigo no Miya	児宮
chijin	地神
chikushō	畜生
chinju	鎮守
chinkon	鎮魂
Chiyosada	千与定
chōbuku	調伏
Chōkan	長寛
Chōkan Chōja	長寛長者
chōkan no kanmon	長寛勘文
chōmoto	帳元
chōri	長吏
Chūbu	中部
Chūdai Hachiyōin	中台八葉院
chūdan	中壇
Chūyūki	中右記
Daibyakushin Bosatsu	大白身菩薩
Daigoji	醍醐寺
Daigo Sanbōin	醍醐三宝院
Daihishin Ōji	大悲心王子
Daiitoku Myōō	大威徳明王
daikan	大寒
Dainichi Nyorai [Mahāvairocana -tathāgata]	大日如来

Dainippon Seishinhi	大日本精神碑
Daisen (Hōki)	大山（伯耆）
daisendatsu	大先達
danna [dāna]	檀那
darani [dhāraṇi]	陀羅尼
Daranikyō [dhāraṇi sūtra]	陀羅尼経
Deguchi Onisaburō	出口王仁三郎
dōji [kumāra]	童子
dōjō	道場
Dōkō	道興
dokyō	読経
dōnyū	導入
Dorotsuji	洞辻
doshū	度衆
dōsojin	道祖神
dōzoku	同族
Eikō	永興
Eikyūji	永久寺
eki	易
ekijin	疫神
ema	絵馬
engaku [pratyekabuddha]	縁覚
En'i	円伊
Enkun keiseiki	役君形生記
Enma	閻魔
ennen	延年
En no Gyōja	役行者
En no Ozunu	役小角
fuda	札
Fudaraku-sen [Potalaka]	補陀洛山
Fudō Myōō [Acala]	不動明王
Fugen Bosatsu [Samantabhadra -bodhisattva]	普賢菩薩
fuji-kō	富士講
Fujishiro	藤代
Fujiwara	藤原
fuju	符呪
fujushū	符呪集
fujutsu	巫術
Fukan	普寛
Fukūkensaku Kannon [Amogh- apāśāvalokiteśvara-bodhisattva]	不空羂索観音

fuku wa uchi	福は内
Fusōkyō	扶桑教
fuyu no mine	冬の峰
gaki [preta]	餓鬼
gakuryo	学侶
gakusō	学僧
gakutō	学頭
gakutōdai	学頭代
ganmon	願文
Gedatsukai	解脱会
Gedatsu Kongō	解脱金剛
Gedatsu Kongō Hōtō	解脱金剛宝塔
gekkei	月経
gen	験
genja	験者
genjutsu	験術
genki	元気
genkurabe	験競べ
genpuku	元服
Genri Kenkyūkai	原理研究会
genyaku	現益
genze riyaku	現世利益
geppō	月報
gessui	月水
ginshari	銀舎利
GLA	ジー・エル・エー
gō [karma]	業
Gobangaseki	五番ヶ関
Gochi Nyorai	五智如来
godanhō	五壇法
gogyō	五行
gohei	御幣
gohō	護法
gohō shugyō	五法修業
Gohōsoku	五法則
Gohō Zenshin	護法善神
gōkuyō	業供養
goma [homa]	護摩
gongyō	勤行
gō no hakari	業秤
Goreichi	御霊地

gorin	五輪
Gorin Hōtō	五輪宝塔
goryō	御霊
Goryū	五流
Goshirakawa Hōō	後白河法皇
Gosho Ōji	五所王子
Goshugo Ōkami	御守護大神
Gotai Ōji	五体王子
Gotoba Jōkō	後鳥羽上皇
Gotobiki iwa	ゴトビキ岩
gyōja	行者
Gyōja denki	行者伝記
Hachidai Kongō Dōji	八大金剛童子
Hachidai Ryūō [aṣṭa nāga-rājāḥ]	八大竜王
Hachiman	八幡
haku	魄
hanaku no mine	花供の峰
hana matsuri	花祭
Hannya shingyo [Prajñāpāramitā-hṛdaya-sūtra]	般若心経
harai	祓い
hare	ハレ
haru no higan	春の彼岸
hashiramatsu	柱松
hashiramoto goma	柱源護摩
hashiri nawa	走縄
hatsumōde	初詣
Hayatama no Kami	速玉神
hihō	秘法
Hijiri no Miya	聖宮
Hikosan	英彦山
Hikōyasha	飛行夜叉
himachi	日待
himitsushū	秘密集
hina matsuri	雛祭り
hiōgi	檜扇
Hiraoka Yoshifumi	平岡好文
Hirō Gongen	飛滝権現
hisshiki	引敷
hitogata	人形
Hitokoto Nushi no Kami	一言主神

Hito no Michi Kyōdan (PL)	ひとのみち教団（PL）
hi-tsuki-hoshi no matsuri	日・月・星の祭
Hiyoshi Taisha	日吉大社
hōhei	奉幣
Hōjūjiden	法住寺殿
Hoki naiden	簠簋内伝
Hokkai Kyōdō Kumiai	北海協同組合
hokkyō	法橋
Hōkyōintō	宝篋印塔
hōkyu	法弓
Hōnen	法然
hongaku	本覚
hongaku shisō	本覚思想
Hongū (Kumano)	本宮（熊野）
honji suijaku	本地垂迹
honke	本家
honsendatsu	本先達
Honshū	本州
hora	法螺
Hori Ichirō	堀一郎
hōshin	報身
hōshu	法主
hosshin [dharma-kāya]	法身
Hosshinmon	発心門
hotoke	ホトケ
hōza	法座
ichii	櫟（一位）
Ichiman	一万
ichi no shuku	一の宿
ie	家
Iesu no Hakobune	イエスの方舟
ikiryō	生霊
Imakumano Sha	新熊野社
Inabane Ōji	稲葉根王子
Inamuragatake	稲村ヶ岳
Inari	稲荷
inge	院家
inzō [mudrā]	印相
irataka no juzu	苛高数珠
Ise	伊勢
Ishizuchi	石鎚

Isonokami Ōji	石上王子
Itō Rokurōbei	伊藤六郎兵衛
Izanagi no Mikoto	伊弉諾尊
Izanami no Mikoto	伊弉冉尊
Jakkōkutsu	寂光窟
jarei	邪霊
jashin	邪神
jigoku	地獄
Jihi Daiken Ō	慈悲大顕王
Jihi Mojo	慈悲母女
Jihi Shin Ō	慈悲神王
jikkai shugyō	十界修行
Jikkōkyō	実行教
Jinja Honchō	神社本庁
Jinshadaishō	深沙大将
Jinushigami	地主神
Jinzen	深仙
Jinzen kanjō	深仙灌頂
Jippōin	実報院
jisha bugyō	寺社奉行
Jishū	時宗
jisō	寺僧
Jitsui	実意
Jizō Bosatsu [Kṣitigarbha-bodhisa-ttva]	地蔵菩薩
Jōbon	上品
Jōdo wasan	浄土和讃
Jōjōin (Nyaku Ōji)	乗々院（若王子）
joya	除夜
Jōzō	淨蔵
Jūichimen Kannon [Ekadaśamukha-avalokiteśvara-bodhisattva]	十一面観音
Jūman	十万
junnengyōji	准年行事
Jūshin'in	住心院
ka [phala]	果
kagen	下弦
kagura	神楽
kai no o	螺緒
kaji [adhiṣṭhāna]	加持
kajikitō	加持祈禱

Kakumei	覚明
Kakusan	覚讃
kami	神
kamidana	神棚
Kanda Myōjin	神田明神
Kane no Mitake	金の御岳
kanjō [abhiṣeka]	灌頂
Kanjō Jūgosho	勧請十五所
kanmangi	カンマン衣
kannabi	神奈備
kannazuki	神無月
Kanro Dai Ō	甘露大王
kanshasai	感謝祭
kariage matsuri	刈上祭
Kashihara Jingū	橿原神宮
Kashō [Kāśyapa]	迦葉
kasō	家相
kasumi	霞
katabako	肩箱
katen [Agni]	火天
katendan	火天壇
Katsuragi	葛城
kaza matsuri	風祭
Kazan Hōō	花山法皇
kei kuyō	敬供養
kemu gyō	烟行
kengyō	検校
kenzoku [parivāra]	眷屬
kenzokushin	眷屬神
kesagashira	袈裟頭
Ketsumimiko no Kami	家津美御子神
ki	気
kidan	祈壇
kikkyō	吉凶
kikō	気候
kikyūtai	希求態
kimon	鬼門
Kinbusen	金峯山
Kinbusen Shugen Honshū	金峯山修験本宗
Kinki	近畿
ki o otosu	気を落す

ki o ushinau	気を失う
kirigami	切紙
Kirume Ōji	切目王子
Kishimoto Hideo	岸本英夫
Kisoontake-kō	木曽御嶽講
Kitamotojuku	北本宿
Kitamoto Shi	北本市
kitō	祈禱
kō	講
Kōdō Kyōdan	孝道教団
kōfuku	幸福
kogi	小木
kogomebana	小米花
kohijiri	小聖
Kojiki	古事記
Kōjin	荒神
kokugaku	国学
Kokūzō Bosatsu [Ākāśa-garbha -bodhisattva]	虚空蔵菩薩
Komori no Miya	子守宮
kon	魂
Kongō Dōjihō	金剛童子法
kongōkai [vajra-dhātu]	金剛界
Kongō Zaō Gongen	金剛蔵王権現
kongōzue	金剛杖
Konoe Masaie	近衛政家
konpon sendatsu	根本先達
koshimaki	腰巻
Kōshō Dōji	香精童子
koshōgatsu	小正月
kuchiyose	口寄
kudoku	功徳
kuji	九字
Kūkai	空海
kūki	空気
Kumano bettōkeizu	熊野別当系図
Kumano Fusumi no Kami	熊野夫須美神
Kumano Gongen	熊野権現
Kumano Gongen gosuijaku engi	熊野権現御垂迹縁起
Kumano Hayatama no Kami	熊野速玉神
Kumano Jūnisho Gongen	熊野十二所権現

Kumano *mōde*	熊野詣
Kumano Musubi no Kami	熊野牟須美神
Kumanosan ryakki	熊野山略記
Kumano Sansho Gongen	熊野三所権現
Kumano Sanzan	熊野三山
kumi	組
Kuni no Tokotachi no Kami	国之常立神
kuyō fuda	供養札
kuyōhō	供養法
kuyōtō	供養塔
kyahan	脚絆
kyōzuka	経塚
Mahikari Kyōdan	真光教団
maikyō	埋経
majinai	呪い
Makadakoku [Magadha]	摩掲陀国
makura ishi	枕石
mandō	満堂
mangetsu	満月
Man'yōshū	万葉集
Manzan Gohō	満山護法
mappō	末法
matagi	マタギ
matsu hijiri	松聖
Matsuno Junkō	松野純孝
Meiji Kongō	米持金剛
mibarai	身祓い
michi	道
michi no sendatsu	道の先達
Mikkyō	密教
Miko	巫女
minami-okugake	南奥駆
mineiri	峰入
minkan shinkō	民間信仰
Minoosan	箕面山
Misatoshi	御諭し
misoka yamabushi	晦山伏
Mitsumine san	三峰山
Miwayama	三輪山
Miyazaki Ken	宮崎県
mizu matsuri	水祭

mochi	餅
Mochizuki Shinkō	望月信亨
Monju Bosatsu [Mañjuśri-bod-hisattva]	文殊菩薩
mono	モノ
monzeki	門跡
Moralogy (Dōtoku Kagaku)	モラロジー（道徳科学）
Moto no Oyagami (Nichigetsu Sengen Daibosatsu)	もとの親神（日月仙元大菩薩）
Motoori Norinaga	本居宣長
muenbotoke	無縁仏
muenrei	無縁霊
mukaebi	迎火
mura	村
mushi okuri	虫送り
musubi	むすび
Myōhōzan Amidaji	妙法山阿弥陀寺
Myōken Bosatsu	妙見菩薩
Nachi	那智
Nagata Hideaki	永田英明
nagatoko	長床
nagatokoshū	長床衆
Nagatoko Shukurō Goryū	長床宿老五流
Nakagusuku Mura	中城村
Nakamura Hajime	中村元
Naka no Goze	中御前
nanban-ibushi	南蛮いぶし
Nara Ken	奈良県
natsu no mine	夏の峰
nayami	悩み
nenbutsu hijiri	念仏聖
nenbutsu-kō	念仏講
nengyōji	年行事
nenjūgyōji	年中行事
Nihon Bukkyō Kenkyūkai	日本仏教研究会
Nihon shoki	日本書紀
niiname sai	新嘗祭
nijūsanya-ko	二十三夜講
ningen	人間
ni no shuku	二の宿
Nishida Kitarō	西田幾太郎

Nishi no Goze	西御前
Nishiyama Ryōshi	西山猟師
Noborito	登戸
Nyaku Ōji	若王子
Nyaku Ōjisha	若王子社
Nyoirin Kannon [Cintāmaṇi-cakra -avalokiteśvara-bodhisattva]	如意輪観音
nyoraidō	如来堂
nyūboku	乳木
nyūbu shugyō	入峰修行
nyūjō	入定
ōbarai	大祓
ogamiya	拝み屋
oi	笈
oikaragaki	笈絡
ōji	王子
okage	御蔭
Okano Eizō (Seiken)	岡野英蔵（聖憲）
Okano Makitarō	岡野牧太郎
Okayama Ken	岡山県
Okinawa	沖縄
okiyome	お浄め
okoze	おこぜ
Oku-gun	邑久郡
okuribi	送火
omikuji	御籤
ominaeshi	女郎花
Ōmine kaie mangyō jizai shidai	大峰界会万行自在次第
Ōminesan	大峰山
Ōmotokyō	大本教
ondamatsuri	御田祭
oni	鬼
oni wa soto	鬼はそと
Onmyōdō	陰陽道
Onmyōji	陰陽師
onozukara	おのずから
Ontake-kō	御岳講
oshi	御師
oshi monjo	御師文書
ōshin	応身
oshirabe	御調べ

oshirasama	オシラサマ
Ōshō	応照
ōshuku	大宿
Otohime	乙姫
Oyagami	親神
Ōyu no Hara	大湯原
Ozasa	小笹
P.L.Kyōdan	PL教団
Ragyō	裸行
raiden	礼殿
reichi	霊地
reifu	霊符
reikon	霊魂
ri kuyō	理供養
Risshō Kōsei Kai	立正佼成会
risshū	立秋
risshun	立春
rittō	立冬
riyaku	利益
rokudai [ṣaḍ dhātavaḥ]	六大
rokudō	六道
Roku Jizō	六地蔵
Rōnobō	廊之坊
Ryōbu mondō hishō	両峰問答秘鈔
Ryōsho Gongen	両所権垷
Ryōyu	良瑜
Ryūgū	龍宮
Ryūju [Nāgārjuna]	龍樹
Ryū no Taki	龍の滝
Ryūō	龍王
sai no kami	塞の神
saitō goma	採（柴）灯護摩
sakaki	榊
Sakugami	作神
samidare	五月雨
Sanbōin (Daigo)	三宝院（醍醐）
Sanjōgatake	山上ヶ岳
Sanjō-kō	山上講
sanmitsu	三密
san no shuku	三の宿
Sansha Ōkuchishin Ōkami	三社大口神大神

Sansho Gongen	三所権現
Santoku Daimyōjin	三徳大明神
sanzu no kawa	三途の川
sato shugen	里修験
satsuki	五月
sawari	障り
Seichō no Ie	生長の家
seigantai	請願態
Seigantoji	青岸渡寺
seijin shiki	成人式
seirei	精霊
sekki	節季
Senchaku hongan nenbutsu shū	選択本願念仏集
sendatsu	先達
Sengen Daibosatsu	仙元大菩薩
sennin	仙人
Sennyūji	泉涌寺
senryakushu	浅略趣
setendan	世天壇
setsubun	節分
shakujō	錫杖
shasō	社僧
shiba-uchi	柴打
shichifuku sokushō	七福即生
shichi go san	七五三
shichinan sokumetsu	七難即滅
shichiya	七夜
Shiiba Mura	椎葉村
shikkō	執行
Shimada Kenshō	島田顕祥
shimenawa	注連縄
Shimo Kasaka Mura	下笠加村
shinbutsu	神仏
shinbutsu shūgō	神仏習合
shingon [mantra]	真言
Shingū (Kumano)	新宮（熊野）
shinkan	神官
Shinkō	真行
shinkō kankei shugoshin	信仰関係守護神
Shinnyoen	真如苑
Shinra Myōjin	新羅明神

shinrei	神霊
Shinreikyō	神霊教
shinshoku	神職
Shintōshū	神道集
shiogori	潮垢離
shiryō	死霊
shishi	獅子
shisō	思想
shizen	自然
shizen kagaku	自然科学
shizen kankyō	自然環境
shōdaisendatsu	正大先達
shōen	荘園
shōgatsu	正月
Shōgoin	聖護院
shōjinya	精進屋
Shōjōden	証誠殿
shōkan	小寒
shōkanjō [abhiṣeka]	正灌頂
Shōkannon [Avalokiteśvara-bod-hisattva]	正観音
Shokokusōkesagashira	諸国総袈裟頭
shomin shūkyō	庶民宗教
shōmon [śrāvaka]	声聞
shonanoka	初七日
shōryōbune	精霊舟
Shōryoshū	性霊集
shōshi no matsuri	小祠の祭
shosonbō	諸尊法
Shoson yōshō	諸尊要鈔
Shōtokuhi	頌徳碑
Shugendō	修験道
shugenja	修験者
Shugen jinpi gyōhō fujushū	修験深秘行法符呪集
Shugen saishō e'insanmayahō rokudan	修験最勝慧印三昧耶法　六壇
Shugen shinanshō	修験指南鈔
Shugen shūyō hiketsushū	修験修要秘決集
shugo	守護
shugyō	修行
shūhō	修法
shuhōdōjō	修法道場

shūkaku sai	収穫祭
Shūkongōjin [vajra-dhara]	執金剛神
shura [asura]	修羅
shuto	衆徒
Sōka Gakkai	創価学会
sokusai goma	息災護摩
sokushin jōbutsu	即身成仏
sokushin sokubutsu	即身即仏
sōryo	僧侶
sosenshin	祖先神
Sugawara no Michizane	菅原道真
suijin sai	水神祭
surikae no ronri	摩り替えの論理
suzukake	鈴懸
taian	大安
taiinreki	太陰暦
taijūtai	諦住態
Taira no Masakado	平将門
taizōkai [garbha-dhātu]	胎蔵界
Takagi Hiroo	高木宏夫
Takakuraji no Mikoto	高倉下命
Takatori Masao	高取正男
takigomori-shū	滝籠衆
Takijiri	滝尻
Taki no Miya	滝宮
takusen	託宣
tama	魂
Tamonji	多聞寺
Tamura Yoshirō	田村芳朗
tanabata	七夕
tango no sekku	端午の節句
tanjō	誕生
ta no kami	田の神
tatari	祟り
taue matsuri	田植祭
ten	天
tenchi	天地
tengu	天狗
Tenjin Chigi Ōmikami	天神地祇大神
Tenkawa	天河
tenki	天気

Tenmangū	天満宮
Tenmantenjin	天満天神
Tenpushin	天父神
Tenrikyō	天理教
Tenri Ō no Mikoto	天理王命
Tōgyoshin	統御神
tōji	冬至
tokin	頭巾
toki no sendatsu	時の先達
tokko [vajra-pounder]	独鈷
tokogatame	床堅
tokōsanjō	床散杖
Tokumitsukyō	徳光教
tomobiki	友引
tomurai	弔い
tomurai age	弔いあげ
tondo	トンド
toshidama	年玉
toshigami	歳神
toshigomori	年籠
toshi iwai	年祝い
Tōtōmi	遠江
Tōzan Shōdaisendatsushū	当山正大先達衆
tsuchi no e	戊
tsugomori	晦日
tsukikomori (tsugomori)	月隠（晦日）
tsuki machi	月待
tsukimi	月見
tsukimi dango	月見団子
tsukimono otoshi	憑物おとし
tsukitachi (tsuitachi)	月立ち（朔日）
Tsukiyomi no Mikoto	月読尊
tsumadachi gyō	爪立行
Tsurugaoka Hachimangū	鶴岡八幡宮
tsuya	通夜
ubugami	産神
ubuishi	産石
uchinaru shizen	内なる自然
uchū	宇宙
Uda Jōkō	宇多上皇
ujigami	氏神

Ukemochi no Kami	保食神
unsei	運勢
uretsuki tōba	梢付塔婆
wakamiya	若宮
Wakamiya Nyoichi Ōji	若宮女一王子
Wakayama Ken	和歌山県
waraji	草鞋
Yahanmēutaki	ヤハンメー御嶽
yakudoshi	厄年
yakujin	厄神
Yakushi Nyorai [Bhaiṣajya-guru]	薬師如来
yamabushi	山伏
yama no kami	山の神
yamayuki	山行き
yamayuri	山百合
Yanagawa Keiichi	柳川啓一
Yanagita Kunio	柳田国男
Yasha [yakṣa]	夜叉
yashikigami	屋敷神
Yatagarasu	八咫烏
yorigitō	憑祈禱
Yorozu Mitama Matsuri Tō	万霊魂祭塔
yōshuku	曜宿
yōshukudan	曜宿段
yugyō	遊行
yuigesa	結袈裟
Yunomine	湯峰
yūrei	幽霊
Yuzuruhasan	諭鶴羽山
zadankai	座談会
zaichi sendatsu	在地先達
Zendō	禅洞
Zenji no Miya	禅師宮
Zenki	前鬼
Zenrinji	禅林寺
Zōmyō	増命
zōni	雑煮
Zōyo	増誉

Bibliography

(A) Works in Western Languages

Anesaki, Masaharu. *Religious Life of the Japanese People.* Revised by Kishimoto Hideo. Tokyo: Kokusai Bunka Shinkōkai, 1961.

Ashkenazi, Michael. *Matsuri: Festivals of a Japanese Town.* Honolulu: University of Hawaii Press, 1993.

Asquith, Pamela J., and Arne Kalland, eds. *Japanese Images of Nature: Cultural Perspectives.* Richmond, Surrey: Curzon Press, 1997.

Averbuch, Irit. *The Gods Come Dancing: A Study of the Japanese Ritual Dance of Yamabushi Kagura.* Cornell East Asian Series 79. Ithaca, NY: Cornell University Press, 1995.

Bellah, Robert N. *Tokugawa Religion: The Values of Pre-industrial Japan.* Glencoe, Ill.: Free Press, 1957.

Blacker, Carmen. *The Catalpa Bow: A Study of Shamanistic Practices in Japan.* London: Allen and Unwin, 1975.

———. "Initiation in Shugendō: The Passage Through the Ten States of Existence." In *Initiation,* edited by C. J. Bleeker. Leiden: E. J. Brill, 1965.

Bohner, Hermann, trans. "Honchō-shinsen-Den." *Monumenta Nipponica* 13.1–2 (1957):129–52.

Bownas, Geoffrey. *Japanese Rainmaking and Other Folk Practices.* London: George Allen and Unwin, 1963.

Casal, Ugo. *The Five Sacred Festivals of Ancient Japan: Their Symbolism and Historical Development.* Monumenta Nipponica Monograph 26. Tokyo: Sophia University Press and Charles E. Tuttle Co., 1967.

———. "The Yamabushi." *Mitteilungen der Deutschen Gesellschaft für Natur- und Völkerkunde Ostasiens* 46 (1965):1–45.

Coward, Maurice. "Japanese Festivals: A Preliminary Semiotic Analysis in Time Out of Time." In *Essays on the Festival,* edited by Alessandro Falassic. Albuquerque, NM: University of New Mexico Press, 1987.

Davis, Winston B. *Japanese Religion and Society, Paradigms of Structure and Change.* Albany: State University of New York Press, 1992.

———. *Toward Modernity: A Developmental Typology of Popular Religious Affiliations in Japan.* Cornell East Asia Papers 12. Ithaca, NY: Cornell China-Japan Program, 1977.

de Visser, M. W. "The Tengu." *Transactions of the Asiatic Society of Japan* 36 (Part II) (1908):25–99.

Dorson, Richard M., ed. *Studies in Japanese Folklore*. Chief translator, Yasuyo Ishiwara. Bloomington: Indiana University Press, 1963.

Dräger, Walter, and Helmut Erlinghagens, trans. "No Katsuragi." *Monumenta Nipponica* 5.2 (1947):437–65.

Earhart, H. Byron. "The Celebration of *Haru-yama* (Spring Mountain): An Example of Folk Religious Practices in Contemporary Japan." *Asian Folklore Studies* 27.1 (1968):1–18.

———. "Four Ritual Periods of Haguro Shugendō in Northeastern Japan." *History of Religions* 5.1 (Summer 1965):93–113.

———. *Gedatsukai and Religion in Contemporary Japan: Returning to the Center*. Bloomington: Indiana University Press, 1989.

———. "Gedatsukai: One Life History and its Significance for Interpreting Japanese New Religions." *Japanese Journal of Religious Studies* 7.2–3 (1980):227–57.

———. "The Ideal of Nature in Japanese Religion and its Possible Significance for Environmental Concerns." *Contemporary Religions in Japan* 2.1–2 (March–June 1970):1–26.

———. "The Interpretation of the New Religions of Japan as Historical Phenomena." *Journal of the American Academy of Religion* 37.3 (September 1969):237–48.

———. "Ishikozume: Ritual Execution in Japanese Religion. Especially in Shugendō." *Numen* 13.2 (August 1966):116–27.

———. *Japanese Religion: Unity and Diversity*. 3d ed. Belmont, CA: Wadsworth, 1982.

———. *Religion in the Japanese Experience: Sources and Interpretations*. 2d ed. Belmont, CA: Wadsworth, 1996.

———. *A Religious Study of the Mount Haguro Sect of Shugendō: An Example of Japanese Mountain Religion*. Tokyo: Sophia University, 1970.

———. "Shugendō. The Tradition of En No Gyōja, and Mikkyō Influence." In *Studies of Esoteric Buddhism and Tantrism*, edited by Kōyasan University. Kōyasan: Kōyasan University, 1965.

———. "The Significance of the 'New Religions' for Understanding Japanese Religions." *KBS Bulletin on Japanese Culture* 101 (April–May 1970):1–9.

———. "Toward a Theory of the Formation of the Japanese New Religions: A Case Study of Gedatsukai." *History of Religions* 20.1–2 (1980):175–97.

———. "Toward a Unified Interpretation of Japanese Religion." In *The History of Religions: Essays on the Problem of Understanding*, edited by Joseph M. Kitagawa. Chicago: University of Chicago Press, 1967.

Eliade, Mircea. "Berge, heilige." In *Die Religion in Geschichte und Gegenwart*. Vol. 1, 3d ed., edited by Hans Frhr. von Campenhausen et al. Tubingen: Mohr, 1956.

———. *Shamanism: Archaic Techniques of Ecstasy*. Translated by W. T. Trask. Rev. ed. Bollingen Series 76. Princeton, NJ: Princeton University Press, 1972.

Embree, John F. *Suye Mura*. Chicago: University of Chicago Press, 1960.

Fairchild, William P. "Shamanism in Japan." *Folklore Studies* 21 (1952):1–122.

Gennep, Arnold van. *The Rites of Passage*. Translated by Monika B. Vizedom and Gabrielle L. Caffee. Chicago: University of Chicago Press, 1960; originally published as *Les rites de passage* (1909).

Guth, Christine, with Haruki Kageyama. *Shintō Arts: Nature, Gods and Man in Japan*. New York: Japan Society, 1976.

Hardacre, Helen. "The Postwar Development of Studies of Japanese Religions." In *The Postwar Development of Japanese Studies in the United States*. London: Brill, 1998.

Honda Yasuji. "Yamabushi Kagura and Bangaku: Performance in Japanese Middle Ages and Contemporary Folk Performance." Translated by Frank Hoff. *Educational Theater Journal* (May 1974).

Hori Ichirō. *Folk Religion in Japan: Continuity and Change.* Edited and translated by Joseph M. Kitagawa and Alan Miller. Chicago: University of Chicago Press, 1968.

———. "Japanese Folk-Beliefs." *The American Anthropologist*, n.s., 61.3 (June 1959):405–24.

———. "Mountains and Their Importance for the Idea of the Other World in Japanese Folk Religion." *History of Religions* 6.1 (1966):1–23.

———. "On the Concept of *Hijiri* (Holy Man)." *Numen* 5.2 (1958):128–60; 5.3 (1958):199–232.

———. "Self-mummified Buddhas in Japan. An Aspect of the Shugen-dō (Mountain Asceticism) Sect." *History of Religions* 1.2 (Winter 1961):222–42.

———, ed. *Japanese Religion.* Translated by Abe Yoshiya and David Reid. Tokyo: Kodansha International, 1972.

Ikegami Hiromasa. "The Significance of Mountains in the Popular Belief in Japan." In *Religious Studies in Japan*, edited by Japanese Association for Religious Studies. Tokyo: Maruzen, 1959.

Immoos, Thomas. *Das Tanzritual der Yamabushi: Ein Ritual der Wiedergeburt in den Yamabushi Kagura.* Tokyo: Deutsche Gesellschaft für Natur- und Völkerkunde Ostasiens, 1968.

Inoue Nobutaka, ed. *Kami.* Contemporary Papers on Japanese Religion 4. Tokyo: Institute for Japanese Culture and Classics, Kokugakuin University, 1998.

———, ed. *Matsuri: Festival and Rite in Japanese Life.* Translated by Norman Havens. Contemporary Papers on Japanese Religion 1. Tokyo: Institute for Japanese Culture and Classics, Kokugakuin University, 1988.

———, ed. *New Religions.* Translated by Norman Havens. Contemporary Papers on Japanese Religion 2. Tokyo: Institute for Japanese Culture and Classics, Kokugakuin University, 1991.

Ishida Eiichirō. "Mother and Son Deities." *History of Religions* 4.1 (1964):30–52.

Ishida Mosaku. "About the Hanging-Buddha of Zaō-Gongen." *Religions in Japan at Present* 1 (1962):30.

Ishii Kenji. "The Secularization of Religion in the City." *Japanese Journal of Religious Studies* 13.2–3 (1986):193–209.

———. "Transformation of a Japanese New Religion in American Society. A Case Study of Gedatsu Church of America." In *Japanese Religions in California: A Report on Research Within and Without the Japanese American Community*, edited by Yanagawa Keiichi. Tokyo: Department of Religious Studies, University of Tokyo, 1983.

Japanese-English Buddhist Dictionary. Rev. ed. Tokyo: Daitō Shuppansha, 1991.

Kaneko Satoru. "Dimensions of Religiosity among Believers in Japanese Folk Religion." *Journal for the Scientific Study Of Religion* 29.1 (March 1990):1–18.

Kidder, Jonathan E. *Japan Before Buddhism.* New York: Praeger, 1959.

Kishida Eizan. *The Character and Doctrine of Gedatsu Kongo.* Translated by Louis K. Itō. San Francisco: Gedatsu Church of America, 1969.

Kishimoto Hideo. "The Role of Mountains in the Religious Life of the Japanese People." In *Proceedings of the Ninth International Congress for the History of Religions*, edited by International Association for the History of Religions. Tokyo: Maruzen, 1960.

————, ed. *Japanese Religion in the Meiji Era.* Translated by John F. Howes. Tokyo: Ōbunsha, 1956.

Kitagawa, Joseph M. *On Understanding Japanese Religion.* Princeton, NJ: Princeton University Press, 1987.

————. *Religion in Japanese History.* New York: Columbia University Press, 1966.

————. "Three Types of Pilgrimage in Japan." In *Studies in Mysticism and Religion Presented to Gershom G. Scholem,* edited by E. E. Urbach, R. J. Zwi Werblowsky and Ch. Wirszubski. Jerusalem: Magnes Press, 1967.

Kiyota, Minoru. *Gedatsukai: Its Theory and Practice.* Los Angeles-Tokyo: Buddhist Books International, 1982.

————. *Shingon Buddhism: Theory and Practice.* Los Angeles-Tokyo: Buddhist Books International, 1978.

————, ed. *Japanese Buddhism: Its Traditions, New Religions and Interaction with Christianity.* Los Angeles-Tokyo: Buddhist Books International, 1987.

Kurata Ichirō. "Yama-no-kami (Mountain Deities)." *Contemporary Japan* 10 (1940):1304–12.

Lebra, Takie Sugiyama. "Self-Reconstruction in Japanese Religious Psychotherapy." In *Cultural Conceptions of Mental Health and Therapy,* edited by A. J. Marsella and G. M. White. The Hague: D. Reidel, 1982.

————. "Taking the Role of the Supernatural Other: Spirit Possession in a Japanese Healing Cult." In *Cultural Bound Syndromes: Ethnopsychiatry and Alternate Therapies,* edited by William P. Lebra. Mental Health Research in Asia and the Pacific 4. Honolulu: East-west Center Press, 1976.

Mabuchi Tōichi. "Spiritual Predominance of the Sister." In *Ryukyuan Culture and Society,* edited by Allan H. Smith. Honolulu: University of Hawaii Press, 1964.

Marcure, Kenneth A. "The Danka System." *Monumenta Nipponica* 40.1 (1985):39–67.

Matsudaira Narimitsu. "The Concept of Tamashii in Japan." In *Studies in Japanese Folklore,* edited by R. M. Dorson. Bloomington: Indiana University Press, 1963.

Miyake Hitoshi. *The Structure of Folk Religion in Japan.* Tokyo: Keiō Tsūshin, 1974.

Morioka Kiyomi. "Ancestor Worship in Contemporary Japan: Continuity and Change." In *Religion and Family in East Asia,* edited by George A. Devos and Takao Sofue. Los Angeles: University of California Press, 1984.

————. *Religion in Changing Japanese Society.* Tokyo: University of Tokyo Press, 1975.

———— and William H. Newell, eds. *The Sociology of Japanese Religion.* Leiden: E. J. Brill, 1968.

Mullins, Mark R., Shimazono Susumu, and Paul L. Swanson, eds. *Religion and Society in Modern Japan: Selected Readings.* Berkeley, CA: Asian Humanities Press, 1993.

Murakami Shigeyoshi. *Japanese Religion in the Modern Century.* Translated by H. Byron Earhart. Tokyo: University of Tokyo Press, 1980.

Muraoka Tsunetsugu. *Studies in Shintō Thought.* Translated by Delmer M. Brown and James T. Araki. Tokyo: Ministry of Education, 1964.

Nakane Chie. *Japanese Society.* Berkeley: University of California Press, 1970.

Naumann, Nelly. "Yama no Kami—die japanische Berggottheit." Teil I: Grundvorstellungen. Teil II: Zusätzliche Vorstellungen. *Asian Folklore Studies* 22 (1963):133–366; 23 (1964):48–199.

Nelson, John. *A Year in the Life of a Shintō Shrine.* Seattle: University of Washington Press, 1995.

Newell, William H., ed. *Ancestors.* The Hague: Mouton, 1976.

Nosco, Peter, ed. *The Emperor System and Religion in Japan.* Special issue of *Japanese Journal of Religious Studies* 17.2–3 (June–September 1990).

Ohnuki-Tierney, Emiko. *Illness and Culture in Contemporary Japan: An Anthropological View.* Cambridge: Cambridge University Press, 1984.

———. *The Monkey as Mirror: Symbolic Transformation in Japanese History and Ritual.* Princeton, NJ: Princeton University Press, 1987.

Ooms, Herman. "A Structural Analysis of Japanese Ancestral Rites and Beliefs." In *Ancestors,* edited by William H. Newell. The Hague: Mouton, 1976.

Ōto Tokihiko. *Folklore in Japanese Life and Customs.* Tokyo: Society for the Promotion of Science, 1963.

Ouwehand, C. *Namazu-e and Their Themes: An Interpretative Approach to Some Aspects of Japanese Folk Religion.* Leiden: E. J. Brill, 1964.

Philippi, Donald, trans. *Kojiki.* Tokyo: University of Tokyo Press, 1968.

———, trans. *Norito: A New Translation of the Ancient Japanese Ritual Prayers.* Tokyo: Institute for Japanese Culture and Classics, Kokugakuin University, 1959.

Plutschow, Herbert. "The Fear of Evil Spirits in Japanese Culture." *Transactions of the Asiatic Society of Japan.* 3d ser., vol. 18 (1983):133–51.

Reader, Ian. "Back to the Future: Images of Nostalgia and Renewal in a Japanese Religious Context." *Japanese Journal of Religious Studies* 14.4 (1987):287–303.

———. *Religion in Contemporary Japan.* Honolulu: University of Hawaii Press, 1991.

Renondeau, Gaston. *Le Shugendō: histoire, doctrine et rites des anachorètes dits Yamabushi.* Cahiers de la Société Asiatique 18. Paris: Imprimerie Nationale, 1965.

Rotermund, Hartmut O. "Die Legende des En no Gyōja." *Oriens Extremus* 12 (1965):221–41.

———. "Notizen zur Gesellschaftlichen Stellung Pilgender Yamabushi der späten Edozeit." *Oriens Extremus* 12.1–2 (1979):133–51.

———. *Die Yamabushi. Aspekte ihres Glaubens, Lebens und ihrer sozialen Funktion, im Japanischen Mittelalter.* Monographien zur Völkerunde 5. Hamburg: Kommissionsverlag Cram, de Gruyter & Co., 1968.

Sakurai Tokutarō. "Japanese Folk Religion and the Regulation of Social Life: The Interrelation of Ke, Kegare, and Hare." *Komazawa Journal of Sociology* 16 (March 1984):62–77.

Schurhammer, George. "Die Yamabushis; nach gedruckten und ungedruckten Berichten des 16. und 17. Jahrhunderts." *Zeitschrift für Missionwissenschaft und Religionswissenschaft* 12 (1922):206–28.

Segawa Kiyoko. "Menstrual Taboos Imposed on Women." In *Studies in Japanese Folklore,* edited by R. M. Dorson. Bloomington: Indiana University Press, 1963.

Shimazono Susumu. "The Living Kami Idea in the New Religions of Japan." *Japanese Journal of Religious Studies* 6.3 (September 1979):389–412.

Smith, Robert J. *Ancestor Worship in Contemporary Japan.* Stanford, CA: Stanford University Press, 1974.

Sonoda Minoru. "The Traditional Festival in Urban Society." *Japanese Journal of Religious Studies* 2.2–3 (1975):103–36.

Statler, Oliver. *Japanese Pilgrimage.* New York: William Morrow and Co., 1983.

Swanson, Paul L. "Shugendō and the Yoshino-Kumano Pilgrimage: An Example of Mountain Pilgrimage." *Monumenta Nipponica* 36.1 (1981):55–84.

Tsushima Michihito, Nishiyama Shigeru, Shimazono Susumu, and Shiramizu Hiroko. "The Vitalistic Conception of Salvation in Japanese New Religions:

An Aspect of Modern Religious Consciousness." *Japanese Journal of Religious Studies* 6.1–2 (March–June 1979):139–61.

Tubielewicz, Jolanta. *Superstitions, Magic and Mantric Practices in the Heian Period.* Warszawa: Wydawnictwa Uniwersytetu Warszawskietgo, 1980.

Tyler, Royall, and Paul L. Swanson, eds. *Shugendō and Mountain Religion in Japan.* Special issue of *Japanese Journal of Religious Studies* 16.1–2 (June–September 1989).

Waddell, L. A. "The Dhāraṇī Cult in Buddhism, its Origin, Deified Literature and Images." *Ostasiatische Zeitschrift* 1 (1912–13):155–95.

Yanagita Kunio. *About Our Ancestors.* Translated by Fanny Hagin Mayer and Ishiwara Yasuyo. Tokyo: Society for the Promotion of Science, 1970.

———, comp. *Japanese Folklore Dictionary.* Translated by Masanori Takatsuka and edited by George K. Brady. Kentucky Microcards Series A, no. 18. Lexington: University of Kentucky Press, 1968.

———. *The Legend of Tōno.* Translated by Ronald A. Morse. Tokyo: The Japan Foundation, 1975.

Yoshida Teigo. "The Stranger as God: The Place of the Outsider in Japanese Folk Religion." *Ethnology* 20.2 (April 1981):87–99.

(B) WORKS IN JAPANESE

Akada Mitsuo. *Sorei shinkō to takaikan.* Kyoto: Jinmon Shoin, 1986.

———, ed. *Sorei shinkō.* Minshū Shūkyōshi Kenkyū Sōsho 26. Tokyo: Yūzankaku, 1991.

——— and Komatsu Kazuhiko, eds. *Kami to reikon no minzoku.* Kōza Nihon no Minzokugaku 7. Tokyo: Yūzankaku, 1997.

Amano Kanmei. *Shugendō no shinzui.* Tokyo: Kōsei Shuppansha, 1980.

Amino Yoshihiko. *Muen, kugai, raku—Nihon chūsei no jiyū to heiwa.* Tokyo: Heibonsha, 1978.

———. *Nihon shakai no rekishi.* 3 vols. Tokyo: Iwanami Shoten, 1997.

Bukkyō Minzokugaku Taikei Henshūiinkai, ed. *Bukkyō minzokugaku taikei.* 8 vols. Tokyo: Meicho Shuppan, 1986–93: 1, *Bukkyō minzokugaku no shomondai* (Henshūiinkai, ed.); 2, *Hijiri to minshū* (Hagiwara Tatsuo and Shinno Toshikazu, eds.); 3, *Seichi to takaikan* (Sakurai Tokutarō, ed.); 4, *Sosen saishi to sōho* (Fujii Masao, ed.); 5, *Bukkyō geinō to bijutsu* (Suzuki Shōei, ed.); 6, *Bukkyō Nenjūgyōji* (Itō Yuishin, ed.); 7, *Tera to chiiki shakai* (Togawa Anshō, ed.); 8, *Zokushin to bukkyō* (Miyata Noboru and Sakamoto Kaname, eds.).

Bunkachō, ed. *Nihon minzoku chizu.* 7 vols. Tokyo: Kokudō Chiri Kyōkai, 1968–80: 1, 2, *Nenjūgyōji;* 3, *Shinkō;* 4, *Shakai seikatsu;* 5, *Shussan yukuji;* 6, *Kon'in;* 7, *Sōsei bosei.*

Chiba Masashi. *Matsuri no hōshakaigaku.* Tokyo: Kōbundō, 1970.

Chiba Tokuji. *Nyōbō to yama no kami.* Osaka: Sakaiya Tosho, 1983.

Chūjo Shinzen. *Shugendō no buchū shugyō.* Kyoto: Sanmitsudō Shoten, 1987.

———. *Shugendō no kyōri.* Kyoto: Sanmitsudō Shoten, 1975.

Doi Takuji et al., eds. *Sōsō bosei kenkyū shūsei.* 5 vols. Tokyo: Meicho Shuppan, 1979: 1, *Sōhō* (Doi Takuji and Sato Yoneji, eds.); 2, *Sōsō girei* (Inoguchi Shōji, ed.); 3, *Senzo kuyō* (Takeda Chōshu, ed.); 4, *Haka no shūzoku* (Mogami Takayoshi, ed.); 5, *Haka no rekishi* (Uwai Hisayoshi, ed.).

Earhart, H. Byron and Miyake Hitoshi, eds. *Dentōteki shūkyō no saisei–Gedatsukai no shisō to kōdō.* Tokyo: Meicho Shuppan, 1983.

Fujii Masao. *Gendaijin no shinkō kōzō.* Tokyo: Hyōronsha, 1974.

———. *Sosen saishi no girei kōzō to minzoku.* Tokyo: Kōbundō, 1992.

Fujii Masao, Tamamuro Fumio, Miyake Hitoshi, Miyata Noboru, and Kiuchi Gyōei, eds. "Genze riyaku kankei bunken mokuroku." *Nihon bukkyō* 34 (1972):42–47.

Fujita Sadaoki. *Kinsei Shugendō no chiikiteki tenkai.* Nihon Shūkyō Minzokugaku Sōsho 3. Tokyo: Iwata Shoten, 1996.

Gorai Shigeru. *Kumano mōde–sanzan no shinkō to bunka.* Kyoto: Tankōsha, 1968.

———. "Shomin shinkō ni okeru metsuzai no ronri." *Shisō* 622 (1976):1–22.

———. *Shugendō nyūmon.* Tokyo: Kadokawa Shoten, 1980.

———. *Shugendō no rekishi to tabi–shūkyō minzoku shūsei.* Tokyo: Kadokawa Shoten, 1995.

———. *Sō to kuyō.* Osaka: Tōhō Shuppan, 1992.

———. *Yama no shūkyō—Shugendō.* Kyoto: Tankōsha, 1970.

———. Sakurai Tokutarō, Ōshima Takehiko, and Miyata Noboru, eds. *Nihon no minzoku shūkyō.* 7 vols. Tokyo: Kōbundō, 1979–80: 1, *Shintō minzokugaku* (Sakurai Tokutarō, ed.); 2, *Bukkyō minzokugaku* (Gorai Shigeru, ed.); 3, *Kami kannen to minzoku* (Gorai Shigeru and Miyata Noboru, eds.); 4, *Fūzoku to zokushin* (Miyata Noboru, ed.); 5, *Minzoku shūkyō to shakai* (Emura Eiichi, Maruyama Kyō, and Sakurai Tokutarō, eds.); 6, *Shūkyō minzoku geinō* (Gorai Shigeru, ed.); 7, *Minkan shūkyō bungei* (Ōshima Takehiko, ed.).

Gyochi. *Konohagoromo, Tōunrokuji hoka.* In *Shugendō shiryō,* edited by Gorai Shigeru. Vol. 1. Tōyōbunko 273. Tokyo: Heibonsha, 1975.

Hagiwara Tatsuo. *Miko to bukkyōshi—Kumano bikuni no shimei to tenkai.* Tokyo: Yoshikawa Kōbunkan, 1983.

Harada Toshiaki. *Kodai Nihon no shinkō to shakai.* Tokyo: Shōkō Shoin, 1948.

———. *Mura no matsuri to seinaru mono.* Tokyo: Chūō Kōronsha, 1980.

———, ed. *Shinkō to minzoku.* Nihon Minzokugaku Taikei 8. Tokyo: Heibonsha, 1959.

Hasebe Hachirō. *Kitō girei no sekai–kami to hotoke no minzokushi.* Tokyo: Meicho Shuppan, 1992.

Hatta Yukio. "Shugendō e'in hōryu no giki to mikkyō 1." *Nihon bukkyō* 40 (1977):29–58.

———. "Shugendō e'in hōryu no giki to mikkyō 2. Kuyōhō, Gomahō." *Mikkyō bunka* 118 (1977):15–43.

———. "Shugendō e'in sōmandara no sekai." *Shūkyō kenkyū* 277 (1977):45–72.

Higo Kazuo. *Nihon ni okeru genshi shinkō no kenkyū.* Tokyo: Tōkai Shobō, 1947.

Hiraoka Jōkai. *Gongen shinkō.* Minshū Shūkyōshi Kenkyū Sōsho 23. Tokyo: Yūzankaku, 1991.

Honda Yasuji. *Yamabushi kagura bungaku.* Sendai: Saitō Hōonkai, 1942.

Hori Ichirō. *Minkan shinkō.* Tokyo: Iwanami Shoten, 1951.

———. *Nihon no shamanizumu.* Tokyo: Kōdansha, 1971.

———. "Nyonin kinsei." In *Hori Ichirō Chōsakushū.* Vol. 5. Tokyo: Miraisha, 1987.

———. *Wagakuni minkan shinkōshi no kenkyū.* 2 vols. Tokyo: Sōgensha, 1953.

Ienaga Saburō. *Nihon shisōshi ni okeru shūkyōteki shizenkan no tenkai.* Tokyo: Sōgensha, 1944.

Iguchi Takao. *Kurashi no kisetsu.* Nihon no Minzoku 2. Tokyo: Yūraku Shuppan, 1976.

Ikegami Hiromasa. *Shūkyō minzokugaku no kenkyū.* Tokyo: Meicho Shuppan, 1991.
Ikebe Wataru. *Kodai jinjashi ronkō.* Tokyo: Yoshikawa Kōbunkan, 1987.
Imamura Michio. *Nihon no minkan iryō.* Tokyo: Kōbundō, 1983.
Inoguchi Shōji. *Nihon no zokushin.* Tokyo: Kōbundō, 1975.
————, ed. *Jinsei girei.* Kōza Nihon no Minzoku 3. Tokyo: Yūseidō, 1978.
Inoue Nobutaka et al., eds. *Shinshūkyō kenkyū chōsa handobukku.* Tokyo: Yūzankaku, 1981.
Inoue Nobutaka, Kōmoto Mitsugi, Tsushima Michihito, Nakamaki Hirochika, and Nishiyama Shigeru, eds. *Shinshūkyō jiten.* Tokyo: Kōbundō, 1994.
Inoue Toshio. *Yama no tami, kawa no tami—Nihon chūsei no seikatsu to shinkō.* Tokyo: Heibonsha, 1981.
Ishida Mosaku and Yajima Kyōsuke. "Kinbusen kyōzuka ibutsu no kenkyū." *Teishitsu Hakubutsukan Gakuhō* 8 (1937):1–178. Reprint, Tokyo: Tōkyōdō Shuppan, 1979.
Ishizuka Takatoshi. *Nihon no tsukimono.* Tokyo: Miraisha, 1950.
Itō Mikiharu. *Inasaku girei no kenkyū—Nichi-Ryū dōsoron no saikentō.* Tokyo: Jiritsu Shobō, 1978.
Iwasaki Toshio. *Honpō shōshi no kenkyū.* Fukushima: Iwasaki Hakase Gakuironbun Shuppan Kōenkai, 1963. Reprint, Tokyo: Meicho Shuppan, 1977.
————, Kurabayashi Masatsugu, Tsuboi Hirofumi, Misaki Haruo, Yanagawa Keiichi, and Ishida Takehisa, eds. *Nihon saishi kenkyū shūsei.* 5 vols. Tokyo: Meicho Shuppan, 1976–78: 1, *Matsuri no kigen to tenkai*; 2, *Saishi kenkyū no saikōsei*; 3, 4, 5, *Matsuri no shokeitai.*
Iwashina Kōichiro. *Yama no minzoku.* Tokyo: Iwasaki Bijutsu Shuppan, 1968.
Kamei Munetada. *Goma no rekishiteki kenkyū.* Tokyo: Sankibō, 1967.
Kanaoka Shūyū. *Mikkyō no tetsugaku.* Kyoto: Heirakuji Shoten, 1969.
Kaneko Takezō, ed. *Shizen—rinrigakuteki kōsatsu.* Tokyo: Ibunsha, 1979.
Katō Kyūzo, ed. *Nihon no shamanizumu to sono shūhen—Nihon bunka no genzō o motomete.* Tokyo: Nihon Hōsō Shuppan Kyōkai, 1984.
Kimura Hiroshi. *Shi-bukkyō to minzoku.* Tokyo: Meicho Shuppan, 1989.
Kinkiminzoku Gakkaihen. *Yamato no minzoku.* Nara: Yamato Taimuzusha, 1959.
Kishimoto Hideo. "Sangaku shūkyō—Dewa Sanzan ni okeru shūkyōteki shugyō ni tsuite." In *Shūkyō genshō no shosō.* Tokyo: Kaname Shobō, 1949.
————. "Shinkō to shugyō no shinri." In *Kishimoto Hideo shū.* Vol. 3. Tokyo: Keiseisha, 1975.
————. *Shi o mitsumeru kokoro—gan to tatakatta jūnenkan.* Tokyo: Kōdansha, 1964.
Kizu Yuzuru. *Nyonin kinsei.* Osaka: Kaihō Shuppansha, 1993.
Kodama Yōichi. *Kumano sanzan keizaishi.* Tokyo: Yūhikaku, 1941. Reprint, Tokyo: Kaiteiban, 1954.
Kokugakuin Daigaku Nihon Bunka Kenkyūsho, ed. *Shintō jiten.* Tokyo: Kōbundō, 1994.
Kokugakuin Daigaku Nihon Minzoku Kenkyū Taikei Henshūiinkai, ed. *Nihon minzoku kenkyū taikei.* 10 vols. Tokyo: Kokugakuin Daigaku, 1982–83: 2, *Shinkō denshō*; 3, *Shūki denshō*; 4, *Roshō denshō.*
Komatsu Kazuhiko. *Hyōrei shinkō ron.* Tokyo: Dentō to Gendaisha, 1982.
————. *Kamigami no seishinshi.* Tokyo: Dentō to Gendaisha, 1978.
————, ed. *Hyōrei shinkō.* Minshū Shūkyōshi Kenkyū Sōsho 30. Tokyo: Yūzankaku, 1992.
Kondō Yoshihiro. *Nihon no oni.* Tokyo: Ōfūsha, 1966.

Konno Ensuke. *Gendai no meishin.* Tokyo: Shakaishisōsha, 1961.

Kurabayashi Masatsugu. *Matsuri no kōzō.* Tokyo: Nihon Hōsō Shuppan Kyōkai, 1975.

Kuroda Toshio. *Jisha seiryoku—mō hitotsu no chūsei shakai.* Tokyo: Iwanami Shoten, 1980.

————. *Nihon chūsei no kokka to shūkyō.* Tokyo: Iwanami Shoten, 1975.

Makida Shigeru. *Jinsei no rekishi.* Nihon no Minzoku 5. Tokyo: Kawade Shobō Shinsha, 1965.

Matsumoto Ryūshin. *Chūsei ni okeru honjimono no kenkyū.* Tokyo: Kyūko Shoin, 1996.

Matsuoka Minoru. "Shugendō to minzoku, saitō goma to hiwatari." *Nihon minzokugaku* 97 (1975):26–35.

Matsutani Miyoko. *Ano yo e itta hanashi, shi no hanashi, umare kawari.* Gendai Minwa Kō 5. Tokyo: Tatekaze Shobō, 1986.

Minegishi Sumio and Fukuda Ajio, eds. *Ie to mura no girei.* Nihon Rekishi Minzoku Ronshū 16. Tokyo: Yoshikawa Kōbunkan, 1993.

Miyagi Taimen, ed. *Jinzen kanjō.* Special issue of *Honzan shugen* 11 (1965).

————, ed. *Katsuragi kanjō.* Special issue of *Honzan shugen* 23 (1968).

Miyaji Naoichi. "Gohō." In *Shintōshi.* Vol. 2. Tokyo: Risōsha, 1959.

————. *Kumano Sanzan no shiteki kenkyū.* Tokyo: Kokumin Shinkō Kenkyūsho, 1954.

Miyake Hitoshi. *Kumano Shugen.* Nihon Rekishi Sōsho 48. Tokyo: Yoshikawa Kōbunkan, 1992.

————. *Minzoku shūkyō e no izanai.* Tokyo: Keiō Tsūshin, 1990.

————. *Nihon no minzoku shūkyō.* Tokyo: Kōdansha, 1994.

————. *Ōmine Shugendō no kenkyū.* Tokyo: Kōsei Shuppansha, 1988.

————. *Seikatsu no naka no shūkyō.* Tokyo: Nihon Hōsō Shuppan Kyōkai, 1980.

————. *Shugendō girei no kenkyū.* 2d ed., rev. Tokyo: Shunjūsha, 1985.

————. *Shugendō shisō no kenkyū.* Tokyo: Shunjūsha, 1985.

————. *Shugendō soshiki no kenkyū.* Tokyo: Shunjūsha, 1999.

————. *Shugendō to Nihon shūkyō.* Tokyo: Shunjūsha, 1996.

————. "Shugendō to shomin seikatsu—Shugen jinpi gyōhō fujushū o chūshin to shite." In *Sangaku shūkyō to minkan shinkō no kenkyū,* edited by Sakurai Tokutarō. Sangaku Shūkyōshi Kenkyū Sōsho 6. Tokyo: Meicho Shuppan, 1976.

————. *Shugendō—yamabushi no rekishi to shisō.* Tokyo: Kyōikusha, 1978.

————. *Shūkyō minzokugaku.* Tokyo: Tōkyō Daigaku Shuppankai, 1989.

————. *Shūkyō minzokugaku e no shōtai.* Tokyo: Maruzen, 1992.

————. *Yamabushi—sono kōdō to soshiki.* Tokyo: Hyōronsha, 1973.

————, ed. *Kumano shinkō.* Minshū Shūkyōshi Sōsho 21. Tokyo: Yūzankaku, 1990.

————, ed. *Minzoku to girei.* Taikei Bukkyō to Nihonjin 9. Tokyo: Shunjūsha, 1986.

————, ed. *Mitake shinkō.* Minshū Shūkyōshi Sōsho 6. Tokyo: Yūzankaku, 1985.

————, ed. *Shugendō jiten.* Tokyo: Tōkyōdō Shuppan, 1986.

————, ed. *Shugendō shosō kaidai.* Nihon Daizōkyō 99, 100. Tokyo: Suzuki Gakujutsu Zaidan, Kōdansha, 1977.

————, ed. *Yama no matsuri to geinō.* 2 vols. Tokyo: Hirakawa Shuppansha, 1984.

Miyamoto Kesao, ed. "Sangaku shūkyō bunken sōmokuroku." In *Sangaku shūkyō to minkan shinkō no kenkyū,* edited by Sakurai Tokutarō. Sangaku Shūkyōshi Kenkyū Sōsho 6. Tokyo: Meicho Shuppan, 1976.

————. *Sato Shugen no kenkyū.* Tokyo: Yoshikawa Kōbunkan, 1984.

————. *Tengu to shugenja.* Kyoto: Jinmon Shoin, 1989.

Miyata Noboru. *Ikigami shinkō—hito o kami ni matsuru shūzoku.* Tokyo: Hanawa Shobō, 1970.

————. *Koyomi to saiji—Nihonjin no kisetsu kankaku.* Nihon Minzoku Bunka Taikei 9. Tokyo: Shōgakkan, 1984.

————. *Miroku shinkō no kenkyū.* Tokyo: Miraisha, 1970.

————. *Onna no reiryoku to ie no kami.* Kyoto: Jinmon Shoin, 1983.

————. *Reikon no minzokugaku.* Tokyo: Nihon Editāzu Sukūru Shuppanbu, 1988.

————. *Yama to sato no shinkōshi.* Tokyo: Yoshikawa Kōbunkan, 1993.

———— and Tsukamoto Manabu. *Minkan shinkō to minshū shūkyō.* Nihon Rekishi Minzoku Ronshū 10. Tokyo: Yoshikawa Kōbunkan, 1994.

————, ed. *Kami to hotoke—minzoku shūkyō no shosō.* Nihon Minzoku Bunka Taikei 4. Tokyo: Shōgakkan, 1983.

————. Yamaji Kōzō, Fukuda Ajio, Miyamoto Kesao, and Komatsu Kazuhiko, eds. *Minzokugaku bunken kaidai.* Tokyo: Meicho Shuppan, 1980.

Mogami Takeyoshi. *Mairibaka.* Tokyo: Kokon Shoin, 1956.

————. *Reikon no yukue.* Tokyo: Meicho Shuppan, 1984.

Mori Tsuyoshi. *Shugendō kasumi shoku no shiteki kenkyū.* Tokyo: Meicho Shuppan, 1989.

Morioka Kiyomi. *Kesshi no sedai to isho.* Tokyo: Shinchi Shobō, 1991. Reprint, Tokyo: Yoshikawa Kōbunkan, 1995.

————, ed. *Hendōki no ningen to shakai.* Tokyo: Miraisha, 1978.

Murakami Shigeyoshi. *Kinsei minshū shūkyōshi no kenkyū.* Kyoto: Hōzōkan, 1963.

————. *Nihon shūkyō jiten.* Tokyo: Kōdansha, 1978.

Murakami Toshio. *Shugendō no hattatsu.* Tokyo: Unebi Shobō, 1943. Reprint, Tokyo: Meicho Shuppan, 1978.

Muratake Seiichi. *Saishi kūkan no kōzō—shakai jinruigaku nōto.* Tokyo: Tōkyō Daigaku Shuppankai, 1984.

Murayama Shūichi. *Chūsei Nihonjin no shūkyō to seikatsu.* Tokyo: Meguro Shobō, 1948.

————. *Nihon onmyōdōshi gaisetsu.* Tokyo: Hanawa Shobō, 1981.

————. *Shugen no sekai.* Kyoto: Jinmon Shoin, 1992.

————. *Shugendō.* Shintō Taikei 75. Tokyo: Shintō Taikei Hensankai, 1988.

————. *Tenjin goryō shinkō.* Tokyo: Hanawa Shobō, 1996.

————. *Yamabushi no rekishi.* Tokyo: Hanawa Shobō, 1970.

Nagano Tadashi. *Hikosan Shugendō no rekishi chirigakuteki kenkyū.* Tokyo: Meicho Shuppan, 1987.

Nakano Tatsue, ed. *Shugendō shōso.* 3 vols. Nihon Daizōkyō 46–48. Tokyo: Ryūbunkan, 1916–19.

Nakayama Seiden. "Tendai hongaku shisō to shinbutsu konkō shisō—toku ni hashiramoto goma o chūshin to shite." *Indogaku bukkyō kenkyū* 23.2 (1975):368–71.

Namihira Emiko. *Byōki to chiryō no bunka jinruigaku.* Tokyo: Uminarisha, 1984.

————. *Kegare.* Tokyo: Tōkyōdō Shuppan, 1985.

————. *Yamai to shi no bunka—gendai iryō no jinruigaku.* Tokyo: Asahi Shinbunsha, 1990.

Nanri Michiko. *Onryō to shugen no setsuwa.* Tokyo: Perikansha, 1996.

Negishi Kennosuke. *Iryō minzoku gakuron.* Tokyo: Yūzankaku, 1991.

Nihon Bukkyō Kenkyūkai, ed. *Nihon shūkyō no genze riyaku.* Tokyo: Daizō Shuppan, 1970.

Nihon Minzoku Gakkai, ed. *Nihon no minzokugaku 1964–1983.* Tokyo: Kōbundō, 1986.

Nishida Nagao. "Kumano tsukumo ōji." In *Shintōshi kenkyū*. Tokyo: Hanawa Shobō, 1966.

Nishiguchi Junko. *Onna no chikara—kodai no josei to bukkyō*. Tokyo: Heibonsha, 1967.

Nishitsunoi Masanori. *Nenjūgyōji jiten*. Tokyo: Tōkyōdō Shuppan, 1958.

Niiya Shigehiko, Shimazono Susumu, Tanabe Shintarō, and Yumiyama Tatsuya. *Iyashi to wakai—gendai ni okeru keā no shosō*. Tokyo: Haavesutasha, 1995.

Nomoto Kenichi. *Kamigami no fūkei*. Tokyo: Hakusuisha, 1990.

Nyonin kinsei. Special issue of *Ashinaka* 53 (1956).

Ōbayashi Taryō. "Taiyō to tsuki—kodaijin no uchūkan to shiseikan." In *Taiyō to tsuki—kodaijin no uchūkan to shiseikan*. Nihon Minzoku Bunka Taikei 2. Tokyo: Shōgakkan, 1983.

Oguchi Iichi. *Nihon shūkyō no shakaiteki seikaku*. Tokyo: Tōkyō Daigaku Shuppankai, 1953.

———, ed. *Shūkyō to shinkō no shinrigaku*. Tokyo: Kawade Shobō, 1956.

Ohnuki-Tierney, Emiko. *Nihonjin no byōkikan—shōcho jinruigakuteki kōsatsu*. Tokyo: Iwanami Shoten, 1985.

Okada Shigekiyo. *Kodai no imi—Nihonjin no kisō shinkō*. Tokyo: Kokusho Kankōkai, 1982.

Ōmori Shōzō et al., eds. *Shizen to kosumosu*. Shin Iwanami Kōza Tetsugaku 5. Tokyo: Iwanami Shoten, 1985.

Ōmachi Tokuzō. *Kon'in no minzokugaku*. Tokyo: Iwasaki Bijutsusha, 1967.

Ono Yasuhiro. *Sukui no kōzō—shinkō chiryōshi josetsu*. Tokyo: Kōdosha, 1977.

———, Shimode Sekiyo, Sugiyama Shigetsugu, Suzuki Norihisa, Sonoda Minoru, Nara Yasuhiro, Bitō Masahide, Fujii Masao, Miyake Hitoshi, and Miyata Noboru, eds. *Nihon shūkyō jiten*. Tokyo: Kōbundō, 1985.

Ooms, Herman. *Sosen sūhai no shinborizumu*. Tokyo: Kōbundō, 1987.

Origuchi Shinobu. *Kodai kenkyū*. 3 vols. Tokyo: Ōokayama Shoten, 1927–30. Reprinted in *Origuchi Shinobu zenshū*. Tokyo: Chūō Kōronsha, 1954–55.

Ōshima Takehiko. *Nenjūgyōji kōza*. Nihon no Minzoku 6. Tokyo: Yūseidō, 1979.

———, Ōmori Shiro, Gotō Shuku, Saitō Shōji, Muratake Seiichi and Yoshida Mitsukuni, eds. *Nihon o shiru jiten*. Tokyo: Shakai Shisōsha, 1979.

Ōto Yuki. *Ko yarai—Sanyuku no minzoku*. Tokyo: Iwasaki Bijutsusha, 1941.

Ōtsuka Minzoku Gakkai, ed. *Nihon minzoku jiten*. Tokyo: Kōbundō, 1972.

Sakurai Tokutarō. *Minkan shinkō to gendai shakai—ningen to jujutsu*. Tokyo: Hyōronsha, 1972.

———. *Nihon no shamanizumu*. 2 vols. Tokyo: Yoshikawa Kōbunkan, 1974–77.

———. *Shinkō*. Kōza Nihon no Minzoku 7. Tokyo: Yūseidō, 1979.

———. *Shinkō densho*. Nihon Minzokugaku Kōza 3. Tokyo: Asakura Shoten, 1976.

———, Hagiwara Tatsuo, and Miyata Noboru, eds. *Jisha engi*. Nihon Shisō Taikei 20. Tokyo: Iwanami Shoten, 1975.

———. ed. *Minkan shinkō jiten*. Tokyo: Tōkyōdō Shuppan, 1980.

———, ed. *Shamanizumu no sekai*. Tokyo: Shunjūsha, 1978.

Sakurai Yoshirō. *Kamigami no henbō engi no sekai kara*. Tokyo: Tōkyō Daigaku Shuppankai, 1976.

———. *Kami to hotoke*. Taikei Bukkyō to Nihonjin 1. Tokyo: Shunjūsha, 1985.

Sangaku Shūkyōshi Kenkyū Sōsho. Edited by Wakamori Tarō et al. 18 vols. Tokyo: Meicho Shuppan, 1975–84: 1, *Sangaku shūyō no seiritsu to tenkai*. (Wakamori Tarō, ed.); 2, *Hieizan to Tendai bukkyō* (Murayama Shūichi, ed.); 3, *Kōyasan to shingon mikkyō* (Gorai Shigeru, ed.); 4, *Yoshino Kumano shinkō no kenkyū* (Gorai

Shigeru, ed.); 5, *Dewa sanzan to Tōhoku shugen no kenkyū* (Togawa Anshō, ed.); 6, *Sangaku shūkyō to minkan shinkō no kenkyū* (Sakurai Tokutarō, ed.); 7, *Tōhoku reizan to Shugendō* (Gakkō Yoshihiro, ed.); 8, *Nikkōsan to kantō no Shugendō* (Miyata Noboru, Miyamoto Kesao, eds.); 9, *Fuji-ontake to Chūbu Reizan* (Suzuki Shōei, ed.); 10, *Hakusan-Tateyama to hokuriku Shugendō* (Takase Shigeo, ed.); 11, *Kinki reizan to Shugendō* (Gorai Shigeru, ed.); 12, *Daisen ishizuchi to saigoku Shugendō* (Miyake Hitoshi, ed.); 13, *Hikosan to Kyūshū no Shugendō* (Nakano Hatayoshi, ed.); 14, 15, *Shugendō no bijutsu, Geinō bungaku* I, II; 16, *Shugendō no densho bunka*; 17, 18, *Shugendō shiryōshu* I, II (Gorai Shigeru, ed.).

Sasaki Kōkan. *Shamanizumu—ekusutashī to hyōrei no bunka*. Tokyo: Chūō Kōronsha, 1980.

Sawa Ryūken, ed. *Butsuzō jiten*. Tokyo: Yoshikawa Kōbunkan, 1962.

Segawa Kiyoko. *Wakamono to musume o meguru minzoku*. Tokyo: Miraisha, 1973.

Seki Keigo, ed. *Nihon mukashibanashi kenkyū shūsei*. 5 vols. Tokyo: Meicho Shuppan, 1984–85.

Shibata Minoru. *Chūsei shomin shinkō no kenkyū*. Tokyo: Kadokawa Shoten, 1966.

———. *Goryō shinkō*. Minshū Shūkyōshi Kenkyū Sōsho 5. Tokyo: Yūzankaku, 1984.

Shigematsu Toshimi, Yamada Ryūshin, and Okumura Masahiro. *Kubote shugen no sekai*. Fukuoka: Ashi Shobō, 1983.

Shimazono Susumu. *Gendai kyūsaishūkyō*. Tokyo: Seikyūsha, 1992.

Shimazu Dendō. *Hagurosan Shugendō teiyō*. Tokyo: Koyūkan, 1942.

Shinjo Tsunezo. *Shinkō shaji sankei no shakai—keizaishiteki kenkyū*. Tokyo: Hanawa Shobō, 1982.

Shintani Takanori. *Ryōbosei to takaikan*. Tokyo: Yoshikawa Kōbunkan, 1991.

———. *Sei to shi no minzokushi*. Tokyo: Mokujisha, 1986.

Shizen. Manuscripts prepared for the Fourth Public Symposium of the Philosophy Division, Science Council of Japan, 1994.

Shugendō Shugyō Taikei Hensan Iinkai (Miyake Hitoshi et al.), ed. *Shugendō shugyō taikei*. Tokyo: Kokusho Kankōkai, 1994.

Shutō Yoshiki. *Kinbusen*. Yoshino: Kinbusenji, 1985.

Sonoda Minoru. *Matsuri no genshōgaku*. Tokyo: Kōbundō, 1990.

Sugawara Jusei. *Ontake gyōja no uchūkan*. Gendai Shūkyō 5. Tokyo: Shunjūsha, 1982.

Suzuki Masataka. *Yama to kami to hito—sangaku shinkō to Shugendō no sekai*. Kyoto: Tankōsha, 1991.

Suzuki Shōei. "Sangaku shinkō, Shugendō to shamanizumu no kankei—gohōtobi no kōsatsu o megutte." *Ōtani shigaku* 8 (1961):27–43.

———. "Shugendō tōzanha no kyōdan soshiki to nyūbu." In *Yoshino Kumano shinkō no kenkyū*, edited by Gorai Shigeru. Sangaku Shūkyōshi Kenkyū Sōsho 4. Tokyo: Meicho Shuppan, 1975.

Takagi Hiroo. "Nihonjin no shūkyō seikatsu no jittai." In *Nihonjin no shūkyō seikatsu*. Tokyo: Sōbunsha, 1955.

———. *Shinkō shūkyō*. Tokyo: Kōdansha, 1958.

Takai Kankai. *Mikkyō jiso taikei*. Kyoto: Takai Zenchizankeshu, Chosaku Kankōkai, 1953.

Takano Toshihiko. *Kinsei Nihon no kokka kenryoku to shūkyō*. Tokyo: Tōkyō Daigaku Shuppankai, 1988.

Takase Shigeo. *Kodai sangaku shinkō no shiteki kōsatsu*. Tokyo: Kadokawa Shoten, 1969.

Takatori Masao. *Minkan shinkōshi no kenkyū*. Kyoto: Hōzōkan, 1982.

————. *Shintō no seiritsu.* Tokyo: Heibonsha, 1979.

Takeda Chōshu. *Minzoku bukkyō to sosen shinkō.* Tokyo: Tōkyō Daigaku Shuppankai, 1971.

————. *Sosen sūhai.* Kyoto: Heirakuji Shoten, 1957.

Takigawa Masajiro, ed. *Kumano.* Tokyo: Chihōshi Kenkyūsho, 1957.

Tamamuro Fumio, Hirano Eiji, Miyake Hitoshi, and Miyata Noboru, eds. *Minkan shinkō chōsa seiri handobukku.* 2 vols. Tokyo: Yūzankaku, 1987.

Tamamuro Taijō. "Chibyō shūkyo no keifu." *Nihon rekishi* 186 (1963):2–15.

————. "Edo jidai no yamabushi kenkyū josetsu." In *Bukkyōgaku no shomondai,* edited by Buttan Nisengohyakunen Kinengakkai. Tokyo: Iwanami Shoten, 1935.

————. *Kitō bukkyō no kenkyū.* Tokyo: Shinjinbutsu Ōraisha, 1971.

Tamura Yoshirō. *Kamakura shin bukkyō shisō no kenkyū.* Kyoto: Heirakuji Shoten, 1965.

————. *Tendai hongakuron.* Nihon Shisō Taikei 9. Tokyo: Iwanami Shoten, 1973.

Tanabe Saburōsuke. *Shinbutsu shūgō to shugen.* Zusetsu, Nihon no Bukkyō 6. Tokyo: Shinchōsha, 1989.

Tanaka Hisao, ed. *Fudō shinkō.* Minshū Shūkyōshi Kenkyū Sōsho 25. Tokyo: Yūzankaku, 1993.

————. *Sosen saishi no kenkyū.* Tokyo: Kōbundō, 1978.

Tanaka Sen'ichi. *Nenjūgyōji no kenkyū.* Tokyo: Ōfūsha, 1992.

Toganoo Shōun. *Himitsu jiso no kenkyū.* Wakayama: Kōyasan Mikkyō Bunka Kenkyūsho, 1975.

————. *Mandara no kenkyū.* Wakayama: Kōyasan Mikkyō Bunka Kenkyūsho, 1927.

Togawa Anshō. *Shinpan Dewa Sanzan Shugendō no kenkyū.* Tokyo: Kōsei Shuppansha, 1986.

————. "Shugendō haguroha goi kaisetsu." *Kokugakuin zasshi* 46.11 (1940):143–69.

————. *Shugendō to minzoku.* Tokyo: Iwasaki Bijutsu Shuppan, 1972.

Tsuboi Hirofumi. "Nihonjin no seishikan; minzokugaku kara mita Nihon." In *Oka Masao koki kinen ronbonshū.* Tokyo: Kawade Shobō Shinsha, 1970.

————. *Yakudoshi; Toshiiwai.* Nihon Minzokugaku Taikei 4. Tokyo: Heibonsha, 1959.

Tsuda Sōkichi. "En no Gyōja densetsu kō." *Shichō* 1.3 (1931):1–32. Reprinted in *Tsuda Sōkichi zenshū.* Vol. 9. Tokyo: Iwanami Shoten, 1964.

Ueda Noriyuki. *Iyashi no jidai o hiraku.* Kyoto: Hōzōkan, 1997.

Ui Hakuju. *Konsaisu bukkyō jiten.* Tokyo: Daitō Shuppansha, 1938.

Umehara Masaki. "Gedatsukai." In *Shinshūkyō no sekai.* Vol. 3. Tokyo: Daizō Shuppan, 1978.

————, Sasaki Kōkan, Abe Toshiharu, and Miyata Noboru, eds. *Sukui.* Tokyo: Kōbundō, 1975.

Umehara Takeshi. *Nihonjin no ano yo kan.* Tokyo: Chūō Kōronsha, 1989.

Ushikubo Kōzen. *Shugendō kōyō.* Tokyo: Meicho Shuppan, 1980.

Ushiyama Yoshiyuki. "Nyonin kinsei sairon." *Sangaku Shugen* 17 (1996):1–11.

Wakamori Tarō. *Shugendōshi kenkyū.* Tokyo: Kawade Shobō, 1947. Reprint, Tōyō Bunkō 211. Tokyo: Heibonsha, 1972.

————. *Yamabushi—nyūbu, shugyō, juhō.* Tokyo: Chūō Kōronsha, 1964.

Wakimoto Tsuneya. *Shi no hikaku shūkyōgaku.* Gendai no Shūkyō 3. Tokyo: Iwanami Shoten, 1997.

Watanabe Shōko. *Fudō Myōō.* Tokyo: Asahi Shinbunsha, 1975.

Yajima Kyōsuke. "Shugendō no yōgu ni tsuite, butsugu." In *Bukkyō kōkōgaku kōza,* edited by Ishida Mosaku. Vol. 5. Tokyo: Yūzankaku, 1976.

Yamaori Tetsuo. *Nihonjin no reikonkan.* Tokyo: Kawade Shobō Shinsha, 1976.

———, and Miyamoto Kesao, eds. *Saiji to jujutsu.* Nihon Rekishi Minzoku Ronshū 9. Tokyo: Yoshikawa Kōbunkan, 1994.

———, ed. *Yūgyō to hyōhaku.* Taikei Bukkyō to Nihonjin 6. Tokyo: Shunjūsha, 1986.

Yanabu Akira. *Honyaku no shisō: shizen to neichyā.* Tokyo: Heibonsha, 1977.

Yanagawa Keiichi. *Matsuri to girei no shūkyōgaku.* Tokyo: Chikuma Shobō, 1987.

Yanagita Kunio. "Gohō dōji." *Kyōdo kenkyū* 2.11 (1915):641–54. Reprinted in *Teihon Yanagita Kunio shū.* Vol. 9. Tokyo: Chikuma Shobō, 1962.

———. *Imo no chikara.* Tokyo: Sōbunsha, 1940. Reprinted in *Teihon Yanagita Kunio shū.* Vol. 10. Tokyo: Chikuma Shobō, 1962.

———. *Senzo no hanashi.* Tokyo: Chikuma Shobō, 1946. Reprinted in *Teihon Yanagita Kunio shū.* Vol. 10. Tokyo: Chikuma Shobō, 1962.

———, ed. *Bunrui saishi shūzoku goi.* Tokyo: Kadokawa Shoten, 1963.

——— and Kokugakuin Daigaku Hōgengakkai, eds. *Kinki shūzoku goi.* Tokyo: Kadokawa Shoten, 1938.

———, ed. *Saiji shūzoku goi.* Tokyo: Minkan Denshō no Kai, 1939.

——— and Hashiura Yasuo, eds. *Sanyuku shūzoku goi.* Tokyo: Aiyukukai, 1939.

———, ed. *Sōsō shūzoku goi.* Tokyo: Minkan Denshō no Kai, 1937.

Yasumaru Yoshio. *Nihon no kindaika to minshū shisō.* Tokyo: Aoki Shoten, 1974.

Yoshida Teigo. *Masho no bunkashi.* Tokyo: Kenkyūsha, 1959.

———. *Nihon no tsukimono—shakai-jinruigakuteki kōsatsu.* Tokyo: Chūō Kōronsha, 1972.

———. *Shūkyō jinruigaku.* Tokyo: Tokyō Daigaku Shuppankai, 1982.

——— and Ayabe Tsuneo. "Seinan Nihon ni okeru chitsujo to henka." *Kyūshū Daigaku Kyōyōgakubu Hikaku Kyōiku Bunka Kenkyū Shisetsu kiyō* 18 (1967):1–106.

Yuasa Yasuo, ed. *Mitsugi to shugyō.* Taikei Bukkyō to Nihonjin 3. Tokyo: Shunjūsha, 1989.

Zenitani Osamu. "Ōminesan no nyonin kaikin mondai tsuiokuki." *Jinben* 724 (1970):37–44.

(C) A BASIC BIBLIOGRAPHY OF FOLK RELIGION IN JAPAN

Dictionaries and Other Reference Works

Bunkachō, ed. (The Agency for Cultural Affairs, Government of Japan). *Nihon minzoku chizu* (Atlas of Japanese folk culture). 7 vols. Tokyo: Kokudō Chiri Kyōkai, 1968–80: 1, 2, *Nenjūgyōji* (Annual events); 3, *Shinkō* (Worship); 4, *Shakai seikatsu* (Social life); 5, *Shussan ikuji* (Childbirth and care of children); 6, *Kon'in* (Marriage); 7, *Sōsei bosei* (Funerals and gravestones).

Minzokugaku Kenkyūjo, ed. (Institute for the Study of Folklore). *Minzokugaku jiten* (Folklore dictionary). General editor, Yanagita Kunio. Tokyo: Tōkyōdō Shuppan, 1951.

Minzokugaku Kenkyūjo, ed. (Institute for the Study of Folklore). *Sōgō minzoku goi* (Collection of folklore vocabulary). 5 vols. General editor, Yanagita Kunio. Tokyo: Heibonsha, 1955–56.

Nihon Minzoku Gakkai, ed. (The Folklore Society of Japan). *Nihon minzokugaku* (Bulletin of the Folklore Society of Japan). Tokyo, bimonthly, since 1958.

Nihon Minzokugaku Kyōkai, ed. (Association for Japanese Ethnology). *Nihon shakai minzoku jiten* (Dictionary of folklore in Japan). 4 vols. Tokyo: Seibundō Shinkōsha, 1952–57.

Tsuboi Yōbun and Inoguchi Shōji. *Nihon minzokugaku no chōsa hōhō, bunken mokuroku, sōsakuin* (Research method of Japanese folklore studies, bibliography, and general index). Nihon Minzokugaku Taikei 13 (Series on Japanese folklore). Tokyo: Heibonsha, 1960.

General

Hori Ichirō. *Minkan shinkō* (Folk beliefs). Tokyo: Iwanami Shoten, 1951.

———. *Wagakuni minkan shinkōshi no kenkyū*. (A study of the history of Japanese folk religion). 2 vols. Tokyo: Sōgensha, 1953, 1955.

Katō Totsudō. *Minkan shinkōshi* (History of folk beliefs). Tokyo: Heigo Shuppansha, 1925.

Nihon Minzokugaku Taikei (Series on Japanese folklore). Edited by Omachi Tokuzō et al. 13 vols. Tokyo: Heibonsha, 1958–60.

Origuchi Shinobu Kinenkai, ed. (The Commemorative Committee for Dr. Origuchi's Works). *Origuchi Shinobu zenshū*. (Collected works of Origuchi Shinobu). 31 vols., and one additional vol. Tokyo: Chūō Kōronsha, 1954–59.

Yanagita Kunio. *Yanagita Kunio shū* (Works of Yanagita Kunio, the standard edition). 25 vols., and 3 additional vols. Tokyo: Chikuma Shobō, 1962–64.

Worldview and Folktales

Harada Toshiaki, ed. *Shinkō to minzoku* (Beliefs and folklore). Nihon Minzokugaku Taikei 8 (Series on Japanese folklore). Tokyo: Heibonsha, 1959.

Seki Keigo. *Nihon mukashibanashi shūsei* (A collection of Japanese folk tales). 3 parts in 6 vols. Tokyo: Kadokawa Shoten, 1950–58. Part I: *Dōbutsu mukashibanashi* (Animal tales), 1950. Part II: *Honkaku mukashibanashi* (Ordinary folk tales), vol. 1, 2, 1953, vol. 3, 1955. Part III: *Waraibanashi* (Jokes and anecdotes), vol. 1, 1957, vol. 2, 1958.

Takeda Chōshū. *Sosen sūhai: minzoku to rekishi* (Ancestor worship: folklore and history). Kyoto: Heirakuji Shoten, 1957.

Shrines and Festivals

Harada Toshiaki. *Jinja: minzokugaku no tachiba kara miru* (Shrine: from the viewpoint of folklore). Nihon Rekishi Shinsho (New series on Japanese history). Tokyo: Shibundō, 1961.

Hayakawa Kōtarō. *Hanamatsuri* (Flower festival). 2 vols. Tokyo: Oka Shoten, 1930.

Higo Kazuo. *Miyaza no kenkyū* (A study on Miyaza). Tokyo: Kōbundō, 1941.

Matsudaira Narimitsu. *Matsuri* (Festival). Tokyo: Nikkō Shoin, 1943.

Wakamori Tarō. *Chūsei kyōdōtai no kenkyū* (Studies on medieval cooperative organizations). Tokyo: Kōbundō, 1950.

———. *Miho jinja no kenkyū* (A study on the Miho Shrine). Tokyo: Kōbundō, 1955.

Calendar and Annual Events

Minzokugaku Kenkyūjo, ed. (Institute for the Study of Folklore). *Nenjūgyōji zusetsu* (An illustrated explanatory book of annual events). General editor, Yanagita Kunio. Tokyo: Iwasaki Shoten, 1953.

Miyamoto Tsuneichi. *Minkan reki* (Popular calendar). Tokyo: Rokuninsha, 1942.
Nishitsunoi Masayoshi, ed. *Nenjūgyōji jiten* (Dictionary of annual events). Tokyo: Tōkyōdō Shuppan, 1958.
Sakai Usaku. *Ine no matsuri* (Rice festival). Tokyo: Iwasaki Shoten, 1958.
Sakurada Katsunori, ed. *Seikatsu to minzoku* II (Life and folklore, part II). Nihon Minzokugaku Taikei 7 (Series on Japanese folklore). Tokyo: Heibonsha, 1959.
Wakamori Tarō. *Nenjūgyōji* (Annual events). Tokyo: Shibundō, 1957.

Rites of Passage

Inoguchi Shōji. *Bukkyō izen* (Before Buddhism). Minzoku Sensho (Selected works on folklore). Tokyo: Kokon Shoin, 1954.
Mogami Takayoshi. *Mairibaka: ryōbosei no tankyū* (Tombs for rites: studies on the dual tomb system). Tokyo: Kokon Shoin, 1956.
Sakurada Katsunori, ed. *Shakai to minzoku* II (Society and folklore, part II). Nihon Minzokugaku Taikei 4 (Series on Japanese Folklore). Tokyo: Heibonsha, 1959.

Superstition

Ishizuka Takatoshi. *Nihon no tsukimono* (Posessed spirits in Japan). Tokyo: Miraisha, 1959.
Meishin Chōsa Kyōgikai, ed. (The Committee for the Research in Superstition). *Nihon no zokushin* (Popular beliefs in Japan). 3 vols. Tokyo: Gihōdō, 1949–55.

Folk Religion and Society

Ariga Kizaemon. *Sonraku seikatsu* (Village life). Tokyo: Kunitachi Shoin, 1948.
Inoue Yoritoshi. *Kyoto koshū-shi* (Record of traditional practices in Kyoto). Osaka: Ōsakakanyū Shinshokukai, 1940. Reprint, Tokyo: Chijin Shokan, 1943.
Kubo Noritada. *Kōshin shinkō no kenkyū: nitchū shūkyō-bunka kōshō-shi* (A study on the Kōshin-belief: history of religio-cultural relations between China and Japan). Tokyo: Nihon Gakujutsu Shinkōkai (The Japan Society for the Promotion of Scientific Research), 1961.
Nakayama Tarō. *Nihon fujoshi* (History of Japanese sibyls). Tokyo: Ōokayama Shoten, 1930.
―――. *Nihon mōjinshi* (The history of the blind in Japan). Tokyo: Seikōkan, 1934.
Sakurai Tokutarō. *Kō shūdan seiritsu katei no kenkyū* (A study on the development of the *kō* organization). Tokyo: Yoshikawa Kōbunkan, 1962.
Takahashi Bonsen. *Kakushi Nenbutsu kō* (A study on Kakushi Nenbutsu). Vol. 1. Tokyo: Nihon Gakujutsu Shinkōtai (The Japan Society for the Promotion of Scientific Research), 1956.
Takeuchi Toshimi, ed. *Nōson shinkōshi: Kōshin Nenbutsu hen* (Record of religious life in villages). Higashi Chikuma-gun Shi (Records of Higashi Chikuma district). Separate volume 2. Tokyo: Rokuninsha, 1943.

Shugendō

Miyaji Naokazu. *Kumano sanzan no shiteki kenkyū* (Historical study of the three sacred mountains in Kumono). Tokyo: Kokumin Shinkō Kenkyūsho (Institute for National Beliefs), 1954.
Miyake Hitoshi. *Shugendō girei no kenkyū* (A study of religious rituals in Shugendō). Tokyo: Shunjūsha, 1970.

Murakami Toshio. *Shugendō no hattatsu* (The development of Shugendō). Tokyo:
    Unebi Shobō, 1943.
Wakamori Tarō. *Shugendōshi kenkyū* (Studies in the history of Shugendō). Tokyo:
    Kawade Shobō, 1943.

Index